# A Jubilee Printing Celebration!

*From The Mountains Came The Light* was written in 1987. That was my Dad's 50th year in the pulpit. It was a year of Jubilee, a year of celebrating the goodness of God!

This year, 2016, is my 50th wedding anniversary. Muzette and I were married on July 1, 1966.

This year is the 50th Anniversary of Trinity Baptist Church in Asheville, NC. Trinity was founded by Ralph Sexton, Sr. on October 2, 1966.

This year, 2016, will be my 50th teaching tour to the Holy Land! On November 8, we will again walk where Jesus walked!

Leviticus 25:10 speaks of the fiftieth year as a "year of Jubilee," a year of remembrance and celebration.

This year is the Jubilee year for Trinity Baptist, Ralph and Muzette, and Ralph Sexton Ministries in the Holy Land.

We celebrate and remember by reprinting Dad's life story and adding an EPILOGUE from many friends!

Yours in His Service,

Ralph H. Sexton, Jr.
John 3:30

Long before his twentieth birthday, Ralph Sexton, Sr. was preaching the gospel of Jesus Christ and seeing souls saved. This year, 1987, is his 50th year in the pulpit. At the age of 67, he feels he has several more years to go and will make the most of it for the Kingdom of God.

Ralph Sexton's story is a serious story of a man's serious work for the Lord, but at times it is humorous to the point of evoking guffaws. Ralph Sexton believes that the Lord has a great sense of humor, and Sexton himself certainly has one. He has had to exercise it often enough in his work.

If you looked across the width and breadth of this nation, you would find Ralph Sexton to be one of the few remaining exponents of the Old-Time Religion. It fills his body and permeates his soul. As such, this work is the story of the Old-Time Religion in modern times.

Within these pages are the account of how Ralph and his brother Lee were called to preached, just as clearly as if God had met with them in the road and told them what He wanted them to do.

They were called into the hedgerows and byways, and they faithfully preached the Word in those places. They preached in tents and had the canvas come down around their ears in the midst of a violent storm. They preached on the streets of many cities and towns, and for doing that they paid the price in their hometown. Three times they were jailed in Asheville, North Carolina for "disturbing the peace", knowing that the only "peace" they disturbed was that of sinner men.

This is a marvelous love story of a man who prayed for a wife for seven years, and the wife who almost had to run a gantlet to get to the altar to marry the man she loved.

The Ralph Sextons are real people who live in a real world, and they have spent their waking hours trying to make it a better world for you and me.

Bob Terrell
Asheville, NC
1987

It isn't every man who gets to commit his life's story to paper and see it printed in book form. Bob Terrell and I discussed the writing of my life's story for a number of years, and I am indebted to him for doing it for me.

We met more than fifty times at Holiday Inn West in Asheville, North Carolina, and after lunch and fellowship managed to tape an hour or two of the story. Bob then put all of this together in the way I feel only he can do, for he is an expert writer who understands what he writes about.

Bob has written more than fifteen books, and at least four were "as told to" books in which he figuratively had to become the person he wrote about. He had to learn to think, to talk, and to act like the persons about whom he wrote.

This is the first time he had to become a preacher. I think he was a good one.

Ralph Sexton, Sr.
Asheville, North Carolina

# THE RALPH SEXTON STORY

## —From The Mountains Came The Light

*The trials, triumphs, and good times of a mountain preacher*

**with BOB TERRELL**

OTHER BOOKS BY BOB TERRELL

J. D. Sumner—Gospel Music Is My Life!
Fun Is Where You Find It!
Holy Land: A Journey Into Time
A Touch of Terrell
Billy Graham in Hungary
Grandpa's Town
Woody (with Barbara Shelton)
Old Gold
The Peace That Passeth Understanding
(with Connie Hopper)
Disorder in the Court!
(with Marcellus Buchanan)
Billy Graham in the Soviet Union
Keep 'em Laughing
Papa Coke (with Sanders Rowland)

# CONTENTS

"Because he hath set his love upon me, therefore will I deliver him: I will set him on high, because he hath known my name."

*Psalm 91:14*

# — 1 —

# A Boy's World

Although I don't remember a thing about it, I first saw the light of day on September 14, 1919, in a little house on Sassafras Gap. To pinpoint the location exactly, Sassafras Gap is on Elk Mountain just beyond Buzzard Rock. If you don't know where that is, it's about seven or eight miles north as the crow flies from Pack Square, the center of Asheville, North Carolina. I was a mountaineer by birth, and I wouldn't take anything for that heritage. It is priceless to me.

All of that mountain was planted in orchard during World War I, and my father, Charles Harrison Sexton, hired out to a Dr. Carroll to look after the orchard during the war. My dad missed the war. He was expecting to be drafted in the next call late in 1918, but the war ended on November 11 and he didn't have to go.

My mother was Mary Elizabeth Shetley, and she, like my father, was a typical mountaineer. She was part Cherokee Indian, so I have some of the blood of that great Indian nation in my veins.

I was sixth in a line of nine children born to my parents, six boys and three girls. The second daughter, Henrietta, was stillborn. The other eight of us are still alive at this writing, and we are, in descending order: Evelyn Lindberg, Paul, Perry, Lee, me, Raymond, Ethel Hyatt, and Frank. The eight of us have experienced almost six hundred years of living, and we are thankful to God for that. What a blessing!—that God would give one family that much life.

We were not reared in a strong Christian home, but we were like other mountain people: We had strong principles and good morals. We believed in Christ and truly loved God, but were not Christians in the way we are today. Our home was strict, though not like a military camp. Mountaineers didn't do a lot of talking, but we did a lot of living—family living. We didn't have a family altar, and we didn't sit down and pray together, but our parents taught us respect for others and respect for other people's property. They taught us manners and grace. They wanted all those traits to be instilled in each one of us.

My brother Lee, which is short for Leroy, remembers when I was five or six months old and our father built a little one-room Sunday School over on Ox Creek. Coming up the mountain from Asheville, a visitor came first to Buzzard Rock, then Sassafras Gap where he crossed the mountain, and the first creek on the other side of the mountain was Ox Creek. If we looked out the front door of that Sunday School, we saw Mount Mitchell. Ralph Poole, who ran Poole Dry Cleaners in Asheville, came over each week and taught Sunday School.

Our growing-up time was rough on us. Daddy was a cleaner and dyer by trade, but he couldn't always get work, especially after our nation was plunged into the Great Depression.

We lived on the mountain in Sassafras Gap until I was about five years old. Then we moved to the Asheville side of the mountain into a two-story house on Beaverdam Road, where the road forked at Webb's orchard. It was about that time that I remember first coming to Asheville. My dad drove my sister and me to town in a buggy drawn by two mules. I recall my father tying the mules on Lexington Avenue in front of the stores, and I remember riding in that buggy through the Grace section of North Asheville.

Most of my childhood memories, however, come from depression times. The problem then, especially for mountain folk, was that of real survival. At first we had to get along as get-along can. There were no handouts. We didn't have all that modern-day welfare. We were taught that if we didn't work we didn't eat, and there were times when we went hungry for lack of enough food. We spent most of our time scrounging for things the family could eat—but we scrounged honestly. Finally, the government instituted a welfare program called "commodities," but even then we mostly worked for what we ate.

Through the depression we moved many times. We lived in most sections of Buncombe County and even in adjoining counties. My father couldn't always find cleaning work; so he sharecropped. He could rent a farm for ten or twelve dollars a month, but we seldom came up with that kind of cash. There were so many kids that Daddy simply paid the rent by sharecropping and we all worked in the fields. We usually raised good crops and gave part of them for rent. Many mountain families lived that way. It gave us a feeling of independence.

When the banks failed in 1929, things got really rough. We kids went to the fields and picked berries, gathered apples, and worked for the neighbors gathering leaves and bedding barns. We did anything we could to get food for the table.

It was during that time that we resorted to commodities. We rode to town to get the commodities, and there in line were always a number of people our parents knew. Times were hard, indeed, but people managed to laugh about them. Mountaineers had a lot of laughs over grapefruits then. Most didn't know what grapefruits were, or at least pretended not to know, and they laughed about how they ate the fruits.

"My Martha didn't know how to fix these things," I overheard a tall mountaineer say, pointing to a pile of grapefruit. "When I took the first ones home, she boiled 'em and boiled 'em and never could get the blamed things tender enough to eat." Another vowed his wife boiled a grapefruit till it exploded, blowing seeds all over the kitchen.

No one we knew thought about cursing his luck and burning the city. We simply accepted the lot in life that had been cast to us and made the most of it. And we laughed a lot. And looked for work. The Three Mountaineers in Asheville made rugs out of "loopings," which were the cut-off tops of stockings; but in order to use them, the loopings had to be strung together. That firm let families take huge quantities of loopings home. I remember Perry going after ours and our entire family spending evenings looping until we had the loops in huge balls. When we took the balls to the factory, we were paid up to nine cents a pound for our work.

We always took the money home to Mama. That was grocery money. Twenty-five cents went a long way at the store if a person bought carefully. Mama often sent me to the store with a dime to buy a nickel's worth of fatback and a nickel's worth of sugar. She fried the fatback, made gravy, and served rice with sugar on it, and we had a good meal.

People didn't give up. They had a determination, and they never quit laughing at life.

Sometimes we didn't live in one place too long because of the living conditions. We moved across Minehole Gap to Fairview one fall and rented an old house. When it rained it was like the old-timers said: It rained inside and leaked outside. We set all of our pots and pans under leaks, and in the daytime when it rained we could even see through the holes in the roof. I remember how we laughed like crazy about that.

We never heard—or at least seldom heard—anyone feeling sorry for himself. People didn't have time for that. Too, we had strong families who were close and loved each other and liked to work together. We went to the fields and picked berries that Mama canned in the old-fashioned way. We built a fire in the back yard and she canned over the open flame in a Number Two wash tub. Those were joyous times.

I remember some of the old cars my dad owned. First was a T-Model Ford he bought in 1925 for $480, then he had a Jewit, an Essex, a Hudson, a Studebaker, and an old Willis Knight. But mostly we didn't have enough money to run a car. My dad could buy insurance policies for a nickel a week. When bill collectors came, Daddy would laugh and say, "Come back Tuesday and I'll tell you when to come back again."

In the fall, we headed for the hills and gathered chestnuts. The blight hadn't taken all the trees then. At one of the old homeplaces where we lived, men came and shook the chestnut trees and we gathered chestnuts by the bucketsful.

Just after Roosevelt became president in early 1933, my brother Lee went to work on the WPA. He worked on Pinnacle Street between Canton and Enka, helping build a road. The government didn't furnish cement, so the gangs built dry bridges with rock and no adhesive. Some of those bridges are still in use.

The WPA had a reputation of standing around leaning on shovels. One of the sayings that went around was something like this: "Those WPA boys work so slow that when fellows go hunting they only shoot at things moving. If they see anything standing still, chances are it's a WPA worker."

Lee made five dollars and a quarter for working three days a week. His was the only money coming in to our family, so he gave the five dollars to Mama and kept the quarter for himself. That was instilled in children then: If a child drew a paycheck, he took it straight to his parents for grocery money.

Most of us kids weren't old enough to work on the WPA, so we hired out elsewhere. We went to the old Bingham Military Academy and set tobacco plants for the owner. He paid us five cents an hour, rain or shine, and when we got our pay we took it straight to Mama and Daddy. We had no other thoughts but that the money belonged to them.

When we moved to Fairview we worked for a Mrs. Daniel Wise. We pulled corn, cleaned the barns, carried leaves and bedded the barns for the cattle—and she didn't pay us in money; she paid in apples. She sent us to the basement to get the apples, and she always said, "Now, be sure you only get the little apples." We were hungry, and I always put big apples in the bottom of my bucket and topped it off with little ones. After the Lord saved me, he reminded me of taking her good apples instead of the small ones, and I looked for her to apologize but could never find her. She is dead now; so I'll have to tell her I'm sorry when I get to heaven.

God surely gave my parents wisdom to rear such a large family in the depression. Those were lean years, but families stuck together, no matter what. That's how a lot of families made it through. Working and playing together, we had a lot of fun. When I think what the divorce rate is today with all the affluence we have, I shudder to think what the divorce rate would be if we had a depression and couples had to face the hard times our parents faced. Families today don't laugh at life enough. They feel sorry for themselves when they feel deprived. If kids don't get everything they want, some of them kill themselves. They've lost the challenge of life. To us, growing up was a matter of survival. People no longer have the pioneer spirit.

We often lived near the railroad during the depression, once in Emma and another time down near Pearson Bridge in Asheville. A common sight was to see whole families traveling together in box cars, going from one place to another place they hoped would treat them better. We often saw a father and mother traveling in the rail cars with small children, even nursing babies. They were looking for work, and what kind of work didn't matter.

They didn't think of separating. Whatever came, they faced it together.

We played beside the railroad and watched trains come through. It was a thrill to see those big engines puffing along, blowing smoke, fireboxes ablaze, engineers sitting in the cabs like kings on their thrones.

When a coal train came through, chunks of coal fell off some of the cars. We kept a lookout for these, and when we found them we took them home for fuel.

Men walked to Craggy where the trains stopped at water tanks, and when the trains pulled out, men swung aboard and climbed into the coal cars. At Pearson Bridge, they kicked off huge chunks of coal, big blocks, and some of them stamped with a Red Diamond or other identifying brand. These blocks were beautiful, I thought, and the best fuel there was for keeping a house warm. Most homes were heated by fireplaces equipped with grates for burning coal. Ashes dropped through the grates, and those hot ashes roasted potatoes to the best taste you could imagine.

The men who threw coal off the cars had to ride on into the Asheville yards before the train slowed to a hopping-off speed. Then they ran back to Pearson Bridge, collected their coal, and took it home. When we were in the vicinity and saw a coal train coming in, we ran to Pearson Bridge, picked up the coal the men kicked off the train, and hid it somewhere along the river where they couldn't find it. When they quit looking for it, figuring someone had taken it already, we came out of hiding, retrieved the coal and took it home. That was a means of staying warm in the winter—a matter of survival.

I loved the steam engines and their whistles. When the great engineer, Mike O'Conner, pulled the Carolina Special out of the Asheville yards, bound for Cincinnati, people stopped everything and went out to watch him pass, playing a tune on the whistle.

At home each of us had to help with chores, such as

washing dishes. The only dishwashers were the two-legged kind you raised rather than bought. It didn't matter a bit that we were boys, we all took turns. One night when Lee and I were washing dishes we heard a knock at the back door. That's where hoboes and tramps came, always to the back door, looking for warm meals and other handouts. Lee opened the door and a man stood there who said he was hungry and did we have anything we could spare him to eat? There were seldom leftovers—we had too many mouths to feed at our house—but this night Mama had made some cherry pies. They were still hot, very hot, and she had left them on the back of the stove to stay warm. Lee told the old man to hold out his hands and he slid one of those hot cherry pies out of the pan into the fellow's hands. You should have seen him dancing and running around the kitchen, shifting that pie from one hot hand to the other—but he wasn't about to turn it loose. He ran into the night throwing that pie from one hand to the other.

Those were hard but happy days for children growing up. We had a lot of fun. We made a lot of memories.

Through the depression, we made money in various ways; a quarter here, a half-dollar there, and it kept us going.

Along the railroad tracks where the river paralleled the rails, the river banks were covered with May apples. Some called them "May pops." Asheville still had a number of herb houses that paid good money for many kinds of herbs, and people roamed the mountains looking for certain weeds and plants they could dry and sell to the herb houses.

Maxie Ellenburg lived in a small house beside the river, and we went to his house often. Usually he fed us a glass of cornbread and milk before we went hunting for May apples. We didn't have far to go to find them, and when we did, we dug their roots. When we had a lot we spread them on the tin roof of the old man's barn and dried them.

When we had dried a tow sack full, we took the roots to Spinner's Herb House on Broadway and sold them for twenty-five cents. We always took our share of the money home to Mama for grocery money.

I dug ginsing to sell. One year we went to the Big Bald Mountain on Sandy Mush in northwestern Buncombe County and late in the day we found some pretty good ginsing. It was almost dark, and we were too hungry to make it home without eating. Besides, we didn't want to leave that ginsing to someone else. I had a .22 rifle and when I saw a squirrel I popped him out of the tree. We roasted the squirrel on a spit over an open fire and shared it for supper. Then we slept beside the fire and next morning gathered the ginsing and went home.

Another time, we were in the government forest behind the Biltmore Estate digging ginsing when darkness caught us. We built a fire and for some reason all of us—I don't remember who all was along—got scared of the screech owls hollering. They sounded like lions and tigers, and bears, and especially like panthers. So we built the fire bigger and huddled together and sweated it out till morning.

I wouldn't take anything for growing up in that way of life. We made do, and we survived without frills and extravagances. I think people would be better off today if more had to grow up the way we did.

We found it embarrassing to talk about charity. We never gave a thought to living off the government. Our parents taught us to believe that if a man didn't work, he didn't eat. If one was sick, the story was different; people helped each other. Otherwise, we supported ourselves.

Today people live in central heat, air conditioning, and wall-to-wall carpet. We had those things, too; or, at least, similar things. We had a fireplace and it was situated central to the house; we had cracks in the walls that let in all the air-conditioning we wanted; and sometimes we lived in wall-to-wall mud. Our houses were usually made of logs or clapboard on the outside. There was seldom a ceiling inside, just two-by-fours overhead. Often we could look outside through the cracks in the walls. We papered the walls with newspaper, plastering it on with homemade flour paste, and in the evenings when everyone gathered in for supper, we played games on the wallpaper.

Mealtime was something to behold at our house. With that many boys, our folks said it was just like trying to fill so many silos with legs. It's hard to fill a silo, but God gave our mother a lot of wisdom and knowledge of how to stretch food.

When we could, we raised chickens and hogs and cows and that helped us, but sometimes during the depression we didn't have much food. Mom learned to take a little bit of stuff and stretch it a long way.

We didn't have meals like we have today, never a large variety of food unless the garden had come in and we could have beans and potatoes and corn and stuff like that. Usually we had one major item: beans or potatoes, or, if we were lucky, beans *and* potatoes and corn bread.

We had homemade tables and benches and coal oil lamps. We scampered to the table and while waiting for Mom to get supper ready, we played games, finding words on the newspapers on the wall. Someone spotted a certain word somewhere on the wall and challenged the others to find it. We learned a lot of words while chasing others across the walls.

We could hardly wait for supper, not only because we were hungry, but because of the feeling there: I remember it well, that old wood stove going, the lamp burning, Mom busy with the food. It was so cozy there. After she served the meal and we ate, we lingered at the table to talk. It was dark outside but warm and bright inside with the lamp burning. Suddenly one of the smaller children would nod off to sleep at the table. My older brother Perry went to sleep one night and laid his head in the molasses plate.

Our home was like a circus, and yet it was a lovely place

for all of its lack of material things. Television hadn't been invented, and though we sometimes had an old radio, we didn't listen to it much. Electricity cost too much to waste on frivolities—when we had electrically-wired houses—so we usually entertained ourselves. Nobody tried to eat and watch the Lone Ranger at the same time.

We talked to each other, but we talked in low tones. Nobody shouted or screamed. That old mountain home brought a peace and discipline to us. We enjoyed living.

When we had a hog and hog-killing time came, that was a highlight of our year. We always looked forward to it. On hog-killing day, there were several preliminary chores. We built a large fire and put several big stones in it to heat. While some of us did this, others dug a slanted hole for a barrel, and still others carried water from the creek to fill the barrel. While Daddy killed the hog, we shoveled those hot stones into the water and it sounded like the World War when they hit the water—Crack! Pop!—and when the rocks got the water scalding hot we let that big old hog down in there, soaked him a bit, and hauled him out on a board. All of us then gathered around and scraped him. Then we hung him from a limb of a tree, or from a frame we built expressly for that purpose.

Talk about living! On hog-killing night, we had pork loins that were lip-smacking good. We kids made sausage with an old-fashioned, hand-turned sausage grinder. Kids who haven't gone through times like that have missed something. What joy!

We salted and stored hams and shoulders and middlings and ate pork all winter. Nobody had to coax us out of bed in the mornings. When we woke up Dad had a fire going in the fireplace, and Mom had the kitchen stove going. She didn't have to wake anybody with an alarm clock; the smell of ham frying in the pan brought us over the top of each other, scrambling to get to the kitchen. Mom had ham and red-eye gravy and those big cathead biscuits. Man! That was eating!

We kids slept together, the girls in one room, and the boys in two beds in another room. We slept three boys to the bed, two in ordinary positions and one across the foot of the bed. My lot was usually to sleep at the foot. In the winter there was no heat in our bedrooms and Lee and Perry, with whom I usually slept, pulled the cover off of me and Lee stuck his big feet in my face—and, Brother! if one of them happened to wet the bed, that was disaster!

There used to be a song called "Sleeping At The Foot Of The Bed." That was real to me.

At bedtime we stood around the fireplace warming ourselves. We didn't have jeans, we wore bibbed overalls, and you could tell how warm one was by the amount of steam rising from his overalls.

I remember standing before the fire warming one night before I went to bed, and when I was warm enough I made a dive for the bed. One of my brothers had found a three- or four-foot piece of hose, which he coiled up and placed in my bed. When I plunged into bed and touched that hose, I thought I was in bed with a snake. I came out of bed a lot faster than I went in—and my brothers and sisters laughed like hyenas.

Laughter like that meant a lot to families during those grim depression days.

Another Occasion with a capital O was bath time at our house. This always occurred on Saturday night, not Tuesday or Thursday, always on Saturday. Like most other people without plumbing, we bathed once a week. We carried water into the house, heated it on the stove, then poured it in a wash tub.

Mom worked on a first-come, first-served basis, and whoever got the last water got it mighty dingy. We all used the same water. Mom wasn't about to carry and heat two tubs of water.

We bathed on Saturday night because Mom was getting us ready for the Lord's Day. We moved a lot from place to place, because of the depression, always trying to improve our housing. Perry said, "Every time the wagon backs up, the chickens run and lie down and cross their legs. They know they're going to get tied up again." We moved from one old house to another, all over everywhere.

Whatever community we were in, and whatever church it had, that's the church we went to. When we lived way up in Dula Springs, we went to the old Presbyterian Church because it was handiest. Get our Saturday night bath, sleep well, and walk to church on Sunday morning. When we lived in Canton, we went to the Methodist Church because it was closest.

So we didn't grow up in any one church, just whatever church was handy—but back then we didn't have this awful conflict between the Methodists and Baptists and Presbyterians. They had union meetings in which all churches gathered together for one great revival. There was no feeling of separation. We didn't have the warfare among denominations that we have today.

My mother got us ready early Sunday morning and one of the older brothers or sisters took the younger kids to church. Once in a while my mother and dad went to church, but not often. They were from that old mountain stock, firm in their ways and solid in their convictions, and they seldom took time away from the myriad chores they had to perform to go to church.

The first time I remember going to church was when I was about four and lived on Beaverdam at the foot of Elk Mountain. My oldest sister brought me down to a little white Baptist Church at Lewis Memorial. We walked from the foot of the mountain to the church, a long way, especially for a four-year-old. I remember the sun shining through the windows of the church and hearing "Love Lifted Me." That was the first song I remember ever hearing.

Because of lack of money and transportation and distances involved, sickness and injury were handled differently during the depression. If we were injured, we had to be our own doctors, and medicine was where we found it. When we lived on Elk Mountain and I was four or five years old, Lee and I were in the cow barn and he had a butcher knife, cutting corn with it, but someway he ran that knife up under my knee and cut me. I still have the scar.

Today, they would rush me in an ambulance to the emergency room and hire surgeons to sew me up, but then my mother came running when Lee called frantically and carried me to the house and laid me on the front porch.

"Quickly," she said to Lee, "run in the house and get some soot out of the chimney."

Lee took one look at the blood—I was bleeding like a stuck pig—and fairly flew to the fireplace, scraping a handful of black soot which he rushed to Mom. She packed the soot on the cut and soon it checked the bleeding. Then she spread Cloverine salve over the wound and tied it up. I was immobile for a day or two, but then I went back to business as usual.

Sometimes she poured kerosene oil in cuts like that.

Mother used many of the same remedies that other mothers of that day used: asafetida, camphor, castor oil, mentholatum, and Cloverine salve.

The dictionary calls asafetida an "antispasmodic," which means its good for the spasms, but mothers thought it also warded off the flu, the common cold, whooping cough, the croup, and maybe a lot of other things. There is no question that it warded off people. Asafetida—we called it "asafidity"—was the most evil-smelling concoction known to man, or, more specifically, to little boys. It was a gum resin that came from the drugstore, and mothers made little sacks of white cloth, filled them with asafetida, and tied them around their children's necks in the winter.

I heard of two brothers being attacked point-blank by a skunk one morning, and when they walked into the school room, they smelled so bad that all the other kids crammed their noses into their asafetida bags for a better scent.

Camphor was used for bruises and cuts, and sometimes if we got sick and nauseated, Mother would rub it on our foreheads.

Castor oil was for constipation and colds, and the way Mom administered it I guess she thought it would heal broken bones and the mange and anything else that ailed us. When we saw Mom coming with the castor oil, running didn't help. She always caught us. That stuff was so gaggy I shudder when I think of it, thick and slick and foul-tasting. It seemed Mom could pour a tablespoon so full of castor oil it stood up in the spoon. I don't know how she did it, but she could wrap her leg around a child, manipulate that spoon, put her finger at the back of it, and scrape the spoon so hard with her finger that it took off the shine. She'd push that stuff in my mouth and then make me suck it off her finger, and finally she'd rub my goozle to make sure I swallowed it. There wasn't any trick to swallowing it if you didn't gag. It was so greasy that once you got it started, it slid right on down.

It tickles the fire out of me to think of it now, but it wasn't funny then.

In school we used to get samples of Cloverine salve, and some of the kids were so hungry they'd eat the stuff. As soon as the teacher passed out those little boxes of salve, some of the kids opened them and dug out the salve and ate it.

In the spring we gathered mullen and Mom made a tonic out of it, like tea. I believe it helped us. She'd make catnip tea. And sassafras root, boiled into a tea, made a good tonic.

I still believe those things had healing qualities. People my age are walking proof of it.

We were taught survival. We couldn't run to the hospital every whipstitch. When someone got hurt, we downed him, bound him up, and took care of him. It was as simple as that—most of the time.

We had fun. We cried a lot, but we also laughed a lot. When the war came and boys had to leave home, I think that's why they were so anxious to get back home: They were exceptionally close to their brothers and sisters and parents.

One of the members of our church, H. B. Buckner, survived the Bataan Death March in the Philippines at the start of World War II. He grew up in a Weaverville home that was sound in Christian principles and family love. One Sunday when I preached on Heaven, I got into the message to the part where I talked about things that will make you fight on and give you something to hold to, and I asked Mr. Buckner to come up front and testify. He told how he was forced to march across the Bataan peninsula and how his Japanese captors put several prisoners in a bunch and practiced bayonet drills on them. He said he saw many American boys killed in that manner.

I asked him, "What do you think keeps people steady in times of pressure like that?"

And he replied, "What kept me was my strong desire to come home."

Home life meant something to people then. When he was in the prison camp he said he stole rice from the Japanese and used it for bait to catch rats which he stealthily roasted over a tiny charcoal fire under the floorboards at night. He ate the rats to survive.

"I didn't think I could ever eat a rat," he said, "but when I thought of going home to Mama, I ate them."

That's what home used to mean to people. When I was away at school, I could hardly wait to get back home.

All of my childhood experiences were part of God's training program to prepare me for the ministry. I believe the reason many young men fail in the ministry today is that they aren't properly prepared. Some believe when they finish college that a big church will be waiting for them. They are not prepared to start with nothing.

My happiest childhood memories center around holidays: Christmas, Thanksgiving, Easter, and the Fourth of July. The Fourth was a patriotic time that taught us respect for our flag and country. We were all very patriotic in our family.

Thanksgiving was a big holiday that called for special food and giving special thanks, but it was big to kids because the Christmas season started for us at Thanksgiving. We were mountain folk and things were hard to come by, but if Mama got her hands on some sugar she started baking soon after Thanksgiving. She baked tea cakes, pumpkin pies, and fruit cakes. The air was filled with the wonderful smells of Christmas right on through the month.

There was singing everywhere, and it was wonderful. We had great fun singing Christmas carols as a family. The spirit of joy and anticipation was everywhere. We knew we wouldn't get worldly goods for Christmas, but still we couldn't wait. We lay in those old feather beds and straw ticks and could hardly sleep. We didn't expect to get new toys or bicycles, or even tricycles. We never did. I wanted a tricycle all my life and never got one. I told my congregation not long ago while preaching that I thought I still might get myself a tricycle.

When Christmas finally came, excitement almost overcame us. What an atmosphere! The songs, the anticipation, the family fellowship! We went to a little mountain church for the Christmas play. Those little churches didn't have much, but they managed to give treats to all the children. If I got an orange or a piece of candy, I was thrilled and excited.

Pop got us useful things for Christmas—like overalls. In those years you could buy a pair of overalls for thirty-five cents, and Pop managed to get enough to go around. I liked the ones with the big tag on the back that read "OSH-KOSH." I wouldn't let anyone take that tag off because I wanted everybody to know I had new overalls. I was proud of that tag.

Finding a Christmas tree was one of the joys of Christmas. We boys went to the woods to hunt a tree. Buying a Christmas tree was unheard of. We tramped through the fields until we found the "right" tree, and we cut it and took it home. Then we built a fire and made our own decorations, cutting them out of paper and pasting them together with flour paste. Today, people buy bags full of decorations and hang them on artificial trees. We didn't have the money, and nobody sold Christmas trees. People longed for affluency. After we finally got an old Gramophone and a few records, we played "Silent Night" at Christmastime, and thought we had moved up in the world.

Easter was also a great time. When we lived at Dula Springs near Weaverville, we rented a farm and paid the rent by sharecropping. We had two or three hundred white leghorn hens that were prolific egg-layers. We kids had to feed the chickens and take care of them. My mother always wondered why egg production dropped off as Easter neared. My older brothers, Paul, Perry, and Lee, hid an old-fashioned five-gallon milk can in the straw in the barn loft, and they slipped into the barn and took so many eggs a day and put them secretly in the milk can. On Easter Sunday morning they carried that can into the house and Mom suddenly knew why the hens hadn't been laying as many eggs. The milk can was full of eggs. We boiled them, dyed some, and ate the most. Boiled eggs were a treat.

Besides holidays, there were other special times in our lives.

The first radio I remember our family having was when we lived in Oakley and I was in about the third grade. We listened to the radio sparingly but got to stay up on Saturday night to hear the Grand Ole Opry. I really enjoyed that.

On occasion I remember my daddy saying, "Now, boys, let's get this corn laid by before the Fourth of July and I'll take you fishing." We worked like Trojans to lay that corn by, and sure enough, Daddy took us fishing on the Fourth of July.

Swimming was no problem. We didn't have access to swimming pools like children do today, so we made our own. We dammed up the creek to make it deep enough to swim. Then we went in wearing nothing but overalls. We hollered and jumped in, and the snakes and bullfrogs went one way and we went the other. Those were good times. We worked hard at home for the privilege of going swimming.

When I started to school in 1925, we lived in the Clyde Community in Haywood County. I remember my first school day vividly. My mother had made my overcoat and pinned it with a safety pin. I was so proud of it I wouldn't take it off.

My brother Paul had given Lee a French harp to take me to school. Lee led me over the old wooden bridge that crossed the Pigeon River, and when we got to the door of my classroom, he pushed me in and said, "Here he is," and left.

I was scared to death, but I had a kind teacher who soon settled all of us down. We studied together and learned to read and write, and school became fun in a strange sort of way. Like most boys, if I had had my way I probably wouldn't have gone—but I did enjoy it. After a time I got better acquainted and learned about Caldwell's Store at the end of the bridge. We crawled under the porch where chickens laid eggs, and we took the eggs and traded them to Mr. Caldwell for candy.

I soon became an expert on various schools. We moved so often I felt I knew more about schools than anyone else.

At Dula Springs we had a one-room school and in that room, one teacher taught about thirty-five kids who stretched over seven grades. We had a wood stove, and we boys had to cut wood and bring it to school to keep the building warm. Finally, a little coal room was added to the back of the school and the county furnished coal, which we had to carry in to keep the fire going.

In a corner of that schoolroom was a water cooler with a communal cup hanging on its side. We all drank out of that cup, and when one had a cold everybody caught it. The teacher usually designated a couple of boys to fill the cooler with water each morning, and one day the teacher kept hearing strange noises coming from that corner. When she finally opened the cooler, she found two bullfrogs in it. We had been drinking bullfrog water all day.

High school was fun too, but most of us were serious about learning. Basketball was big in Buncombe County then, and I played on the Emma High team. The game was a lot slower then than now; a high team score was in the twenties. I enjoyed basketball but didn't have the desire to pursue it beyond high school. I can see now in retrospect that God had other plans for my life than in the sports world. Ball playing and other sports were for fun then.

I was graduated from Emma High School in the Class of 1937. There were seventeen in our graduating class. S. O. Wilde was principal. I tied with Helen Muse, who is now Helen Brown, for the second highest scholastic standing in the class and we served the graduating class as co-salutatorians. Arnold Huffman finished number one and was valedictorian. Our graduation exercises were held in a little building at the entrance to Rhododendron Park. My dad spent six dollars for a secondhand suit for me to wear to graduation.

When the master of ceremonies asked the salutatorian to step forward that night, we had it prearranged and Helen and I both stepped forward, then faked an argument over who was the salutatorian. Finally, it was announced that we had tied.

We each received a gift, something special that was in keeping with our personalities. My gift was a little box of axle grease. I never could stand for my hair to be in my eyes and when playing ball or doing anything that jostled my hair, I kept brushing it back. A note attached to my axle grease read, "Maybe this will keep your hair in place—A whole box of axle grease."

It is true that we remember the little things in life.

When I finished high school, the end of the depression was in sight, but so was the start of another world war. Little by little, work began picking up. My dad was again in the cleaning and dyeing business and I know he must have been happy to be finished with sharecropping. Certainly he was happy to bring a weekly paycheck home. Mostly he worked in Asheville, but sometimes he had to go out of town to places like Marion and Valdese to work.

As the world changed, so did we.

## — 2 —

# Drafted by the Lord

My high school class was graduated in April of 1937. We only had eight months of school in a year back then. Four months later my life was turned around forever.

I had been a happy-go-lucky sort of an average boy through school. Nothing particularly special had happened to me. After graduation I got a job at Superior Cleaners on Broadway. I was not necessarily following my daddy's line of work; but that happened to be where Dad worked at the time, and he helped get me on.

I worked six days a week for a dollar a day, and my job included anything that needed doing, from firing the coal boiler to emptying pockets. I had to make sure there were no matches or anything else left in the pockets of garments to be cleaned. I did any job that was needed.

My boss was a kindly Jewish fellow named Jules Heyman. I liked working for him, though I had no notion of making the cleaning and dyeing business my life's work. But at that time I certainly didn't know what I wanted to do.

In August, Dr. William McBirney, an Irish evangelist, hauled a big tent into Asheville and set it up on the empty lots across College Street from Buncombe County Court House. In the tent he opened a revival meeting.

One evening, with my weekly pay in my pocket and plenty of groceries at home because Daddy and my older brother were both working for Mr. Heyman, I went uptown and sauntered up to the ticket booth of the Paramount Theater on College Street just a block away from Dr. McBirney's tent.

I bought a ticket and started in, but a strange thing happened when I went through the swinging doors into the theater. I felt something grab me by the coattail! It jerked so hard I turned to see who had grabbed me—but no one was there. I was the only person going to the show at that moment.

The incident frightened me I wondered what was happening, and I was so upset I left the theater without going on in. I walked down College Street, trying to gather my senses—and suddenly I saw that huge tent. Next thing I knew I was walking in the back of the tent. An end seat on the back row was vacant, so I sat down.

I knew nothing about tent meetings and very little about preaching and things of the church. But I remember that night well. This was one of the early meetings in a revival that lasted six weeks or more.

Dr. McBirney's message was on the soon coming of Christ and the return of the Jews to their homeland. When he began talking about Christ coming and the Jews going back to Israel, I remember wondering what would happen to me.

God worked in a mysterious way that evening. He instilled a thought in my mind: what would I do if Mr. Heyman went back to Israel and closed the cleaners where I worked? When he gets through preaching, I said to myself, I'll go ask him about the Jews going home.

When the service ended, I went to the platform on which Dr. McBirney stood. I started up the steps when he reached his hand down to me. Before I could say a word, he took me by the hand and asked, "Son, do you know Christ?"

I said, "No, sir," and before I could ask what I wanted to ask, he said, "Hold out your hand."

I put my hand out, and he laid a piece of chalk in it. He

had been using the chalk on a blackboard to illustrate his message.

"How did you get that piece of chalk?" he asked.

I looked at the chalk and then at him. "I received it from you," I said.

"That is the same way about Christ," he said kindly. "You have to receive him personally. Will you receive him?"

There it was, laid out before me—the greatest choice of my life.

But I didn't hesitate.

"Yes, sir!" I said. "I'll take Jesus!"

Another preacher stood beside us on the platform. Dr. McBirney beckoned to him. "Tell this preacher what has happened to you," he said to me.

But I was speechless by that time. I was so full of emotion it overcame me. I couldn't say a word to that preacher; so I just looked at him—and then I abruptly left the tent and went home. On the way, it appeared that the stars in the sky were playing leapfrog, and the trees along the way seemed to be clapping their hands and dancing. I had never experienced anything like that. I didn't know enough about spiritual matters to understand what had happened to me, but I knew something had.

When I reached home I was so excited I could hardly go to sleep. I awakened the next morning with a desire in my heart that everybody should be saved and feel what I was then feeling. I told my mother the Lord had saved me last night. I had been reared in a good, moral home with traditional mountain parents, but we were not a steady church-going family. Yet from the time God saved me I had a strong desire to go to church to witness and tell the world about Jesus's saving grace. Nothing else mattered.

My ignorance was so great that I thought any church would do, and I gave consideration to joining the Catholic Church. I thought everyone who went to church was saved. But the Lord directed me to the Gospel Tabernacle of the Missionary Alliance on South French Broad Avenue where one of my sisters went to church. Dr. Julian Bandy was the pastor, and the church had a great group of young people.

God helped Dr. Bandy, a wonderful minister, to establish me in spiritual truths. It was while attending the Gospel Tabernacle that my way became clear in my mind: I felt God was telling me that I should go on to school—to Bible School. Time is short, and I must prepare, I thought.

We lived on Pearson Drive at that time, a nice part of town about a half-mile from downtown Asheville. Even so, there was no way financially I could go to school. We were just emerging from the Depression and were about to enter a world war, though no one knew to what size the conflagration would grow. Most people at that time, however, thought the war would be a big one. Things for us, as for many other families, were still nip-and-tuck.

I believe our footsteps are guided and ordered of the Lord. I believe God directed me to attend the Gospel Tabernacle. I believe God wanted me to go to Bible School. There was such a desire in my heart that it was as the Apostle Paul said, "The love of Christ constraineth me." The love of Christ consumed me; it burned me with a fever—and, thank God, it still does.

I knew I must go on to school, but I didn't understand God's directions completely: I thought I had a desire to be a missionary. I had felt it even when I was in the third grade and read of Stanley and Livingstone.

I worked at the cleaners a while longer, and was so enthused and carried away with serving the Lord that I prayed, "God, whatever you want me to do, I will do."

I learned early in my Christian life—and it was a good and necessary lesson—that if you don't mean to do something, don't tell God you will. When I told him I would do anything he wanted, he spoke to me and said, "Son, there is no family praying in your home. No one says grace at the table. I have given you health and food to eat and you never stop to thank me for it. I want you to call your family to attention and say grace before meals."

I wondered, how will I ever do that? I thought of every way possible to squirm out of my promise to God, but every time I prayed, he said, "You told me you would do anything I asked and I have asked you to start saying grace at the table."

Still I put it off. I prayed and prayed to myself, and each time the family ate I felt more condemned all the time. My joy began to fade. I had promised God that whatever he showed me to do, I would do—but this? This was too hard. To pray before my whole family—Mom and Dad and all my brothers and sisters! That was too much. They would think I had lost my mind. They were already whispering about me and saying I was acting strangely.

Finally, I became so desperate I had to do something, and I knew what I had to do was follow what God told me to do. I put him off another day. I told God if he would let me live till the next day's noon meal, when everybody came in from work to eat, I would call them to attention and ask them to bow their heads. "I'll say grace, Lord," I vowed.

The next day, here they came—the whole bunch. They piled in, sat down, grabbed their forks and began to eat. They didn't give me time to say anything, and I felt as if I were sinking. I couldn't get up the nerve. I just couldn't do it!

I was about to leave the table when a voice said, "You promised to obey me at any cost."

I don't know how I did it, but I just blurted out, "Wait a minute!"

Everybody paused and looked at me, some with food suspended halfway to their mouths.

"Everybody bow your heads," I said. "I am going to pray."

I don't remember what I said, or how I ever said it; but I prayed, and nobody moved a muscle till I was finished.

I had obeyed God, and the greatest feeling of gladness overcame me. I didn't look up from my plate as I ate, and I felt eyes upon me through the meal. I am sure all my brothers and sisters glanced at me occasionally to see if I was all right.

The strangest thing happened after that. My brothers and sisters still rushed to the table, but they wouldn't grab the food. Silently they waited for me to say grace. I felt so good I thought the world had rolled off me. I had obeyed God!

Soon God said, "You told me you would obey me. Now, son, not only did this family not say grace before meals, but there is no family altar in the home."

"How can I do that?" I asked. Saying grace at the noon table was one thing, but calling everybody together for a service—no matter how short—was something else. And that's what it amounted to, a service.

I tried for days to reason with God. After all, I had said grace. How much could he expect of me? How much could he demand of me?

Reasoning didn't work, however; and soon I promised, "All right, God, I'll do it tonight."

But when night came, I began to squirm again. We all sat around in the living room. The only entertainment we had was an old radio, but mostly we read or talked among ourselves. I sat in a corner, Bible in my lap, praying, "Help me, Lord; help me, Lord"—over and over I prayed for help.

When my brothers and sisters began to leave the room and go to bed, I tried to speak but couldn't. Finally Mom and Dad went on to bed and left me alone.

"Oh, I've lied to you, God," I cried. "I don't want to lie to you, Lord; help me!"

"It still isn't too late," God said. "You can go upstairs. They're all up there."

"God help me," I said to myself. "I don't want to go through this again—putting God off, making a vow to him and not doing it." I jumped to my feet and pounded up the stairs. I ran into Dad's bedroom while he was taking off his clothes, standing there in his long-handled underwear. He looked so funny, but to him I'm sure I looked even funnier.

"What do you want?" he asked.

"Daddy, I want to pray," I said.

I didn't give him time to say yea, nay, or why. I fell down and prayed like the woods were on fire. I said "Amen!!" with an extra exclamation point and tore out of the room and went back downstairs.

We didn't get around to a regular daily family altar, but we had it occasionally, and it was never a hard thing for me to do after that. Once you obey God, he moves on other people who are involved, and it becomes easier to obey him.

Lee was two year older than I, and he wasn't saved. Every time I said grace at the table or prayed at our occasional family altar, I called Lee's name and said, "Lord, don't let him eat, drink, or sleep till he gets saved," and I knew Lee wished I would eat somewhere else. But God put Lee under conviction and he, too, was saved before 1937 ended. He found God in a revival run by Dr. Mordecai Ham, the revivalist in whose Charlotte meeting Billy Graham had been saved in 1934. Later Lee and I worked together in the ministry, and Lee always said it was the prayers I had said over him that led him to conviction and salvation. I am proud of that.

Most of my people and a lot of others thought I had gone overboard and become a religious fanatic. I had a tremendous desire to go to school and learn more about the Lord and more about life. Everyone thought I was crazy to want to go to school so badly when I knew there was no money for schooling.

The desire to serve God burned in my bones. That's why people thought I had jumped into the deep end of the pool. I did not yet feel a call to preach, but I knew I wanted to be a witness for Christ. I still wanted to me a missionary.

Without money, or even the promise of money, I enrolled in the Bible School in Toccoa, Georgia, in the fall of 1937.

In September, when time came to go to school, I still didn't have the money. The Young People's Class at Gospel Tabernacle made up twelve dollars and gave it to me. Dr. Bandy said the church would try to help me some, but it could not pay for my schooling. I knew there was a way, though; I knew I could work my way through school. I believed God would allow me to do that.

On the morning I was to leave, Lee drove me to the bus station. I was up and packed and ready to go at six o'clock. Lee came in rubbing sleep from his eyes. "But you don't have the money to even go," he said. He thought there was really something wrong with me, to be going to catch a bus to go far away without any money. But he drove me to the station.

I wasn't so sure myself. I knew I couldn't go to school without even a down payment, but I had such a desire that I knew I must go. Boys and girls worked their way through college, and I would have to do that.

The bus went out through Sylva and Franklin and down into Georgia from there. Soon it came to Toccoa and I got off, took my bag and found the Bible School. I told them I didn't have any money but God wanted me to go to school and I was strong and willing to work.

"What have you got for me to do?" I asked the registrar.

Without hesitation, she asked, "Can you milk?"

When I was eight years old, my mother taught me to milk. She took me out in the field with a bucket and showed me how to milk a cow. When I thought I was through, she said, "You're not finished yet; you haven't got the strippings—and that's where the cream is." I have used this illustration many times in preaching, especially in taking up necessary offerings. When taking up an offering for a special project and needing a certain amount, if we didn't get it the first time we passed the plates, I would say that we would pass the plates again and get the strippings.

But learning to milk came in handy that day at Toccoa, and I can see the hand of God in it when my mother took me out and taught me to milk.

I told the registrar, "Yes, ma'am, I can milk."

"Then I believe we have something for you," she said.

The school owned eighteen cows. They were the school's milk supply for its students—and they had to be milked morning and night.

I was given the job of milking all those cows. A young man who lived near the school was hired to help me. We started in the mornings at 4:30. We had big carts with large milk cans on them, and we poured the milk into them. When all the cows were milked, I took the milk to the kitchen, strained it, and washed all the vessels in time to pass inspection before the students came in for breakfast at seven o'clock.

I had no time to waste in the mornings. The man who helped me just milked, then he set his buckets down and left the rest to me.

Getting up at four in the morning was one of the hardest battles of my life. The enemy would attack me over that and tell me, "Look at all these other kids. They're still asleep in bed, their parents pay their way and buy them cars, and they don't have to work."

I would answer, "Get thee behind me, Satan."

But he was persistent. "You say God called you?" he would ask. "Then why do you have to get up at four o'clock and work like you do?"

But the Lord used Satan's arguments as a goad to keep me going. In milking so early in the morning, I had a chance to pray while everyone was still asleep. My prayer life was greatly strengthened by those milk cows. I remember rolling that big cart toward the barn while singing "Nothing Between."

The young man showed up about the same time I did, and we herded all the cows into stalls and fed them. The barn was big and had cracks in the walls. In the cold winter months it was bitterly cold even inside the barn. I was a fast milker because Mother had taught me to milk with both hands, and my hands were strong. When we finished I took the milk to the kitchen and had it ready by 6:30. That's when the bell rang to awaken the campus, and the students came in for breakfast at seven.

After breakfast I had to go back to the barn and clean the stalls and spread sawdust before I went to class. The barn was inspected, too, and if it wasn't clean enough, or the sawdust wasn't evenly distributed, I was in trouble.

In the winter, the dormitory rooms were as cold as the barn. Icicles hung off all the buildings on cold, wet mornings.

R. G. LeTourneau had taken an interest in the school. He had donated some metal buildings and had them welded together. These were used as dorms. The only heating in them were wood-burning stoves at the ends of the hallways. Our rooms were so cold that on the coldest nights I slept in my work clothes. I'd put on my clothes and jacket, put my toboggan on my head, and go to bed praying I wouldn't freeze before four o'clock. For all the good those little stoves did, they might have hung lightning bugs by their tails to give us warmth. It was cold and uncomfortable—but we were all glad to get to go to school. We didn't complain about the cold; we joked about it. And that made a difference. If you have been touched of God, all those hard times become a joy.

I'd wrap up in all my clothes on those cold, cold mornings and head for the barn pushing the milk cart and the Devil would waylay me.

"Are you crazy?" he would ask. "You're a nut! Why don't you get out of here and go home where you belong? You can be the life of the party!"

But I laughed at him and kept going. The Lord gave me a wonderful deliverance in all of this. Since I could milk with both hands, I would set the bucket down and milk a tune. The milk squirting on the sides of the bucket made a wonderful tune, and I sang as I milked. . . . "Since Jesus came into my heart" . . . and I milked that tune. In a little while I would get blessed, and it looked like the cows all had religion and were swaying to the tune. The whole barn lit up and became a place of joy to me.

At one afternoon milking the devil decided to put a stop to my happiness. When I got to the barn, a man led an old red cow to me. The school had bought the cow from him. He said, "Son, here's another one for you." That evening, I had to milk her.

She had one horn broken off and had a mean look in her eye. When the man brought her to me, he had a set of "kickers" in his hand. The kickers were log chains with hooks on both ends. We'd hook them around the cow's legs so she couldn't lift a leg to kick.

"You better use these," he said. "She's a kicker."

I was already pushed for time and I thought I would make better time milking the others and leaving the old red cow for last.

When I got to her, I eyed her carefully, and she eyed me back. When we had each other sized up, I put the kickers on her and started to milk.

I hadn't pulled her three times until she went off like a bomb. She simply exploded at both ends. The kickers saved me from taking a good shot, but when she went up I knew she had to come down. I scrambled out of her way—and she landed with both back feet in the milk bucket. I struggled for several minutes before I got her out of the bucket, then I had to wash the bucket and start all over.

Just as I started milking her again, she cut another flip. This time she came down on my foot. I pushed her and she leaned on me. The harder I pushed the harder she leaned. All the time I thought my foot was broken.

"Oh, God, help me," I prayed, and suddenly I knew how to get her off my foot. I got her by the tail and pulled it away from me, and she stepped off my foot.

I was getting desperate. I couldn't leave the old cow unmilked; but time was running out, and I had to get the milk to the barn.

"Lord, help me," I prayed. "What can I do?"

I looked all around the barn for help. I saw all the cobwebs and the dust and the manure, and suddenly I looked up and there was a spike driven in the side of the wall. And at that moment, God spoke to me:

"Son, you haven't prayed enough about this."

I got off my milk stool and right there beside that kicking old cow I got on my knees and prayed. "Lord, you sent me here. You called me, and I'm doing my best to do what you told me to do. My job is to milk these cows and get the milk ready for the students—but I can't work miracles, Lord, and you can. So show me what to do."

I knew if God didn't work a miracle I'd never be able to milk that old cow—and the man who helped me wouldn't either. He was nowhere around at that moment when I needed him.

I put my hand on that cow and prayed, "God, in Jesus's name, take the kick out of this cow so I can milk her." Then I opened my eyes and looked up and the first thing I saw was the spike in the wall.

God said, "Hang the kickers on that nail."

I climbed up there and hung the kickers on the spike.

The devil joined the conversation. "You're a fool," he said. "If you touch that cow with no kickers on, she'll kill you."

But God said, "Put your bucket under her like you do with the other cows. Milk with both hands, by faith, in the name of Jesus."

I reached out and took that cow with both hands and milked the bucket full. As long as I was at Toccoa Bible School she never kicked another time when I milked her, and when I left the school almost two years later the kickers were still hanging on that spike.

I think so many times, if God can take the kick out of a cow, he can surely take it out of us.

At Toccoa we studied the regular courses of English and history and such, and studied deeply in the Bible. Those Bible courses helped me greatly. The professors there straightened me out on a lot of misconceptions I had about the Scriptures, and when I finished the school in the spring of 1939 I thought I had a pretty solid Bible background.

At Toccoa, I learned other things than studies. I learned how important it is to make restitution for wrongdoings.

While growing up I wasn't a Christian, and I did things that no one would be proud of. When I became a Christian, God blessed me with a joyful spirit. Salvation has always been a joyous, happy experience for me. I have always had the thrill of knowing I am saved and on my way to Heaven.

But there were things in my past. . . .

At Toccoa I often went to the woods to pray, down by the creek. God showed me from the beginning that if I didn't pray I couldn't make it. Stay in the Word, read the Word, and pray.

Before I was saved I worked for the Bingham Military Estate, setting out tobacco plants. Col. McKee was head of the estate. One evening I saw a group of baby turkeys running across the tobacco patch, and I caught one—actually I stole it—and took it home. Ed Burrell, a boyhood friend, and I laughed about the theft, as boys will. I put the baby turkey in a box and thought I would raise it, but after a few days it died.

I forgot all about the turkey until one evening when I prayed in the woods at Toccoa. I told the Lord how much I loved him and how I would go where he wanted me to go and be what he wanted me to be.

Suddenly, in my mind, I saw something in the distance flying toward me. As it got nearer, it got bigger. It kept coming and coming and coming and when I finally recognized it, it was that turkey I had stolen years before. But now it was as big as a B-29 with the landing gear down.

I got quiet and my spirits went down, down, down, just like the plug had been pulled out of my bathtub. All my joy disappeared when that turkey landed squarely on my shoulders.

"Now, son," God said to me, "you stole that turkey from the military estate, and you need to go back to that colonel and tell him what you did. Tell him you're sorry for it."

"But, God," I said, "they have the meanest dogs in the world on that estate."

"You promised you would do whatever I asked," God said. "Now, for my sake, you must go back and correct your wrong. Tell the man you took the turkey and offer to pay him."

"He'll put me in jail," I argued.

God ignored that. "If you are saved," he said, "then you're a new creature and you must straighten out the wrongs in your life."

I was saved, I was forgiven, but I know now that God wanted to teach me obedience.

That turkey continued to grow. It became heavier and heavier, and it sat on my shoulders constantly. When I prayed at night, it sat on my shoulders. When I went to bed, it sat on the bedpost, staring at me. When I got up at four to milk, the turkey was still there. He rode the milk cart to the barn, and while I milked, it strutted around glaring at me.

I felt I would die. My joy was gone, and I wondered what I could do?

God said, "I told you what you have to do."

"But, Lord," I argued again, "I can't go home. I don't have a way. Besides, who would milk these cows?"

The Lord ignored me.

Finally, I was desperate. I said, "Lord, if you'll give me grace and let me borrow a car and help me get home, I will go to the man and straighten it out."

The next thing I knew, I was driving a borrowed car into

Asheville. I was scared, and the devil rode in the front seat with me. "You're crazy," he said. "They'll arrest you and put you in jail."

I drove straight to the estate and pulled up in front of the big house. Here came the dogs, looking like they wanted to eat me alive. I stayed in the car till the colonel came out and called off the dogs. He came to the car, and I said, "Colonel, I have to talk to you."

I got out of the car and told him how the Lord had saved me and how I was in school at Toccoa. The words came in a rush, and he listened patiently.

"I was praying one evening," I said, "and God showed me how I had wronged you. I stole a baby turkey from you once, and I have come to settle with you. I took it home to raise, but it died after a few days. Now I have come to pay you for the turkey."

The colonel smiled and said, "Come in a minute."

He took me into the living room of his beautiful home and asked me to sit down. He called his whole family in and said to me, "Son, tell my family what the Lord has done for you."

He hoped my revelation would be a good lesson for his children; so I told the story again.

God later used all of this to his glory. While preaching in the open air in the West End of Asheville, we didn't have any musical instruments, and Col. McKee's sister, Mrs. Grinnan, sent a pump organ.

That wasn't the only time the Lord took hold of me and made me straighten out wrongs.

I once worked for Sam Hughes in Sam's Produce on Lexington Avenue. He had a store on a corner lot and paid me a dollar a day, six days a week, to deliver groceries on a bicycle. Food was inexpensive, and huge watermelons sold for fifty cents. One day I sold a watermelon and instead of putting the half-dollar in the till, I saw no one was looking and dropped the money in my pocket. "Nobody will ever know," I told myself smugly.

After I straightened out the turkey matter with the colonel, God brought that watermelon back into my life, much the same as he had returned the turkey to me. I saw the melon coming down through the air and thought it was the Goodyear blimp. Again, the joy drained from my soul.

"What about the watermelon?" God asked.

I tried to pray around it, over it, through it—I tried to get by it any way I could, but God blocked my way each time.

"Lord, I'll preach your word," I said.

"What about the watermelon?"

"I'll go into the mission field."

"What about the watermelon?"

I realized God really wanted me to make restitution. It was important to him, and important to me. Still I resisted. I sat at the dinner table with the other students and tried to be happy like them, and all I could see was that watermelon.

God arranged for me to get back home soon after that, and I went to see Sam Hughes. It was a dreary day and business wasn't good. We sat down, and I told him how I had sold the watermelon and kept the money and I had come to pay him back.

Instead of being angry, he looked rather thrilled.

"How about working for me today," he said.

We laughed, and I went to work, and at the end of the day he paid me four times what I had been worth to him. And from that day, he always had great respect for mine and Lee's ministry.

Zacchaeus made restitution. And Sexton made restitution. Restitution doesn't save a person—but it's good and acceptable evidence that the person has been saved.

With my head stuffed full of English and history and literature and all sorts of Biblical facts and ideas, I finished at Toccoa Bible School in the spring of 1939 and returned to Asheville. I was still thinking of becoming a missionary and all through that summer the feeling grew that I should have more schooling.

Our financial situation wasn't that much improved,

however, and I knew that further schooling would be difficult at best. I still attended the Gospel Tabernacle on South French Broad Avenue, and there I learned of the Missionary Training Institute in Nyack, New York. This was a school heavy on missionary studies; so I applied for admission and was accepted.

Here again I applied faith to the problem. I didn't have money to go to school, but I knew I would somehow get it if I had the courage to take these steps without it.

When the time came to go to New York, I had only enough money for my bus ticket. I went to the old bus station on Wall Street in downtown Asheville. The bus for New York left at four in the afternoon. I had my trunk with all my clothes and other belongings in it. I also had a lot of faith, and I thought the money for school would come providentially. I prayed that God would send it before four o'clock.

Yet when four o'clock came and the bus pulled out, bound for New York, I still stood there. The devil really jumped me then. He said, "You *are* a fool. They will tell this about you all over town. Here you stand with a bus ticket in your hand, supposed to be going to college, and you don't have enough money to enroll. You'll be a laughing stock."

As I watched the bus leave, I thought what will I do? As I started walking up College Street, God put a man on my heart. He said, "Son, go see Dr. B. B. Morgan." Dr. Morgan was a member of Gospel Tabernacle. "Go see him," God said, "and maybe you can catch the six o'clock bus to New York."

I ran to the Gennett Building where Dr. Morgan had his office. His nurse knew me, and I was breathless when I told her, "I've got to see Dr. Morgan." She must have thought I had emergency business because she took me in right away, ahead of the patients who waited in the waiting room.

Dr. Morgan sat at his desk.

"Dr. Morgan," I said, "God wants me to go to school, and I have my ticket, but . . ."

That was as far as I got. He pulled out his wallet and said, "How much do you need, Ralph?"

"Forty dollars," I told him. That much would get me enrolled.

He handed me two twenty-dollar bills and I flooded over with joy. After thanking him I ran back to the bus station, and when the six o'clock bus pulled out for New York, I was on it! I said, "Now, Satan, who is the fool?"

When I got to New York another strange thing happened to me. I had to go from Manhattan to Tarrytown, but the bus lines were all on strike. There I stood, a country kid in the middle of New York, hardly able to resist staring at all the tall buildings, and I didn't know how to get out of the city. Since I didn't know what to do and didn't want to waste time, I started handing out gospel tracts on Times Square. I talked to a few people and learned there was a train that went to Tarrytown. I found the station and took the train. Reaching Tarrytown, I had to take the ferry across the Hudson River to Nyack, and from the ferry port I had to pay my transportation to the Institute. I had to spend part of my enrollment money for that.

When I went to enroll, I didn't have enough money and they wouldn't let me register, but they gave me a room. I believe they knew I would get the little money I needed, or else they would make arrangements for me. Anyway, I said, "God sent me, and I'm going to stay."

I stayed two weeks without funds in that dormitory, slipping up in the attic to pray, and looking everywhere for money. After two weeks I began to get desperate, and soon I began to realize that I would have to go back home. But one morning the dean called and said, "Sexton, some money has come for you." I ran to his office and found that Dr. Bandy had sent some money. I grabbed it and ran to the registrar's office, but when the cashier counted my money I still lacked fifty cents. She looked at me and sadly shook her head.

I said, "It's only fifty cents."

"I'm sorry," she said, "I can't let you enroll without it."

I must have looked terrible, for a young fellow named Henry from Mount Airy, North Carolina, overheard our conversation and came over and said, "Here's fifty cents. Take it."

I thanked him and gave the half-dollar to the cashier, and she wrote out a receipt for me to take to the registrar.

"Praise God," I shouted, "I'm enrolled in college."

How blessed it was. Today it would be tough to try to get along like that, but then that was the way a lot of kids went to college. They didn't try to go unless they were serious and meant to make the most of it.

I remained at the Missionary Institute from September till Christmas, and during that time God taught me another thing about making restitution.

Before I was converted, I went fishing with my brother, Lee, and Ed Burrell down below the Craggy Dam on the French Broad River. This was in the depression, and as we walked down through the gorge below the dam, we passed several men fishing for supper on the riverbank.

We carried fishing poles and a tin can that supposedly contained our bait, but we had no bait. In Lee's pocket was a stick of dynamite, a cap, and a short fuse. We were very serious about our fishing that day. When we found a good spot out of sight of all the fishermen, Lee rigged the dynamite, Ed struck a match and lit the fuse, and Lee dropped the bomb in the river. We scurried up the bank like mountain goats, dropped behind big, protective rocks and waited.

The charge didn't go off. After a few minutes, we slowly came out of our hiding places and crept back to the river. We could see the dynamite lying in a backwater and Lee retrieved it and rigged another fuse.

This time we went a little farther down the river to a

point where the water flowed toward us in a curve. Ed lit the fuse again and threw the dynamite into a pool and before we could get to cover the charge went off with a head-splitting THUD!

I have never seen such a sight: fish swapped ends flying through the air, landing to flop a little and then lie still. Others rose to the surface of the river, belly up. The dynamite threw water out of the river onto us. I don't think I ever saw so many fish—big fish, little fish, water dogs, all kinds.

Ed and Lee jumped in the river and began throwing the fish out. I stuffed them in an old tow sack. We picked up all that sack would hold and started back up the gorge.

Those fellows were still fishing.

"Any luck?" one asked.

"Yeah," Lee answered, lugging the bulging sack. "We caught a bunch."

The fellow nodded, pulling at his pipe. "Figured," he said. "I heard you catch 'em."

At Nyack one evening I prayed, "Lord, search me. I don't want anything between my soul and you."

God said, "Remember when you dynamited the fish?"

"Uh Oh!" I said.

"That was wrong," God said. "If everybody fished that way, there would be no fish left."

"Lord, what must I do?" I asked in earnest.

"Write to the sheriff," God said, "and tell him that before you were converted you helped dynamite the river. Tell him straight, tell him you're sorry, and ask for forgiveness. Tell him you're willing to make it right."

I wrote the letter to Sheriff Lawrence Brown of Buncombe County. In later years I knew the sheriff well. He was always a friend to us, but he never mentioned that incident. What was thrilling to me was the joy and peace I had after making something like that right.

Youthful lusts got me into tight situations, and God got me out. There is a verse in Second Timothy, chapter two, verse twenty-two, that reads: "Flee also youthful lusts: but follow righteousness, faith, charity, peace, with them that call on the Lord out of a pure heart." What has kept me through the hard times of my life were prayer and staying in the Word of God.

While I was at Nyack, on August 31, 1939, Germany attacked Poland and the war in Europe began. America was drawn nearer to conflict, and one day the announcement was made that all young men had to register for a draft into the armed services. I remember a line of young men singing, "You're in the Army now. . . ." I signed up at the first call.

At Nyack I studied Bible courses and church administration, and I learned a lot there in a short time that helped me later in my ministry.

Meanwhile, my brother Lee and the Rev. Marion Wyatt continued a street ministry in the West End section of Asheville that we had begun the summer of 1938, and I was drawn back to it. I thought less and less of missionary work and more and more of working in that street ministry. Their ministry was in the open air, and they had borrowed seats from the Asheville baseball park for people to sit on. I felt a thrill when I thought of what Lee and Marion were doing.

I prayed constantly about what God would have me do, and suddenly I felt God was calling me to come back to the work in Asheville. That, I suppose, was my first sure feeling that God might be calling me to preach.

I told God that if it was his will for me to go back home, to let me win souls to him on the way. I left school in December and rode the bus back to Asheville. I prayed with a young man in the bus station in New York and he found the Lord. In Virginia two more men were saved in the bus station while we prayed.

All the way home, I saw people saved. I knew then that I was in God's will. That was an exhilarating experience.

Those were not the first conversions of my ministry,

oddly enough. God gave me souls even before I went to Toccoa.

And then at Toccoa, a fellow named Morgan got the courthouse for a revival and asked me to preach. I had just starting preaching, and I said, "Yes, sir, I will—the Lord willing."

But then I prayed, "God, if you've definitely called me to your work, save somebody this morning in that old courthouse. Put your approval on it, Lord."

When I preached and made the altar call, seventeen people gave their lives to God. Seventeen is the number of victory in the Bible.

I felt God put his approval on my saving souls that morning, and that has been my desire since.

# — 3 —

# West End

In 1937, at a prayer meeting in a home off Waynesville Avenue in West Asheville, North Carolina, I preached my first sermon. But my actual call to preach didn't come until 1939 after I returned from Nyack.

When I came home from Toccoa in the spring of 1939, Lee and I had fashioned a crude altar on the mountainside at a place called Mountain Meadows Inn. We went there to pray. My heart's desire, I thought, even after I returned from Nyack, was to go into mission work, but one day while praying at that mountain altar God told me he wanted me to do the work of an evangelist. As I prayed about it, he gave me a verse of Scripture, Exodus 4:12, which reads, "Now therefore go, and I will be with thy mouth, and teach thee what thou shalt say." I knew when I read that verse that my calling was settled: I was to preach as an evangelist. I never looked back. I never considered missions work again.

Our work in the West End of Asheville had actually begun while I was at Toccoa. Until I came back from Nyack, Lee conducted most of that work, and I helped him while I was at home.

Mostly we preached on street corners and on a vacant lot. We arranged with the City of Asheville to borrow seats from the baseball park, McCormick Field, and put them up on the lot. Then people gathered in the evenings for our services.

We managed to raise $100 and purchased a set of speakers from Montgomery Ward. They came complete with microphones and amplifiers. Without realizing it, we had taken the first solid step in our ministry by obtaining equipment. We both felt locked into the ministry at that point.

When we preached in West End, we used the speakers. We preached a lot from home to home, and doing that we usually didn't use the speakers. Frequently, people announced a prayer meeting in their home to their neighbors and invited us to preach. The houses filled and overflowed into the yards, and we had good times in those meetings. We made a lot of friends who remain faithful to our ministry to this day.

Our speakers were portable; so we carried them all over town. We could even hook them up in a car. *The Asheville Citizen* referred to us occasionally as the "roving evangelists," especially after several readers called to say they heard loud voices in the night and wondered where they came from. A reporter tracked us down and printed in the paper who we were and what we were doing. When the reporter found us, I was using the speakers and preaching on someone's front porch to a yardful of people.

Those speakers were a godsend. Not only did they carry our voices to the multitudes, so to speak, they also gave us confidence in our ministry. With them we could preach to a congregation unseen.

Actually, we didn't realize the power of that amplifier, nor the extent of our ministry until one summer evening when we unwittingly stirred up a sizeable portion of Asheville.

We had the speakers rigged up at a house on a bluff on the west side of the French Broad River. The bluff was an old rock quarry where Westgate Shopping Center was built later. The night was warm, the house was filled with people, and the overflow filled the lawn. Lee had placed the speakers in the yard facing the river.

Across the river from that spot, in places around Riverside Cemetery, lived a sizeable portion of Asheville's black population. We had no idea that the sound from the speakers carried all the way across the river, for at that point the river is wide. But the speakers were equipped with "drivers" and when atmospheric conditions were right you could hear them three miles away.

We learned what a commotion we had created when two police cars rolled into the yard and several policemen emerged, all of whom were stifling laughter.

"Boys," one of the officers said, "could you tone it down a little? You've got half of Asheville on the other side of the river thinking the dead have risen and are preaching and praying."

We learned later that a police car was summoned to the cemetery, but when the officer—apparently a God-fearing man—heard the preaching, which sounded like it was coming from the graveyard, he wouldn't go into the cemetery for anything. The only way they found us was through a State Highway Patrolman driving his Silver Bullet up Riverside Drive who picked up our sound on his radio and located us.

We had unusual experiences in the West End in those early days of our ministry. When Lee, and Marion Wyatt, and I began preaching there, we had only a vacant lot which was used mostly for sandlot baseball games. Ours was a poor ministry (in finances) to a poor people, and we were blessed so many times that it is impossible to recount them.

We ministered to the West End people the best we could with our limited resources. Lee and I often went up in the hills and prayed. We took time to commune with God, and there were places around West End where we could be alone with God.

We occasionally spotted poverty-stricken people who needed help, and we did what we could for them. Lee was big and strong as an ox. I remember once he carried a sack of coal on his back to a destitute woman who lived in a shack with her children. As Lee went up the hill toward her house, other children followed him. When he reached the house there were four kids with him.

Lee took the sack of coal inside the house to the woman, and three of the children went with him. The other stayed outside and in a few minutes, as Lee knelt down in the living room and prayed with the woman, the child outside began yelling, "Lee, c'mon! C'mon, Lee! Let's go, Lee."

That was distracting enough, but was nothing to what occurred inside. The woman had a little cross-eyed girl who knelt beside an old cat that lay beside the stove. When Lee began to pray, the cat began to howl, and the little girl slapped the cat so hard she killed it. Then she began to cry and scream, "Mama, old Pussy's dead! Mama, old Pussy's dead!"

In the midst of Lee's prayer, with the yelling outside and the crying inside, the mother began to laugh, and Lee, who had a great sense of humor, quickly finished the prayer, and he laughed, too.

Each Sunday evening we went to West End for services. When the Lord saved me, one way I knew I was a new creature was that I had a desire to see everybody else saved. From the beginning, I knew without doubt that Jesus died for the souls of men, and I felt a burden for the underdog, the deprived, and the lowly. I believe that's why God caused us to be raised poor. We didn't call ourselves poor; we just thought ours was a way of life. We accepted our lot without question and made the most of it. But in the ministry I felt a burden to minister to all others, regardless of their lot in life.

In West End we had plenty of opportunity. There were a lot of wonderful Christian people down there, but at the same time West End was a haven for bootleggers. Old Swifty King, for instance. I have seen his car sitting there many a time, and it was a sight to behold, the way he had modified it and souped it up.

We lived out on Hendersonville Road, and Lee and I had

to walk or hitchhike everywhere we went, unless we could borrow a car. We almost had to have transportation to haul those speakers around, and it was a glorious day when a West Asheville man named Carson James gave us our first car—a 1934 LaSalle. It had wooden spikes in the wheels and looked like an overgrown piano box, but it ran. We painted signs and slogans all over it, things like "The Wicked Shall Be Turned Into Hell And All Nations That Forget God," and "Jesus Is Coming Soon," and "Prepare to Meet Thy God."

When we were called to help with a funeral, we couldn't help but get tickled. The funeral procession would include a shiny black hearse, of course, and most of the cars following it were black and shiny—and we motored along closely behind looking like a rolling signboard. We had no trouble drawing attention!

On Sundays when we went to West End to preach, we usually mounted the speakers on the car and preached as we drove along. We had a 78-rpm turntable attached to the speakers and could play records. When we reached West End, we sometimes left the speakers on the car, and sometimes took them off and hung them in a tree.

That lot on West End seemed a perfectly good place to preach. When the Lord saved me, I just wanted to preach. I never thought churches should let me preach in them. I knew the Bible said to go into the highways and hedgerows, and I thought that was where I was supposed to preach. We preached a lot on Lexington Avenue in Asheville, and in other places around town. Asheville was crowded with people in those days, and we drew a crowd wherever we preached.

After Carson James gave us the car, we drove to Marshall, Burnsville, and other nearby towns to preach.

We didn't take a collection, but sometimes people gave us money. It was such a joy and thrill to be able to preach and have people listen that we didn't think of money.

People in the crowds were usually surprised at the

number of people who came forward and knelt down on the street curbs and were saved. Mountaineers were humble people. They told us straight out, "No, I am not saved, but I want to be," and they knelt in the street while we prayed with them.

One night, lying in bed at our home on Hendersonville Road, I saw something. I don't know if it was a vision, but I saw that corner lot in West End with seats on it and I saw us preaching. I was young and didn't really know what God was telling me, but I thought he wanted me to stay with the West End ministry and build it as large as we could.

The first thing we did was build a little platform at one end of the lot, big enough for us to stand on to preach and to place one of the speakers. The other speaker we continued to hang in a tree. We arranged to buy the lot for $250 and paid for it in small monthly payments, and a clause was placed in the deed that if the lot was ever used for anything but a church it would revert to the heirs of the original owner. That suited us just fine.

From the start of that ministry, God worked a miracle. The way people came in such numbers was miraculous to us. They often filled all the seats, sat in the aisles and around the back of the seats, and sometimes the crowd spilled off the lot and the overflow sat across the road.

Not any of the streets in West End were paved; they were hard-packed dirt, and all through the summers of 1939 and 1940 as we preached we saw police cars, those long touring cars, cruising by. The officers who drove them looked us over and studied the crowd, no doubt searching for wanted bootleggers. The police cars had big contraptions like hay rakes attached to their fronts. Those were clamps used in chasing bootleggers. They tried to steer in close behind the liquor car and drop the hook to clamp the car's rear bumper.

But we had different ideas for the bootleggers of the West End. We wanted to see them saved by the grace of

God, and we saw a lot of them come to the throne on that dusty old lot.

Some people who knew us may have worried about our working in West End, which had the reputation of being the roughest section of town, and with all the bootleggers down there, people may have thought we were in danger.

But we never felt the slightest danger. Those were great people. There was an amount of danger in our tasks, however, but it came from different sources.

Lee and I passed out a lot of gospel tracts. We went uptown one night to pass out tracts, walked up College Street handing tracts to all the people we met, then turned down Broadway. Lee crossed to the east side of the street and worked down from the Langren Hotel. I walked along the west side, heading north. Halfway down, a fellow came out of a business and without saying a word hit me behind the right ear so hard it shot a knot up there the size of a hen egg. When I turned and looked at him, I knew at that moment that God had indeed saved me. A love for that man filled my heart and I wanted to get him in my arms and pray with him. If God hadn't saved me, I'd have wanted to beat the devil out of him.

He wasn't finished with me, however. He grabbed me and meant to finish me off; but at that moment a little fellow appeared, and he hit that man so hard he cleared the sidewalk and fell in some garbage cans in an alleyway. Some fellows ran out and pulled him back in the building, and I turned around to speak to the little man who had helped me—but he was gone. The attack happened so quickly that before Lee could get across the street, the man had already knocked the soup out of the fellow who attacked me and was gone.

Some men came by on a garbage wagon and when they found what had happened they wanted to go in and clean the place out where my assailant had been taken, but we talked them out of it.

I thought I knew the man who helped me. I told Lee, "I

think it was an insurance man I know by the name of Taylor," but when I went to him and asked, he said, "No, preacher, it wasn't me."

The man had appeared and disappeared. When I thought about it I remembered that in God's Word it says, "The angels of God never leave you." From the moment you're converted they never leave you. And all my life I have thought that God sent an angel to help me that night. I couldn't have handled that man alone.

Over the years that has been true. We've had men draw knives and threaten us in many ways, but God has protected us. I firmly believe there is a ministry of guardian angels.

When I started my ministry I was young and certainly inexperienced. I didn't know anything about preaching; I didn't know how to preach. All I knew was that God had called me to preach his Word, and there was no doubt in my mind that the Book was the Word of God.

When I preached, I took a chapter and preached it verse by verse. If the chapter had sixty-five verses, I preached them all. And if I took three or four minutes for every verse, the people stayed with me till I finished. Sometimes I would still be preaching at ten o'clock and the people would be right there.

A lot of those West End people worked in the cotton mill and had to get up at five in the morning, but if our service went till eleven, they stuck it out. They knew the whistle at the cotton mill would wake them at five. It blew every morning at that time.

I was really thrilled when I found in the Bible that Jesus was coming back soon. When I preached on the second coming, I had the best time. I have preached that the Lord is coming all my life, and I still preach it today.

Two of the bootleggers from West End, Bill McKinney and Noah Radford, came to our meetings almost every time we preached. They wouldn't sit in the chairs where they could be easily seen. They sat across the road, back in the rear of the people, and if they saw police cars cruising through, they simply melted from sight until the cars were gone.

For several meetings I preached on the second coming, and I bore down on it pretty hard. I knew Noah was back there in the dark, and I figured Bill McKinney was probably with him. One night I preached on the second coming and emphasized that the trumpet would sound at any moment. I guess I hammered on that point—the trumpet—till I got it planted in everybody's minds.

Bill McKinney's wife told me that the next morning when the whistle blew at the cotton mill at five o'clock that Bill leaped out of bed and shouted, "Oh, God, the Lord has come—and I'm not saved!" The next time we met, Bill came forward and gave his life to Christ.

Not long after that, God put a hook in Noah Radford's jaw and led him forward to confess his sins at our altar. He went home and poured out all the whiskey he had and told his children that he had gotten saved and they would henceforth live on what they could earn by the sweat of their brows. The Lord always provided for Noah and his family.

When meal time came, Noah told his children to bow their heads. "I don't know much about praying," he said, "but we're going to thank God for this food."

Noah prayed over those beans and bread and one of his little boys told him afterward, "Daddy, the beans tasted better."

We had glorious conversions of that kind in those days. Lives were really changed. I long to see more old-fashioned revivals of that sort today—revivals in which men and women really turn their lives around, and everyone who knows them can tell it.

Noah Radford was one of the most humble men I ever met. He was a good man, good to his family, and I believe that both he and Bill McKinney died in the faith. I preached both of their funerals a few years ago.

## — 4 —

# Building a Tabernacle

One of the reasons I left the institute in Nyack was that God was telling me to go back home and help build some kind of church in West End. He wanted us to build a permanent place of worship on that corner lot.

We had a great need for more permanency. One evening we were going down the street toward West End and someone stopped us at the corner of Clingman and Patton Avenue and said the city had taken the seats from our lot back to town to put them up for a dance.

"There's nothing to sit on down at the lot," the fellow said.

We went on down and put up our speakers at the lot and then we announced over the speakers that the city had taken back the seats but we intended to have services anyway. We asked that people bring something to sit on.

After while, people began to come off those hills, all carrying folding chairs or something to sit on. One fellow brought two nail kegs. Another took a pickup truck and borrowed some seats from a mission on Hendersonville Road. And we went right on with our service. The next day the city brought the ball park seats back to us and we used them until the baseball season started again.

But every time the city needed seats, it took the ones we were using. So one night I told the people, "Let us trust in God and build our own seats. Let us build a church."

A man named Rabbit Taylor who worked at the city incinerator was there that evening. He had told me that he often found the bodies of newborn babies thrown away in shoe boxes or jars at the incinerator. "Preacher," he said, "I just couldn't stand to see them thrown away like that, burned in the incinerator." So there on the bank by the side of the incinerator, he had made his own little cemetery.

On that evening when I mentioned building our own place, Mr. Taylor came forward and said, "Here is a dollar to start the fund."

Someone had a hat and began passing it around and people put what they could afford in the hat. Several dollars were contributed, which we took the next day to Harper's Lumber Yard and when we told Mr. Harper what we wanted, he waved to his stacks of lumber and said, "Take what you need and pay me when you can."

For thirty dollars we bought enough lumber to build fifty benches—and that, along with the platform we had previously built, was the start of our church building in West End.

We already had the plans drawn for a church building. When I was at Nyack, I got a postcard from Lee one day, and on it were the words, "This is the plan:" and under that were drawings for a church building.

Those are the only plans we ever had—on a penny postcard. But that's all God really needs. He knew we were sincere, and that's all he needed. He made a way for us to build what we needed.

On our lot, we drove up stakes at the points where Lee had indicated on that post card that the rock pillars would be in the corners of the building. Tom Worley, a son-in-law of the old mountain preacher, Fate Mc Elreath, had a sawmill at Leicester in which he sawed out green white oak lumber for us. When it dried out, it warped in every direction, but it was all we had, and we made do with it.

Riley Candler, who owned Wright Trucking Company, let us have his truck free of charge to haul stone. He even furnished the gas. Down on the river below the lot on which we were building the mission was an old rock quarry. It was a favorite hang out for some of the town's drinking boys. Lee went to the quarry and made friends with some of the drinkers and when he went back to get a load of rock, they loaded the truck for him. He drove it to the lot, we unloaded it, and he drove back to the quarry where the drinkers loaded up the truck again.

The Rev. Lucius Rumbough, who lived in Weaverville, was a rock mason. He volunteered to lay the stone foundation for us. Lee helped him. Tools were scarce, and Lee used his hand for a trowel. They built the foundation and also a stone pulpit, and when the rock work was finished, we went to work on the lumber.

We nailed the arches together on the ground and swung them up with a rope.

The war was at hand and materials were short. We had no money to buy things with, anyway, so it didn't matter.

We began building at the end of 1939 and held our first service in the building on the first Sunday in June, 1940. The building wasn't finished then, but we couldn't wait. We had no doors or windows in it, and the floor wasn't poured; it was just hard-packed dirt over which we spread sawdust and shavings. All we had was the hull of a building, but it was enough.

We learned then that at an old cafe across the road, men were betting on whether we would get the building up, and when the walls went up they bet on whether we could roof it. We wanted a metal roof, but we couldn't afford the scarce material.

We prayed for material. People called us crazy for building at that time, but God had told us to and we believed he would supply. We didn't know how, but we kept building.

The boys at the cafe told us we couldn't get a roof on that building in any way, and I remember Lee laughing and saying, "Fellows, God owns the cattle on a thousand hills, and if nothing else we'll kill cows and skin them and cover this building with cow hides.

Someone told us that the man who operated Sprinkle's Coal, Feed and Seed Company in Marshall had some metal roofing stored in a warehouse, and we might be able to get some from him. We drove Riley Candler's truck to Marshall and talked with Mr. Sprinkle, and when we told him our story he took us to the warehouse where he had stacks of metal roofing.

"Load up what you need, boys," he said.

We put the roofing aboard the truck, paid him a nominal price, and drove back to Asheville. When we backed that truck on the lot, talk about shouting and praising God! People really cut loose.

There was our roof.

When we got that roof on, I preached the next meeting from First Samuel 17:47, which reads, "And all this assembly shall know that the Lord saveth not with sword and spear, for the battle is the Lord's and he will give you into our hands."

From that time, work progressed steadily until the building was finished. Even then, our battles were not finished. People had watched this miracle in progress, and when it was completed, they came slowly forward, knowing we were just boy preachers, young and inexperienced.

One man came to us and said, "Now that you have the building up, I think we should establish a pulpit committee." We smelled a takeover in progress; so we told him no thanks.

God gave us wisdom.

A fellow came to Lee another day and said, "Lee, God told me to come down here and preach. When can I start?"

Lee said, "Well, God hasn't said anything to me about it."

We did have a lot of visiting preachers at the West End Mission. Among those who preached there were Mordecai

Ham, J. Harold Smith, Sergeant Alvin C. York, and many local preachers.

Some of them were not accustomed to facing the sort of audiences that came to the mission.

I remember one long, lanky preacher. I don't recall his name, but that's unimportant. He did not know that when some of the West End people began drinking they got religious.

This fellow was preaching in a big way, and a fellow about halfway back in the house who had had too much to drink began preaching back at the preacher. Every now and then, the drunk stood up and said a few words and shook his finger at the preacher.

I could tell the preacher was aggravated by the drunk, and after the drunk rose and preached for the third time, the preacher stopped his sermon, rolled up his right sleeve, and shook his finger at the drunk.

"You drunk," he said. "I'm apreachin' here, and I'm agoin' to give you one of three choices. Either sit down and shut up, get up and get out, or I'm acomin' back there and stick this fist so far down your goozle it'll take a major operation to get it out."

The drunk rose shakily to his feet, and steadying himself on the benches, lurched out the back door.

Then the preacher rolled down his sleeve, looked about the audience to see if anyone else wanted to preach, and finished his sermon.

People came to that church in droves. They filled the building, and we had to seat the overflow in the yard to handle the bigger crowds.

We named the building the "Jesus Saves Mission."

The spirit of revival was on us. The fear of God was still strong in America. When I began my tent ministry, I could pitch it anywhere and people came and there was much conviction on the people. Once when I pitched the tent on Allen's Creek in Hazelwood, the conviction was so strong I couldn't preach for three nights. People wanted to be saved. As soon as the service started, they came to the altar, fell on their knees, and prayed to be saved. People were anxious for salvation.

Now I fear the spirit of revival and conviction is leaving the land. That's why I am frightened for us. We're in trouble unless conviction returns to our land.

At our little mission, services were like a continuing camp meeting. People came from far and near. We had three services a day on Sunday—Sunday School and morning worship, then afternoon service at three o'clock, and back at seven thirty for an evening service. The building would be filled for almost every service.

We brought in people to sing, and things like that, but God never let us have anything like entertainment. We were serious about how we conducted our services. We emphasized preaching the Word and built a congregation on that. We stayed in the Word and stayed with the authorized King James Version of the Bible. That is still my ministry today: Stay with the Word. I believe God is sovereign. He gave the Word and he is able to preserve the Word.

# — 5 —

# The Holy Ghost

Soon after I surrendered my life to Christ, I began to hear this truth; that after we are saved it is God's will that we be filled with the Holy Spirit. Dr. Bandy preached this at the Christian Missionary Alliance Church where I attended.

This is not heresy or a new doctrine; it is a command of God. He says in Ephesians to be not drunk with wine wherein is excess but be filled with the Spirit. That is a command. It is not optional. He was talking to the church. We are baptized by the Holy Ghost into Christ when we are saved. But there is that crisis feeling that most of the church world never hears about. That's why some Christian lives are so mundane and drab. Some spend their whole Christian life in the energies of the flesh. They work with their training, with their education only—and it won't work. You must work with more than that. You must work with the Spirit.

Even after God saved me, I was hungry. I kept praying, and I thought, "I know I'm saved, but I feel a hungering." Then I began to hear that the believer should be filled with the Spirit.

When I read the Word, I found it in there.

As a young Christian I had battles with things of the world, and I realized I needed help to live the Christian life. I needed unction, anointing, strength, and power that I didn't have. Early in my Christian life, when I went to church, I thought, "Now, I'm really going to enjoy this," but the enemy jumped me and covered me with a barrage of wrong and evil thoughts, and I sat there and prayed and fought against those evil powers until the service was over.

The devil kicked me around like a football.

"There has to be a victory," I thought. I felt like Paul in Romans when he said, "Who will deliver me from this body of death?" I became so hungry I thought there has to be relief.

Some people advised me, "Just settle down. Don't be too religious." But my heart was hungry and I wasn't satisfied. That crowd wanted to feed me with an eye-dropper, and I knew there was more than that. I knew God had said, "There is a river, the streams whereof shall make glad the City of God." I knew there was more than an eye-dropper and a teaspoonful.

I believe that when God saves you there is an abundant life. Jesus said he came to give life and give it more abundantly. I knew I wanted the abundance of Christ, and I kept praying and became so hungry to be filled with the Spirit I dreamed about it. I dreamed that I was in a meeting and God filled me with the Spirit.

Cal Goodlake, a member of the Wesleyan Church, became a pillar to me. He had a sweet spirit and would talk to me and say, "Yes, son, there is the filling of the Spirit." He had a lot of wisdom, and where some cautioned about fanaticism and wildfire and seeking experiences, Goodlake encouraged me to seek the Spirit.

In Luke, the Scripture says, "If our earthly fathers being evil know how to give us good gifts, how much more will our heavenly father give the Holy Ghost to them that ask him."

I was tired of going to church and trying to enjoy the services. I wanted more than that.

One day four of us—Troy Israel, a Baptist preacher friend; a Methodist preacher; and another man who was a layman; and I—went to the woods to pray. We went outside of Asheville toward Woodfin, which is down the river, and there we scattered away from each other in the woods.

I prayed and to the best of my ability poured out my heart to God. I told him I was tired of being halfhearted and defeated and up and down, and that I wanted to be filled with the Spirit.

After praying that, I got up and walked down through the woods. I looked up through the trees and I remember a still small voice saying, "Son, the work is done."

God cannot lie. He tells us if we ask we will receive. Some people think you have to have a great experience or a tremendous emotional experience to be baptized in the Holy Ghost.

But God simply said, "The work is done."

It seemed as if God had cut off the south end of heaven and dropped it in my soul. The glory of God came and God filled me with his Spirit. When I came to myself I was away up on top of a hill praising God and rejoicing because God had filled me with the Spirit.

From that day to this, the mighty presence of God has been in my heart to guide me. The battles have been fierce and trials have been sore, but in it all he knows the way through the wilderness, and he has never left me.

It has always thrilled me to hear of people being filled with the Spirit. One such fellow we called "Believing Thomas" came here in the forties, driving a 1929 A-Model Ford. On the back of his car, he had written, "Believing Thomas in Your Town, Preaching Jesus Christ, a Mystery to the World and a Puzzle to the Devil." He told me how he was filled with the Spirit. I knew when someone was filled with the Spirit that he was more than the everyday one-two-three Christian, and that God would use him.

He told me he had been saved while serving a term in the Atlanta Federal Penitentiary, and he talked of how hungry he was to be filled with the Spirit. He said he was in a home prayer meeting one night, praying for the Spirit to descend on him, and he said he suddenly felt so blessed that he jumped up and ran through the screen door, taking door and all right out in the yard with him. He ran on down the hillside praising God.

Another fellow who was a blessing to me was a little Dutchman named Dirk. He used to come to Asheville and sit on the park benches in Pritchard Park. He was one of the most joyful men I ever met.

When I was around people like Dirk, I knew they were different. This kind of man did not try to exalt himself or try to bring attention to himself. He rejoiced in the Lord.

I remember Dirk sitting on that park bench across Patton Avenue from the S&W Cafeteria. He had a metal whistle from a box of Crackerjacks which he could hide in his mouth and whistle tunes through it. As people came to the S&W and left it, he whistled tunes like "Amazing Grace," "How Firm A Foundation," and "There Is A Fountain," and people could hear him but couldn't tell where the music was coming from.

He sat there and whistled until he got so blessed he started shaking and had to take the whistle out of his mouth to keep from swallowing it.

Dirk lived in Pennsylvania. He said he knew he was saved but was hungry for the fullness of the Spirit. He began to pray. As he prayed he surrendered his all to Christ, and he patiently waited, knowing that in God's time God would fill him with the Spirit.

One day, he said, he was walking down a street in a strange community when suddenly God came on him and filled him with the Spirit. He was so excited, thrilled, and blessed that he began to turn around and around. The anointing of God was so great that he started to run. He ran up and down the street but couldn't run the feeling off. Instead, the feeling became greater and greater, until finally he ran up some steps, into a strange house, and sat down in the living room floor.

He sat there with his hands up, saying, "Glory, Glory,

Glory!" when the lady of the home stuck her head around the corner of the door and said, "Shout on, Brother! I know what has happened!"

God had sent him into a home where a woman who was Spirit-filled would understand.

Today the problem is people are saved but they have never surrendered to God and have never been filled with the Spirit.

There is a Spirit-filled life; and I have found over the years if it had not been for the fullness of the Spirit, I couldn't have made it through.

## — 6 —

# Jailbirds for Jesus

In 1940 Lee and I were fledglings in the matter of gospel preaching. We had our work at the Mission in West End, but we were young and strong and felt we should do more to further the word of God. I don't know that we went out of our way looking for something to do, but if opportunity knocked, we certainly answered.

Some people in Madison County who had heard me preach called and asked if I would pastor a little church for them. They called it the Sexton Church. It was on the way to Marshall, located way back in the mountains.

I accepted their call and pastored this church for a while, and it was an experience. Things there were a little more primitive than they were in our West End Mission. This was a tiny church with lamps hanging on the walls, no piano, but a Mr. Roberts led the singing with a tuning fork. He would strike that fork on the back of a bench and hum until he got the pitch right. The people would hum with him, and when they had the pitch they would burst into song. It was beautiful. There was such a warmth and closeness among them.

Mountain people are a suspicious lot. A stranger has to prove himself before they will cotton to him. It took a while to gain acceptance by that congregation, but after a few weeks of working closely with them, they began to open up.

I didn't pastor the church long. The strain of communicating that distance was too great, and it took a lot of time away from our work in the West End; so I resigned the church and came back home.

I still felt I wasn't reaching enough people. God called me to evangelize, not to pastor—not at that time. I wanted to reach the masses, and the way to do that then was through radio.

I went on the air for the first time in 1940 on WNCA. The station was in the old Langren Hotel just off Pack Square in the center of Asheville. We were close to war then, and I felt a burden for the young men of the country, and I preached to them as much as possible.

That was my start in electronic evangelization. Through the war years I expanded that ministry greatly.

I still concentrated on face-to-face encounters with people and with the devil. God said to go into the highways and hedges and witness, and we did. We didn't wait for churches to call us to preach. God gave me the burden to preach, and I went out into the streets and preached wherever I was.

Street preaching is not an easy ministry. It is not today, and it was not in 1940. But people accepted street preachers more readily then.

The streets were always filled with people. Downtown was a busy place. Today, at ten in the morning, you could shoot a shotgun up Patton Avenue in downtown Asheville and not hit a soul. Not so then. Patton Avenue was a busy place, always crowded with people. Lexington Avenue was a beehive. All the country people came to Lexington Avenue. At one time the street was called "Mule Alley," so many farmers tied their mules to the street's hitching rails then.

Being just a boy, not yet twenty-one years old, to go to Lexington Avenue and preach was a tough assignment, but I took it on myself, and the Lord showed me what to do. I would borrow a crate from one of the produce stands, mount it and start preaching, and soon a crowd would gather. Brother! When we all got in the Spirit, things happened!

Getting the sermon started was the hardest part. I have often wondered if the Apostle Paul ever had trouble that way. He, too, loved to preach in the market place. Markets are the crossroads of any area.

When I approached Lexington Avenue, I faced a natural fear of wondering who, if anyone, would listen to what I had to say—and what they would think about it. This, of course, was old Lucifer interfering, and I had to shake him off.

When I mounted the crate, I opened the Bible and just started reading. It was amazing how God came to honor his Word when I began to read. He blessed me with boldness and freedom, and it wouldn't be long till I chased Satan behind me and broke the barrier of fear and anxiety—and then I preached.

People were hungry to hear the Word. They gathered around and listened intently. At times I gave an altar call and people knelt in the street to be saved. The spirit of revival was on the people.

The hardest part of street preaching, after getting over the initial fear and getting started, was concentrating on the message. People moved about and talked, and traffic flowed up and down the street, and if God didn't help keep my mind on the subject I had to give up and leave. Friday and Saturday were the best days to preach because everyone came to town on those days. Farmers came to sell produce and do their shopping. Around ten or eleven o'clock on Saturday morning, or Saturday afternoon was a good time to preach.

When I attended the Missionary Training Institute in Nyack in 1939, I did a little street preaching in New Jersey. At the institute, we were encouraged to go out and do personal witnessing. But the reception of street preaching was not the same in the North as it was in the South. Not many people stopped to hear us preach in New Jersey, and those who did had a coldness about them. Street preaching really was tough up there. We probably still don't truly realize what a heritage we have here in the mountains where people through the years have loved old-time preaching and singing.

Now and then, when I preached on Lexington Avenue in Asheville, someone said something smart as he passed on foot, or someone yelled derogatory things from a passing car, but I didn't really worry about things like that. The people in the crowd usually took care of such people. These were mountain people who would not stand for anyone to be disrespectful to the preaching of the Word.

Things are different today. Downtown areas are no longer crowded like they used to be. Most of our commerce has shifted into malls, and in most malls people are not allowed even to hand out gospel tracts.

The tract ministry has always been a great ministry, reaching people who might not be reached otherwise.

Henry Becker, who operated the Victory Book Room, a Christian book store on Pack Square, had a little press on which he ran off gospel tracts. He never charged us for the tracts he printed. That was his ministry. We also got tracts from the Ramdon Tract Society, and when I worked a street ministry I also worked a tract ministry. As I preached, I had young people passing out tracts. Sometimes, after preaching, I found a tract discarded on the sidewalk, but for the most part people kept them.

We always carried tracts with us in the car, and when we passed people walking along the highway, we dropped a tract on the side of the road. In most cases, we looked back and saw the walkers pick up the tract.

In later years, I preached in Haiti and the people there were hungry for anything to read. If I threw out gospel tracts on the roads there, people scrambled to pick them up.

I never took an offering in the street meetings. There were times when people walked up and handed me a bit of money, but I never passed the hat. I didn't want anyone to say I was preaching for a meal ticket, or for money. God always supplied our needs.

I think today of the opportunities men have, those who have been blessed of God, making good money, well fixed financially. Many of them never do anything for the sake of the gospel. I have maintained for years that if those who have finances don't give, God will raise up orphans and widows to carry on his work, and this has been true through the years.

One lady in our church today, Mrs. Ada Rice, has been attending for forty years. She brought up a large family and lived on Hominy Creek in West Asheville. She walked to the Mission in West End and brought all her children, coming Sunday after Sunday and faithfully giving one dollar a week. That was all she could afford. She was one of the most faithful members any church could have. She is still with us and is still faithful in attendance and in giving. People who give faithfully amount to more than one who rushes in and makes a one-time gift. I appreciate faithfulness. Jesus was thrilled over the widow's mite because she gave all.

Street preaching was not without plenty of humor. Lexington Avenue in Asheville was the hub of Western North Carolina's farming market. All the produce stands were painted and well-kept, and in season produce would be stacked high. People came to walk around and enjoy themselves. I was strolling around on Lexington one day after preaching and saw a preacher I knew. He didn't see me. He was smoking a big, black cigar and from the way he puffed the smoke, he must have been enjoying himself.

Now I do not believe that abstinence from tobacco will save us, but God says, "Having therefore these promises, let us cleanse ourselves from all filthiness of the flesh and the spirit, perfecting holiness in the fear of God." I believe that if a man is called of God and intends to preach that he should give up the habits of the flesh.

This preacher didn't see me till I was right at him, and when I spoke to him—with no intention of castigating, certainly—he almost had to wave a hole in the smoke to see me. When he recognized me, that cigar must have seemed as big as a saw log to him. He didn't know what to do with it. He grabbed it out of his mouth, put it behind him, cupped it in his hand, shifted it around, and finally crammed it in his coat pocket.

We talked for a moment, and then he tried to leave; but I kept talking. I wanted to see what would happen with that cigar. He tried again to make an exit, and I got a little long-winded. In a few moments the smoke was moving up inside his coat and coming out his collar. I knew then I'd better let him go, and when he left he was running. He must have extinguished the fire because the next time I saw him he was no worse for wear, although he gave me a sheepish smile.

Preaching in the streets also carried an element of danger of ridicule. Three times Lee and I came to grief.

First was on the Fourth of July in 1940, soon after we moved into the Mission. Most of Asheville gathered at Recreation Park on the Fourth of July to see the fireworks display, and Lee and I decided to take our old LaSalle with the slogans painted all over it and the speakers mounted on top, and go preach to the crowd at the park. Noah Radford rode with us.

As we drove up Patton Avenue, we saw that downtown was almost deserted. Now and then we passed a pedestrian, and when we did, I turned on the loudspeaker and said, "Prepare to meet God," or "Jesus saves," or "Jesus is coming soon." Usually the pedestrian waved at us and we passed on by. As we passed the S&W Cafeteria, several people stood there and I opened the loudspeaker and said, "Jesus saves." A policeman standing on the corner of Church Street stepped into the street and waved us down.

"You boys'll have to quit using them speakers," he said.

"Why?" I asked.

"You're disturbing the peace," he said.

We listened, and all over town we could hear the blast of exploding firecrackers and the louder blast of a portion of a stick of dynamite. I looked around and there weren't a dozen people in sight on the street.

"Who are we disturbing?" I asked. "There's no one here." I didn't want to anger him, but we thought he was stretching a point.

We could still hear firecrackers and gunshots.

"Listen to that," I said to him. "Surely, we're not disturbing anybody when everybody else in town is shooting something."

He opened our back door and climbed into the rear seat beside Noah. "Drive to the police station," he ordered.

Lee drove across the square to the police station where the police turned Noah loose and locked up Lee and me. We were placed in the end cell block of the city jail. The fire department and city jail were adjoined and from the flat roof of the fire department you could look into the cells of the jail.

No sooner had the key turned in the lock than Noah Radford began spreading the word of our arrest through West End. And while he made those rounds, we didn't have anything else to do; so Lee and I started singing "Amazing Grace."

From down the cell block, someone yelled, "Hey, you over there singing: Are you the Sexton boys?"

We were not unfamiliar in the city jail. We made regular rounds talking to the prisoners there.

"Yes," I yelled back, "that's us!"

"What are you doing in jail?" the startled voice called back.

"We're have a camp meeting," I hollered back. "What are you doing in jail?"

The man chuckled. "I belong here," he said.

Through the window we could see firemen climbing out their upstairs window onto the roof, looking toward us.

This was Thursday night; and down in West End Marion Wyatt was getting ready to preach, and Noah Radford was telling everyone that we had been locked in jail.

One of the men from the mission came to the jail to see about us. He brought another man with him, an unsaved man. The police let them into the cell block, and when they got to our cell, the unsaved man fell to his knees and began to pray for salvation. I felt the power of God come into that cell block, and Lee and I began to pray for the sinner man.

Now we really were having a camp meeting. There we were in jail and suddenly a man was saved.

The jailer came running. "Here . . . Here," he said. "You boys make bail and get out of here."

We laughed. "We didn't pay to get in," I said, "and we're not going to pay to get out."

In a few minutes another officer came in. "Boys," he said, engagingly, "how about making bail and leaving?"

"Why should we?"

"We're getting a lot of calls about you," he said. "Word's out that you're in here."

"Sorry," Lee said. "This is not our doing. We didn't ask to be put in here and we're not going to pay you to let us out."

It was soon dark, and there were no lights on in our cell. Another officer came in and put a flashlight beam in our faces.

"You fellows are going to have to make bail and get out," he said.

"No," I said. "We've already told you we're not going to do that."

"Well, then," he said in a compromising tone, "we're going to let you out, but you've got to promise to be back here in the morning to stand trial."

"No, sir," I said. "God called us to preach, and if he tells me to go to Georgia to preach tomorrow, I'll go. We'll promise nothing."

He really wanted us gone. He unlocked the cell door. "Go on," he said. "Git! And try to be back in the morning."

"We may not make it," Lee said.

"We trust you," he said.

When we left, we went straight to the West End Mission. The crowd overflowed the place and filled the street. We walked through the people who slapped us on the back and shouted encouragement to us.

When we reached the platform, the people rejoiced that we were out of jail. Lee told the people, "Yes, we're out, but we've got to stand trial in the morning."

"We want all of you to come to the trial," I said, "and bring your Bibles. Don't bring a little bitty Bible. Bring your family Bible, the biggest one you've got."

Lee and I got to the courtroom early on Friday morning. Sam Cathey, the blind judge, was the presiding judge, and Will Hampton was prosecuting attorney. We did not have a lawyer.

Suddenly, the doors opened and people began to come in to the courtroom, all carrying Bibles. Outside, people streamed across Pack Square, lugging the biggest Bibles they could find. The courtroom filled and people crammed the hallways leading to the room.

"What's going on?" the judge asked.

"Lot of people here," Hampton replied. "The room is full, they've filled the halls and the stairs."

The judge called the court to order and banged his gavel. Hampton said, "You Sexton boys, stand up."

Lee and I stood shoulder to shoulder.

"You are charged with disturbing the peace," Hampton said. "Your honor, these boys were driving up Patton Avenue last night, disturbing the peace by talking over loudspeakers on top of their car."

"Talking?" said the judge. "What were they talking about?"

"They were preaching, your honor."

"I see," said the judge. "Well, see how they plead, Mr. Solicitor."

Hampton turned to us. "How do you plead, boys? Guilty or not guilty?"

"Since God saved us," Lee said, "we are not guilty!"

The solicitor was talking about earthly things and Lee spoke of spiritual things. Confusion was pretty deep in the courtroom by that time.

"Mr. Solicitor," the judge said, "will you bring me the ordinance that covers disturbing the peace by preaching?"

While Hampton looked for the ordinance, Lee asked, "Your honor, can I give you the reason for doing what we did?"

"Go right ahead," Judge Cathey said.

Lee opened his Bible to the 150th Psalm and read it:

"Praise ye the Lord," he read. "Praise God in his sanctuary: praise him in the firmament of his power. Praise him for his mighty acts; praise him according to his excellent greatness. Praise him with the sound of the trumpet: praise him with the psaltery and harp. Praise him with the timbrel and dance: praise him with stringed instruments and organs. Praise him upon the loud cymbals: praise him upon the high sounding cymbals. Let every thing that hath breath praise the Lord. Praise ye the Lord.

"You see, your honor," Lee concluded, "we weren't disturbing the peace. We were only praising God."

Hampton came back into the room and approached the bench. We heard him say, "I can't find that ordinance, Judge. I don't think we have one."

Judge Cathey said, "Well, let's make one."

The crowd began to clap their hands in unison.

"Go get some more officers," Cathey said to Hampton. "Put 'em in here to keep this crowd in order."

When Hampton returned with more officers, Judge Cathey said, "I'm going to put you boys on probation for six months. You'll be free as long as you don't commit any more criminal acts."

The crowd laughed, and we walked out of the courtroom free men. We didn't like being on probation, for that smacked of criminality. But we realized the situation we faced and the condition of that court, so we let it go. We didn't plan to commit any criminal acts, anyway.

After that experience, the Lord put a boldness in us, and in the evenings, following services at the mission, Lee and I cranked up that old LaSalle and drove through different areas of the countryside, preaching through those loudspeakers.

We had stencils of slogans like "Prepare to Meet God," "Jesus Is Coming Soon," and "Jesus Saves." A favorite one was, "Prepare For Eternity." Sometimes we took those stencils along, and while one held the stencil, the other manned the paint brush, and we put those slogans on rocks along the way.

One night were were painting rocks and drove into the town of Spruce Pine about two in the morning. We took a stencil and painted "Jesus Is Coming Soon" on the sidewalk. Just as we finished, a police car eased around the corner and we got back in our car and left. We came back later and painted other slogans on the sidewalks, and next morning when people came downtown, everywhere they looked they saw signs about the coming of the Lord.

We thought that was a great stroke, but looking back, I would say what we did was a bit much. We were young and hot for Jesus, and we thought what we did would bring a lot of attention to him. I'm sure it did.

We cruised slowly through the countryside in that old LaSalle, and occasionally one of us opened the speakers and said, "Jesus is coming soon," or "Where will you spend eternity?" At night, if we said that slowly and deliberately, it sounded as if it came from the heavens. I'll bet we put many an old mountaineer on his knees in the middle of the night.

Once we painted "Prepare to Meet God" on a telephone pole in Weaverville. Not long afterward a bus hit that pole and wrecked. The pole broke and fell across the bus, and one of the passenger said when he opened his eyes, the words, "Prepare to Meet God" stared him in the face.

One man wrote a letter to the "Backtalk" section in *The Asheville Citizen* a few years ago complaining about all the signs written along the roadside. He said there were so many "Prepare to Meet God" signs on the road leading to Lake Lure that he wouldn't drive the road.

The night we painted up the Spruce Pine sidewalks, an officer stopped us as we came back through Weaverville. He cautioned us about talking over the speakers that late at night, but he let us go.

Next morning, however, he came to our home on Hendersonville Road south of Asheville with a warrant for our arrest for disturbing the peace. He told us we had to appear for trial the following Saturday.

Before Saturday we passed word among all the people of West End, and among others we knew, that we wanted them to pray for us, and, if possible, to come to the trial and bring their Bibles, just as we had asked them to do before.

On Saturday when we showed up in Weaverville for trial, I believe the officials there would rather have seen John Dillinger show up than us and those who came with us. The town was filled with Bible-carrying saints praying, preaching, passing out tracts. By the time court started, the people were excited and blessed and thrilled, and some even shouted in the streets. They crowded into the courtroom, overflowed it, and stood around outside.

The judge told us to stand and plead, and we stood and said in unison, "Since God saved us, we are not guilty." That put the court in a tailspin because we were not talking of secular things and the court knew it.

The judge tolled off the charges against us, found us

guilty, and fined us fifty dollar each and court costs. We didn't have fifty dollars between us.

Lee stood up and shouted, "We appeal this to a higher court!"

That angered the judge. He shouted to the court officer: "These are your prisoners. Take 'em away!"

You'd have thought we had just robbed the bank. The officer led us by the arms through that crowd and shoved us in his patrol car. He got under the wheel and headed for Asheville. I looked back and saw all those saints standing on the street, waving their Bibles, rejoicing.

But Lee and I didn't feel like rejoicing very much. The officer brought us to the Buncombe County jail in Asheville where we were booked. They took our possessions, put us on the elevator, and took us to the fifteenth floor to the County Jail.

We had been there many times before preaching and holding services, so we were on familiar ground, but again, just as the day we were locked in the Asheville City Jail, we were on the wrong side of the fence.

Officers shoved us in the "bull pen" and clanged shut the door behind us. We looked around at about thirty hostile faces staring at us.

Immediately, I was reminded of a passage from the Bible, Matthew 10:16–20.

"Behold, I send you forth as sheep in the midst of wolves: be ye therefore wise as serpents, and harmless as doves. But beware of men: for they will deliver you up to the councils, and they will scourge you in their synagogues; and ye shall be brought before governors and kind for my sake, for a testimony against them and the Gentiles. But when they deliver you up, take no thought how or what ye shall speak: for it shall be given you in that same hour what ye shall speak. For it is not ye that speak, but the Spirit of your Father which speaketh in you."

Indeed, we had been cast among wolves, it appeared.

Just the preceding week Lee and I had read a story in *Reader's Digest* about how many men had been killed in "kangaroo courts" across the country. Suddenly that article loomed large in our thoughts. I looked around the room and it was shut tight. I knew no one in control could hear us in the cell. That article had said that prisoners in kangaroo courts were tortured by beating, burning with cigarettes, kicking. . . .

The other prisoners looked us over and one man, obviously the leader of the pack, stepped forward and confronted us. He was a big man, tough looking, with a full cast on his leg. He swung that cast around until he faced us and pointed his finger at us.

"You boys have invaded our privacy," he said, "and since you've done that we're going to try you."

"Is this a Kangaroo Court?" I asked.

He sneered. "Call it what you like," he said, "but if you don't produce a dollar apiece to help buy our cigarettes you'll have to take our punishment."

We refused. We couldn't buy cigarettes for anyone.

He motioned to the other men, who formed two lines about six feet apart, stretching down the room. I knew this was a gantlet and that Lee and I would have to run through it while the men struck or kicked at us.

The leader leaped onto a metal bench beside the north wall of the bullpen and shouted to us, "Okay, give us a dollar each or start through the line." The men in line looked at us eagerly, ugly.

I knew God had promised to be with us, and I knew he had promised never to leave or forsake us—but we were frightened.

"Start crawling," the leader said. "Men, do what you will."

A bit of Scripture came to me: "I am a very present help in time of trouble," and through that God gave me the answer to our dilemma.

I looked at the leader. "We are Christians," I said, "and before we do anything we like to pray over it. Would you let us pray before we go through?"

This apparently took him by surprise. He looked as if a

mule had kicked him. The cell block became so quiet you could have heard a pin drop.

"Well, yes," said the leader, hesitantly, "you boys can pray. Go ahead and pray."

We moved to the metal bench under a window in the north wall, a barred window, and dropped to our knees and began to pray. I am not a believer in long prayers, but we stretched that one out.

We both prayed hard, and in a few minutes I opened my eyes and looked out that window and saw a distant light. It seemed to grow nearer, brighter. Suddenly, the presence of God filled that bull pen! Heaven came down and it looked like the bars had turned to gold. Glory filled that cell block and we rose to our feet and began to shout and praise God.

I didn't care if those men turned to lions. We knew God was there—he had come to rescue us. I believe God looked out over the battlements of Heaven and said, "Come here, Gabriel; my boys are in trouble. Go down and take care of them."

I believe God sent not only his holy presence, but the angels of God to us there in that cell.

The men in the gantlet stood still, and slowly the leader who had been so intent on punishing us turned to the others and said in a muffled voice, "There ain't agoin' to be no court."

Then he balled his fist and said, "Furthermore, the first one of you so-and-so's who says one cuss word in front of these preacher boys will answer to me." He shook his fist at the men.

"Glory to God," I said. "He's using the devil to fight for us now."

One of the men in the line dropped to his knees and cried, "Boys, I am lost. I am not right with God. Would you pray for me?"

He rose and staggered to the bench and fell on his knees again, and God saved him. We shouted wildly in that bull pen. We were having camp meeting again!

"What's going on here?" I heard the shout as the cell block doors slammed open and a jailer rushed in.

He took in the scene quickly. "Here, you Sexton boys," he said. "You're free. Get out of here."

"I was free when I came here," I shouted at him.

"Go on," he said. "Get out of here." He took us downstairs and our belongings were returned to us. But we were told we would have to stand trial in Superior Court. And all we had done was preach! We hadn't shot firecrackers or gunpowder. We hadn't held a street dance. We had not really disturbed the peace. All we were guilty of was preaching the Word. We had been called of God and were sincerely trying to witness and win souls to Christ.

The date for our jury trial was set, and it was the talk of Lexington Avenue. Our dad ran a used clothing store on Lexington at that time. One of the men who had been called for jury duty came to my dad's store and sneered at him, "I've been called for jury duty," he said, "and we're going to convict your boys in the trial." He didn't get to sit on the jury, however; he dropped dead before the trial.

During our trial, the mayor of Weaverville sat with the prosecuting attorney, whispering in his ear. We were found guilty and given probation, but no fine.

My third jail experience came in Asheville after that period of probation had expired. The town had a huge street dance on Battery Park Hill in front of the Grove Arcade Building. The street was blocked off, the music of a live string band blared through big speakers, and hundreds of people snaked around the street, dancing.

I drove uptown from the Mission when I finished preaching. I heard music on Battery Park Hill and drove up to see what was going on. The speakers were not mounted on the LaSalle, but I had a big, round, cardboard megaphone, and when I saw the dancing, I drove around the fringe of the crowd and preached through that megaphone. When I had circled the crowd I drove on down Haywood Street. Halfway down that street, a police officer stopped me.

"Sexton," he said, "I'm going to run you in for disturbing the peace."

I could barely hear him above the din of the street dance. "What for?" I asked.

"You're disturbing the peace again," he said.

"Officer, you can hear that dance music all over town," I said. "I heard it away down Patton Avenue. But with this megaphone, you can barely hear me across the street. Yet I'm the one disturbing the peace?"

He got in the car with me. "Drive to the city jail," he said.

The officer who booked me said, "We're going to stop this street preaching."

"As long as we have our freedom," I said, "we have the right to preach."

"Put him on up there," the officer said, "and I don't care if he stays till the jail rots down on him."

That was on Friday night and I was tired from a long week of work. "Maybe the Lord put me here so I could rest," I told myself.

I stretched out on the springs of the lower bunk. There were no mattresses in the cell. For a while I read my Bible, then I thought I would sleep a while. I heard a jailer coming and he was lugging a mattress. He unlocked my cell and threw the mattress on the floor without saying a word.

Putting the mattress on the lower bunk, I lay down and pillowed my head on my Bible, intending to sleep a while.

In a few moments, I felt something move. Then I felt it again. "What is that?" I asked aloud, sitting up to look. Then I began to sting, and I jumped up.

Staring closely at the mattress, I thought I saw Hitler's army marching through France. I had never seen so many bedbugs in my life. There were enough to carry me off and eat me alive.

I threw the mattress on the top bunk and stretched out on the springs of the lower bunk, and just as I began to relax, I heard a commotion, and two officers unlocked the cell beside me and shoved a drunk in. When the jailers left, the drunk began to shout and scream and raise Cain. He shook the cell bars until they rattled.

The drunk carried on all night and I slept very little, tired as I was. When morning came, all prisoners were run into the bull pen. The jailers allowed me to call home and I told Mom I had spent the night in jail but that I was all right.

"Did they arrest you again for preaching, Son?" she asked.

"Yes, Mama," I said, "but don't worry. They won't hurt me."

Lee and Bly Jackson came to the jail to get me out, but I was taken instead with all the drunks to city court, and Judge Sam Cathey put me on probation again and released me.

Soon after that, we had another brush with the law. One evening when we finished preaching at the Mission, Lee and I took an Indian friend, Holland Burgess, and rode out toward Haywood County. Holland was a Christian. People knew he really loved God. He prayed for us constantly. Holland was a tinker who went door to door sharpening knives, fixing clocks, re-bottoming chairs, doing anything he could for a living. He had a wonderful testimony for the Lord, and we really liked him.

From Waynesville, we drove down Fines Creek, away back into the hills. Lee had an old army bugle someone had given him, and when we came to the top of a hill from which we could see houses in the valleys, we stopped the car and one of us spoke slowly over those speakers, "Prepare to meet thy God!" and Lee blew that bugle like a trumpet. I know it was eerie-sounding, and after we did this a couple of times, we could see lights come on down in the valleys. Dogs began to bark, and horses and cattle in the pastures charged toward us, chasing the sound.

We drove on into Hot Springs and came back across the

mountain to Marshall. When we rolled up to the city limits of Marshall, it was about three in the morning, and at the city limits we saw a roadblock.

"Must be looking for bootleggers," Lee said.

He drove up to the roadblock in that garish old LaSalle with the writing all over it. Several cars sat there, including the sheriff's car, and armed men stood at the barricade.

Before Lee could ask what was going on, the sheriff stepped to the window of our car and said, "You boys come with us."

We followed along to the police station, and the sheriff said, "We've been getting calls all night from people over towards Hot Springs saying the end of time has come. My phone has been ringing off the hook all night. You boys wouldn't know anything about that, would you?"

The sheriff stood with a foot propped on our running board, peering into the car, bawling us out.

"I guess you better get out and come with me," he said and I thought, "Oh, no, he's not going to arrest us, too."

But that Indian stubbed up. Holland didn't ever have much to say, and he didn't say much that night. He just said he wasn't going anywhere and puffed up.

The sheriff looked at him and smoked Lee and me over rather well, then he chuckled and said, "Okay, boys, hit the road, but for goodness sake, stop preaching over them speakers in the middle of the night."

We drove on to Asheville and didn't preach any more—until we were in Buncombe County and out of the Madison County sheriff's jurisdiction.

There is a verse of Scripture that says, "Touch not mine anointed and do my prophets no harm." Maybe the sheriff was thinking about that verse the night he let us go.

No one had anything against us personally during that time of trouble with the law. It was just that the city of Asheville was primarily opposed to preaching on the street—and of course we could understand how those folks out in Madison County would object to our scaring the daylights out of them in the middle of the night.

But in Asheville I was stopped by law officers several times for reading the Bible aloud as I walked along a city street.

"Why don't you go down on Lexington and preach where they need it?" an officer asked me one day.

Later, in the 1960s, Asheville passed an ordinance that allowed preaching on the street only with a permit, and preachers had to go to City Hall to secure the permit. Even with the permit, there were only a few streets designated on which we could preach.

Such an ordinance is understandable if preachers persist in blocking traffic, or disturbing businesses. But preaching has always been part of our American freedom—indeed, it was one of the freedoms on which this nation was founded. The freedom to preach to the public is essential, in the market place or on the street corner. Ordinarily, a man who preaches on the street will not be there long. Street preaching has been a blessing down through the years, reaching a lot of people who would never darken a church door. I have seen people converted on the street who would never have entered a church.

In the communist countries, all preaching is restricted to church property. For a while, that's what Asheville appeared to be trying to do. But wise heads prevailed, and the opposition was overruled to an extent.

# — 7 —

# A Memorable Year

The year 1940, in which I turned twenty-one, was memorable for me. That was the year I began my tent ministry and my electronic ministry.

In the old Langren Hotel at the corner of College and Broadway in Asheville was a radio station, WNCA. I went to see the station manager and he let me go on the air and preach. That was a different kind of preaching—no audience, no singing, preaching to a microphone and an empty studio. But I knew that out there somewhere were people listening, and God gave me the words to say. I had to get accustomed to preaching on the radio, but after a while I felt comfortable.

I didn't know it at the time, but those weeks on WNCA were the start of an electronic ministry that has lasted almost a half century and now encompasses television, which properly used would be the greatest communication medium ever devised. Unfortunately, owing to the amount of pure trash on television, the medium has never reached its potential, and is not likely to until some drastic changes are made.

My love affair with tent preaching has lasted to this day, though I don't preach as much now in tents as I did then. I knew when God saved me that I wanted to tell others about the love of God. I felt nudged to go into the highways and hedgerows, to go and tell. But I didn't want to build on someone else's foundation. I didn't want to go into an established work. I loved the pioneer spirit and wanted to start something of my own on which I could build.

My first tent cost seven or eight hundred dollars. It was fifty feet wide and eighty feet long, supported by two poles. I bought it on time from the Smith Tent and Awning Company in Chattanooga, Tennessee, and trusted that God would supply the money to pay for it through the people to whom I preached. I borrowed half the money and paid it down when I got the tent, and I paid the other half on time. I was fortunate to be able to repay the loan and the remainder of payments with contributions from my tent congregations.

Remember that I had preached on the streets, anywhere in the open air I could find a crowd, in homes, on porches, in yards, and in some churches, including our Mission in West End. Preaching in a tent was new to me, an element of the ministry which I had not tried, but I had not preached long in that first tent until I began to feel a freedom that's hard to express. This was my tent, my church—rather, I knew it was God's tent and his church, but he had permitted me to use and administer it.

Lee and I hauled that tent to Canton and pitched it on a vacant lot across the old iron bridge that spanned the Pigeon River. Lee led the singing and God blessed that meeting. A lot of people were saved. It was a sight how God blessed, and I knew before that meeting ended that this was the work God wanted me to do.

The freedom of preaching in a tent was astounding to me. I was not in a church where others could put their thumbs on me and tell me what I could do or couldn't do. I loved the freedom I found. There is no feeling to match the one that comes from being free in Christ and doing what Christ tells you to.

Our tent could be hauled on a good-sized truck. There were three sections to it. We could have added other thirty-foot sections, but with each additional section another pole was required, and a two-pole tent was big enough for us at the beginning. Later, I owned a five-pole tent, but quite a few men were required to get it up.

We used steel axles from old cars for tent stakes. This was a block and tackle tent. We had to put the poles up first, and we had to get men to help us do that. Then we guyed it off with guy wires, stretched the tent on the ground, laced the sections together and tied them off. Next we put in the side stakes, about seven feet tall, all around the canvas and raised them up. This made the tent resemble a huge bowl. At that point, one or two men had to crawl under the canvas to each mast pole, grasp the block and tackle rope and pull it all together. One man on the outside would guide us to keep the two units pulling together. As we hoisted, the tent rose until it reached the required height, then we tied off the block and tackle ropes and tightened all the outside ropes.

About a day was required to put up the tent. Usually when we went into a community, help was no problem. People were so excited about the revival that they would volunteer, sometimes in droves. Sometimes the women of the community fixed food and fed the workers putting up the tent. It was a wonderful, happy time. People looked forward to tent meetings with great joy. Such revivals brought good spirit into the community, and usually they brought awakening in the local church.

Lee and I worked as hard as anyone putting up the tent. Sometimes we worked right up to starting time, then jumped into our suits in a hurry to start the meeting.

We must have been a sight approaching a community with that tent. We had bought a truck from Fred West, a truck with a train hood on it, sort of like the Shriners used. The truck was equipped with a whistle that sounded much like a train whistle, and on the sides of the truck we had painted "Jesus Saves." We had a lot of fun with that truck. Everybody came running to see if a train was really coming down the highway. Too, the truck gave us a good start with the kids of a community.

The Canton meeting was beautiful. The war was approaching and the spirit of revival was on the land. We never knew what a meeting would produce, and after awhile nothing surprised us. We might plan a two-weeks meeting in a community, and the revival would break out to such extent that we stayed there ten or twelve weeks. We learned never to put a strict time schedule on a meeting. My longest tent revival lacked one week of going five months.

If we didn't have three to five hundred people getting saved or rededicating their lives to Christ during a tent meeting, we thought we weren't having a good meeting.

The Canton meeting was so good that we thought that would be a good place to build something permanent. We met Mr. and Mrs. H. A. Osborne, who owned Osborne Lumber Company in Canton, and they told us about a vacant mill building about a half-mile from our tent. It was owned by a couple in Starr, South Carolina, and was up for sale for five thousand dollars. We bought it for five hundred down and arranged time payments, and for a long while we held regular meetings there. We still owed on it when we let Dr. J. Harold Smith take it over and pay off the rest of the indebtedness. Our tent ministry was growing by leaps and bounds, and we didn't really have time to concentrate on a permanent Canton ministry like we wanted to. Dr. Smith used it for occasional meetings.

In that Canton meeting I had a strange thing happen that I had never experienced before. One evening when I made the altar call, God directed me to a young woman in the crowd. I asked her to give her heart to the Lord, and she told me she wasn't interested. I had not been preaching long enough to handle that, I suppose, for it threw me for a loop. I could not imagine anyone not wanting to give his heart to the Lord, and her response scared me.

I ran from the tent down the street and finally stopped and looked back. "What made her say that?" I wondered aloud, and then I returned to the tent, still somewhat shaken.

The woman never gave her heart to the Lord, but when

she married and had children she sent them to church. One Sunday morning, nearly forty years after that tent meeting, she took her grandchildren to Sunday School, drove out in the country, and with a borrowed gun killed herself.

That was one of the saddest parts of my ministry.

The life of a large tent like that is not too long. Actually, the length of its life depends on a lot of things, mostly care in handling. You really have to take care of it, and especially you must make sure it is absolutely dry before you take it down and pack it away. Canvas will mildew quickly, and then rot. We always patched holes, no matter how small, as soon as we found them, and we carried extra canvas, needles, thread, and glue for patching. Caring for a tent meticulously would stretch its life to five or six years, but usually no longer regardless of how good we cared for it.

From Canton we took the tent to Hazelwood to the corner of Allen's Creek Road and had a wonderful meeting there. When we erected the tent, Lee and I put a lot of shavings on the ground. A furniture company in Hazelwood gave us all the shavings we wanted.

Lee and I worked far into the night before the meeting started, putting up the tent, and instead of driving back home to Asheville, we just lay down in those deep shavings and slept all night like babies. Good mountain air, no worries, no income tax to pay, just rest and sleep.

I had a strange dream that night. I dreamed I was going to heaven. I ran and looked down to see the city, which was blue and gold. I ran toward the city, wearing running trunks, and made good time. Almost to the city, I saw a huge lion. He roared and made a dive at me, scaring me good. I looked at him and this thought came to me: "In the name of Jesus, in the name of Jesus, I rebuke you in the name of Jesus." As I said that, the lion began to shrink. I continued to say it, over and over, until that lion was the size of a kitty cat. Since I was no longer afraid of him, I raced on, and just as I saw the city gates, I thought, "I am nearly home."

Just at that moment, a logger drove his huge truck by the tent, and the noise of the powerful engine awakened me. As I came out of the haze, I felt a momentary anger toward that driver for he had awakened me just before I made it into Heaven. I wanted to shake him.

Hazelwood was a tremendous meeting. Large crowds came and many were saved. Conviction and the fear of God was strong on the people. For three nights in a row, I couldn't preach because conviction was so strong. Before I got to the sermon, people streamed to the altar, fell to their knees, and began to pray for salvation. We ministered to them. People prayed all over that tent. One great old soulwinner from Waynesville was Dick Turpin. He was so humble he would fall to his knees, and as people gathered at the altar praying, he crawled from one to the other, trying to harvest souls.

That meeting produced our first experience with a collapsed tent. One Sunday at sunset just as I stepped to the pulpit to tell the people that I would preach on the soon coming of the Lord, I saw the shavings begin to move. Then I heard something that sounded like a freight train coming up the valley, right through Hazelwood.

The shavings stirred again and the tent began to breathe. If a tent quivers, it's all right, but if it begins to breathe, the canvas going up and coming down, watch out! Something is going to happen.

Something happened that night. The wind caught under the tent and pushed the canvas up from the mast pole and down to the side. The tent split top to bottom—and down it came! With a loud WHOOOOOOOSH! the tent collapsed and the canvas flattened over the people. I didn't have time to get off the platform.

I heard the devil laughing. "What are you going to do now?" he asked. "What are you going to say to all these injured people?"

Indeed, I was afraid a lot of people were hurt, but the only injury in that whole crowd was to a woman who received a few light scratches. That was a miracle because even the tent poles and all the wires had fallen and no one was injured.

Lee and I loaded the canvas on our truck and drove it to Asheville the next morning to the awning company. After they sewed it back, we took it straight back to Hazelwood, erected it again, and went on with the meeting.

World War II struck with a fury that threatened not only the safety but the sanity of the nation. It was hard on the boys who marched off to fight the Japanese, Germans, and Italians, but it was also hard on the folks who stayed behind—the mothers and daddies and brothers and sisters of those who went to war.

My tent ministry grew stronger with the war because people really searched for God. They were sincere in trying to find him.

Lee and I were then veterans of tent warfare with the devil. We seldom took the tent far from home. Since God had called us to minister to our mountain neighbors, we concentrated on them.

The Scripture says, "A prophet is not without honor save in his own country." That does not mean that you have to leave your country. It means that ordinarily if a prophet is raised up in his own country the people are accustomed to him, they do not honor him as they would an outsider. I prayed to go to certain places to preach, and God would say, "No, I have called you to minister to these mountain people. You are one of them; you love and understand them. Preach Christ to them and give them the gospel."

The farthest away I ever took a tent for revival services was Portsmouth, Ohio, and Hammond, Indiana, there on the shores of Lake Michigan. I had a tent for two or three years in Kissimmee, Florida, but only for an annual camp meeting.

Mostly, we preached in Western North Carolina: Canton, Hazelwood, Woodfin, all around Asheville, Hendersonville, Waynesville, Spindale, Leicester.

Our income came entirely from offerings. We had no regular income. And out of what we took in from the offering plates, we paid all of our expenses. We paid for all materials, utilities, help, car and vehicle expense. When we passed the plates whatever came in was what we had. Sometimes we got a hundred or two dollars and sometimes just a few dollars.

We took the tent to Woodfin, just north of Asheville, early in the war. We hired a man named Bishop to watch out for the tent. He stayed at the tent all night, his only companion an old .44-caliber pistol. Mr. Bishop was not a saved man, and while I preached he roamed around the tent, making sure everything was all right.

One night while the service was in progress, he went over to Woodfin High School and in the darkness he overheard a group of boys plotting to cut down the tent that night. They thought it would be funny to cut the ropes and let the tent fall.

Bishop listened until the boys disbanded, then made his way back to the tent and got a young man to stay with him the rest of the night. He placed this fellow at the light switch and told him when he heard Bishop peck on a bench he was to throw the master switch and turn on every light inside and outside the tent.

About one in the morning, Bishop saw the boys coming. They crept up the hill and moved in toward the tent, scattering as they came. Bishop waited until they got to the tent, then pecked on the bench and the other man threw the light switch.

That hilltop lit up like Times Square, and Bishop began shooting his pistol into the air. Startled and frightened, the boys split into two groups. One went down the east side of the hill toward Newbridge, and the other down the west side toward the industrial plants along the river. The group that went west ran through a messy hog lot, splashing and shouting, and kept going without losing speed.

Bishop and his helper rolled on the ground in laughter.

Later in the war, I held a tent meeting in Biltmore and hired Bishop to guard the tent again. On a chilly night Bishop lowered all the side flaps and settled down, making occasional rounds. Around one o'clock, he heard someone moving outside the tent and pulled his .44. Suddenly someone slowly raised the canvas and in a few moments two soldiers and a girl slipped inside, intent on using God's tent for evil purposes. Bishop waited until the trio was inside and flicked on his powerful flashlight. He put the beam in their faces and then shoved the .44 into the beam where they could see it.

"Jest keep crawling," Bishop ordered. "Crawl right over there to that altar and start praying." The three crawled on hands and knees to the altar and began praying at gunpoint. They prayed aloud, stricken with fright.

They slowed down.

"Pray some more," Bishop ordered.

They prayed a while longer.

"Now leave," Bishop said.

They plowed some dust getting out of that tent. They ran.

In the mountains of North Carolina, a preacher can only hold tent meetings from about the first of June until the first of September, Otherwise, the evenings are too cool, and at times there is a risk of snow.

We pitched the tent at Barnardsville School in the northern part of Buncombe County early one spring. We had our second tent then, a sixty by one-hundred-twenty-foot tent with three poles. We hired William Justice to keep the tent while it was up.

The meeting began on the first day of April, and we thought the weather would be all right. But about a week into the meeting, Justice telephoned one morning and said, "Preacher, it snowed here last night and there's snow on the tent.

Snow on a tent is heavy and dangerous.

"Fire the smudge pots," I told him.

We had some old Salamanders like the ones used in Florida to protect orchards from frost. They use kerosene and once lighted it forms a gas so that they actually become gas heaters.

Justice fired those pots inside the tent and before long all the snow melted off the canvas and flowed to the ground. He left the heaters up and staked wire in a circle around them to keep people from getting burned, and we continued with the meeting through the cold spell by firing the pots each afternoon and when the people gathered in the evenings, that tent was as warm as home.

Tent meetings cut to the basics of religion, and that's where people lived during the war. Tent meetings were times of relaxation and a place away from the daily cares of people.

A tent was also a place for making things right with God, and people took advantage of that.

In 1944 I had a tent meeting on an empty lot in West Asheville, and before long it broke out into a real revival. The tent filled every night, and people stood five and six deep around the tent on the outside. They rode the trolley buses to the meetings.

During that meeting we saw people fall at the altar by the scores. They lined the area from side to side, lying prostrate in the shavings, praying and crying to God to save their boys in the service. They prayed especially for the boys who were in the fighting, and they prayed that God would bring about the end of the war. I saw that altar so wet with tears I thought we'd have to mop it up. The people promised God, "If you will send my husband, my son, my sweetheart back, we'll serve you. We'll be in church every Sunday. We will honor you."

But the sad part of it was that when President Truman announced the war was over in 1945, America went on the greatest spree of drinking, dancing, sex and drug orgies, and hell-raising the nation had ever seen. We lied to God, and America has gone down spiritually ever since. What frightens me today is that we seem to be going down economically, educationally, and in other ways, too.

With limited income during those early years in the tent, we were happy when the people decided to "pound" the preacher. Each person brought something for the preacher on a designated night—a can of food, a jar of pickles, a pound of sugar, a slab of meat—and for a lot of mountain preachers during those days pounding made the difference between eating and not eating.

When my children came along a few years later and we received a pounding, they danced for joy. They were as excited to see what the pounding brought as they were on Christmas morning to see what Santa brought.

Once when I had a tent pitched at Georgetown, the people gave us such a pounding that a Mr. Ledford, who had been saved in that meeting, had to bring his pickup truck to haul the stuff home for us.

Today, preachers live on salaries. Nobody hears of a pounding any more. Poundings gave everyone a chance to participate. They added a warm and personal touch to the ministry.

The fellowship was great at those tent meetings. When we pitched the tent in any community, right away people invited us to their homes for meals. We went in the late afternoons for supper and fellowshipped with the family before the service began that night. Such visits produced indescribable times of warmth and fellowship. Soon a revival became like a great family meeting because the preacher was acquainted with the people, even with their children.

The spirit of healing was great in these meetings, not physical healings but spiritual ones. People who were mad at each other healed differences. Sometimes we saw people who had not spoken in years wrap their arms about each other and make up. A lot of restitutions were made in these meetings.

On Sunday afternoons we had "dinner on the ground" at the tent and everybody in the community filled long tables with food. We had great times.

The singing in these meetings was wonderful. Then we didn't have to bring singers in. People in each community sang—and beautifully, too.

# — 8 —

# On the Air

When the war broke out I thought a long time about what I should do. At first I thought I should be a conscientious objector because I knew I could never bring myself to kill anyone. But after praying a lot and thinking about it, I decided the course of the conscientious objector was not for me. A man should fight for his country, I reasoned. Too, I was doing God's work, and if it were not for God we wouldn't have a country.

My next thought after settling that problem was of where I could be of greatest service. "Lord," I prayed, "where can I be of service to my country and win the greatest number of souls for you?"

Although I was not yet ordained, I was given a ministerial exemption from the draft because I was preaching as much as any preacher in Buncombe County. That settled the question for me. I knew God wanted me at home to win souls for Him and to aid the war effort through morale-building and such.

I was ordained into the ministry December 10, 1944. The Rev. Tom Connor ordained me at his church, Riverside Baptist Church in Woodfin. The ordaining Council was W. T. Connor, moderator; W. M. Jervis, clerk; and Clay Barnes, Charles F. Rogers, B. N. Rogers, and Harry Dycus, preachers.

At the start of the war, God showed me a way that I could minister both to the people at home and to the servicemen in the states and overseas. That was through radio.

It was a miracle that I got on the radio to begin with. I had to be cleared by the Ministerial Association in Asheville, and I was sure that would take a miracle. A lot of local ministers had looked askance at my ministry, especially after I had been cast in jail the second or third time. Too, I was just a rough mountain boy preacher who had not been to the seminary. I thought it was unlikely that they would let me go on the air.

Miracles do happen, however, and early one morning I drove down to Pearson Drive where the Episcopal minister lived who headed the ministerial association. He invited me into his living room, and I explained that God had called me to go on the radio and preach, and I asked for the permission of the association.

He was a kindly man. He smiled at me and said, "I don't see why not. Of course you have our permission."

"Lord, I thank you," I said when I left his house. "I didn't expect it to be that easy."

This was 1942, in the early days of the United States' participation in the war. I had been on WNCA a few weeks in 1940, and now I wanted to go on WWNC, the city's biggest station and one of the nation's pioneer stations. WWNC reached a long way; it was a very powerful radio station. Its offices and studios were on the third floor of the new Citizen-Times building on O. Henry Avenue. I knew if I could get on that station I could reach parents and families of a lot of men in service.

The station manager, Cecil Hoskins, told me I would have to give an audition to show them what type of programming I wanted to do. I got James W. Roseborough as pianist and Bly Jackson to sing, and I prayed over what I should do. God seemed to tell me to let them play and sing and then for me to brag on Jesus.

I preached a simple message on Jesus, just exalting his holy name, and the station accepted me. At first I preached once a week on the air, but before long the station asked me to preach seven days a week. My program was at six-thirty in the morning, and I did the program live each day.

I cast about for a name for the program and finally settled on "Send The Light." That was the title of one of the great songs in the hymn book of the Missionary Alliance Church.

The light is Christ, and it is our job to tell it. God has honored the name all these years and he gets the glory for all that has been done to spread the gospel through my radio and television ministry. My television show today is called "Send The Light."

My great desire in going on the radio was to reach as many servicemen as possible. Once on the air, I began making daily appeals for everyone to send us the names of their loved ones in service. We compiled these names on a mailing list which grew to great proportions as the months went by. Before long, we had more than six thousand names of men in all branches of service, scattered around the world.

Once a month, we mimeographed one of my messages, word for word—nothing fancy, just typed and mimeographed—and we mailed these messages to the servicemen on our list throughout the world. At the end of the message, we printed the altar call just as I had made it.

The response was overwhelming. Thousands of servicemen wrote to us, expressing their gratitude for our interest and for the gospel messages we sent to them in their great time of need.

The boys in foxholes received them. Sailors on ships all over the globe got them. I began to see why God left me at home. If every serviceman shared his letter with several others, those monthly messages reached thirty or forty thousand military men. In no way could I have reached that many by going into service as a chaplain or whatever. I felt I was truly doing what God wanted me to.

One soldier wrote that he was in the front lines and a jeep bringing up the mail hit a land mine and was blown to kingdom come. He said the only thing that escaped the resulting fire was one of our messages of salvation.

The tough part of that job was when a letter came back with a big red block on the front, containing the words, "Deceased—Killed in Action." That really shook us.

I continued this ministry through the war, and working daily at the radio station was fun. Jim Lorick was the WWNC engineer assigned to me. He was a cut-up. While I preached live on the air, Jim would pile things on his head and slowly peep over the door at me, trying to distract and tickle me. He did it for fun—and he was funny, very funny. But he never broke me up. God used him to help me, because I learned not to be distracted by things around me when I preached.

After I was married in 1944, my wife Jacque helped me with the daily broadcast. She read a verse of Scripture and said a prayer, and I preached.

One morning Jim Lorick and another engineer, Bill Robinson, teamed up for a stunt that capped the stack. They scared the daylights out of me.

Jim and Bill came in early and ran the clock forward three or four minutes. When Jacque and I got to the studio and looked at the clock, we hurried to get our things together and promptly when the clock said six-thirty, I stepped up to the microphone and prepared to speak as soon as the theme song, "Send The Light," went off.

To my great surprise and absolute horror, when Jim, seated behind a control panel, said, "Now here is Ralph Sexton. . . ." and turned up the music, "Send The Light" didn't come forth, but the strains of a comical war song entitled "Flat Foot Floogie" blared from the monitors.

I was supposed to follow a bit of the theme song by saying "Good morning," but when Lorick toned down the music, I was stricken. I tried to speak and couldn't say a word.

Lorick sat poker-faced behind the control panel looking at me, and I was thinking, "I'm ruined! I'm ruined!"

Suddenly Lorick and Robinson burst into laughter. They danced around the studio, slapping their legs and pointing at me, and tears ran down their cheeks. I knew then they had played a joke on me. Suddenly Lorick dashed for the control panel again and began turning knobs and flipping switches—and we were on sure enough. I was still so shaken I'm sure I stumbled over several words until I regained my composure. Jim Lorick, who became a close friend, never ceased to enjoy telling others of that incident.

When I had to be away, we cut programs in advance for airing on certain days. That was before tape was perfected, possibly before it was invented, I don't know. There were some old wire recorders in use, but tape hadn't come in yet. We recorded programs for future broadcast on "transcriptions." These were large recording discs, about the size of a long-play album today.

I was ready to preach a revival in Portsmouth, Ohio, in May of 1944. Lee had taken the tent up and found a crew to help erect it, and I cut transcriptions to be used while I was gone. Jim Lorick came to me and said, "Preacher, D-Day is coming. We don't know exactly when, but I believe we're on the verge of invading Europe. It may be while you're gone. Don't you think you ought to cut a special program we can play that day if you're not here?"

I agreed, and we cut the transcription. I started the program with, "Ladies and gentlemen, our boys are going ashore in Europe right now. They're being mowed down, shelled and blown apart. . . . If they ever needed our prayers, it's now. Let us pray for them." After the prayer, I brought the message, aimed at D-Day occurrences.

On the morning of June 6, 1944, the Allies poured 156,000 men ashore at Normandy in France, and the invasion of Europe was on. At six-thirty that morning, Jim Lorick played the transcription I had cut. It ran for thirty minutes with no interruptions.

The people back home got my D-Day message while I was hundreds of miles away, preaching in Ohio.

Many good things happened to us during the war years. Everything was scarce. Tires and gasoline were almost impossible to get, especially tires, and in my work I had to travel quite a bit. We had rationing coupons and could only buy what we had coupons for.

At lot of these old mountain boys had farms and saw mills. They had tractors and other farm equipment, and they received coupons from the rationing boards for tires and gasoline with which to operate their machinery. They knew I went from church to church preaching and they came to our meetings and put ration coupons in the collection plate. Sometimes they also put money. They knew I needed the gasoline those coupons would permit me to buy, and they knew I couldn't run forever on threadbare tires.

I drove for a purpose, not only to preach, but also to take news of the war into some backwoods areas. We didn't have television; World War II was not fought in our living rooms like the Vietnam War was. God worked it out for me to secure motion picture films made in the front lines—films of actual fighting. They showed the realities of war, and showed exactly what our fighting forces were going through.

Wherever I went to show these films, I first preached and then showed the movies, and people filled the buildings. They were hungry for that kind of news. Sometimes some of the people fled the building in the middle of the film; they couldn't take it. I didn't want to use the films to torture anyone, especially a poor old mountain mother whose sons were in the thick of the fighting, but I told them their sons were going through it and we needed to see enough of the films to let us know it was time to pray and get hold of God.

Getting a projector to show these films was another

miracle. Because of the war, it was impossible to buy anything like a projector, but we learned of a man in Chicago who had projectors to sell to churches, and when I contacted him he said he could sell me a fine projector for five hundred dollars.

We knew we had to have a projector because we felt God wanted this ministry for the families of servicemen, but we didn't have anything like five hundred dollars. We prayed hard for the money, and one day Lee and I were on our knees in the West End Mission praying that somehow God would send the money for the projector; and we heard someone come in.

When we got up we saw it was Noah Radford, the reformed bootlegger who had gone to work for the railroad and was doing fine. We had no idea that Noah had that kind of money, either, but he said, "Boys, if you will meet me at the Post Office in the morning, I will have the money for your projector." We met him at the specified time and he counted out five hundred dollars. We wired it to Chicago and in just a few days the projector arrived. It was all the man had claimed it to be. We used it for the entire war, up and down the countryside, in churches and tents and everywhere we went—and God and Noah Radford were responsible for the fulfillment of that portion of our ministry.

# — 9 —

# Wedding Bells

Asheville was a lively city during World War II. It was filled with saints and sinners. We pitched the tent in various places around town during the war, trying our best to help sinners see the light.

In 1944 we took the tent to Biltmore and erected it on a lot in north Biltmore. Like the others, this meeting started fast. Hundreds flocked to the altar, and we could feel God's hand on every meeting.

Appalachian Hall, a naval hospital, was nearby, and some of the sailors stationed there came to the meetings. One night one of them got gloriously saved. He was so happy he shouted, "Praise God! I want to be baptized!"

We were happy with him. "Fine," I said. "We'll baptize you."

"I mean right now," he said.

"Now?" I looked at my watch and it was ten o'clock. "Come on, then; we'll baptize you right now."

The Swannanoa River was just across the street. Several people went with us, and Lee and I climbed down the river bank and found a place deep enough to baptize him. While people held flashlights on us we took that sailor into the river and baptized him in the name of the Father, and of the Son, and of the Holy Ghost!

Several cars coming down Biltmore Avenue saw the bobbing flashlights and stopped, thinking someone had run off the road into the river. Most of the people in those cars stayed with us, rejoicing until we had the sailor baptized.

For six years I had been preaching, and I was extremely busy with street preaching, tent meetings, radio, and especially with my ministry to servicemen. I had never given serious thought to marriage. I thought I didn't have time for marriage, and told myself that I would just devote my life to preaching and doing God's work.

Down by the river, Lee and I had built an altar, where down on our knees many battles were won. At this altar, I prayed about marriage. My thoughts were that God agreed with me that I should just preach and not worry about a wife, but every time I started to make a vow to God that I would never marry, God always stopped me.

After a few rejections of my vow, I prayed, "Lord, if it is your will that I marry, then I want you to pick out my life's companion that together we can serve the Lord and win the lost and walk hand in hand with Jesus. I am leaving this to you, Lord."

So I continued to preach and gave little further thought to marriage. I was twenty-four, twenty-five years old at the time.

Dr. J. Harold Smith was a friend of mine. I had known him since 1938 when he had his gospel tent in Asheville. Weldon Johnson and I had kept his tent for him, and later I had been in several meetings with him. I told him I was never going to marry, and he laughed every time I mentioned it.

"Ralph," he said one day, "one of these days the love bug will bite you and when it does, wherever I am, you call me and I'll come and perform the ceremony."

"You're wrong, Preacher," I said. "There's not going to be any ceremony."

"One of these days . . ." he said. "Just call me."

One day the Lord told me to go uptown in front of Central Methodist Church and pray. I thought this a strange request. A lot of people would say I was out of my mind, but I believed that obedience to God was more important than anything.

God said, "You go uptown in front of that church, kneel down and pray that I will save someone out of that church and call them into my service."

I didn't know anyone at the Methodist church downtown and I fought with that thing.

"Lord," I said, "there are people uptown who'll think I'm crazy." Some already did, I knew. "Lord," I continued, "they will say: 'That preacher has lost his mind; I saw him on the sidewalk praying.'"

Had I stopped to think this thing through I would have realized that thousands of people had seen me praying on the sidewalks of Asheville the last six years, but I was in a wrestling mood and I wrestled with God. Finally, I realized that God had a reason for asking me to do this.

I told one of the old saints of West Asheville, Mrs. Fred Felmet, who ran Felmet Brothers Grocery, what God had burdened me to do, and she said without pause, "I'll go with you."

We went to town and when we arrived in front of the Methodist Church, a beautiful, gray, stone structure on Church Street, I didn't tarry. I have come to obey God, I thought, and I am going to get it done.

I dropped to my knees, Mrs. Felmet beside me, and I prayed, "God, in Christ's name, save someone out of this church. I don't know who, Lord, but save them and call them into your service. In Christ's name, Amen."

And I left there.

It is strange, how the hand of God works. I didn't know then that I was praying for my wife.

Jacqueline Buckner lived with her parents, Albert and Hester Buckner, on Pearson Drive. Her father was a night watchman for the downtown banks. The Buckners were good members of Central Methodist Church. Jacque was nineteen years old and had been deeply involved in church work since she was fifteen.

That was the summer I had my tent in Biltmore, 1944, and the meeting was going well. My list of names of servicemen continued to grow, the radio ministry thrived, and each morning I announced on the radio that services would be held that night in the tent in Biltmore.

Hester Buckner listened to my radio program. Her son, Bobby, was a tail gunner in Europe, and she wanted prayers said for him. Jacque was in the midst of a long recovery from rheumatic fever. She had been confined for so long her mother was looking for interesting places to take her, hoping that keeping her amused would speed her recovery.

One morning Hester asked Jacque, "That preacher who has the soldier ministry has his tent in Biltmore. Would you like to go hear him tonight?"

"Yes," Jacque answered. "That might be fun." She thought it would be a lark. Having never been to a tent meeting, she thought it would be something different to do. She knew it was a different world, different in religion, in social life, in everything. Yes, she wanted to go.

The two rode the trolley to Biltmore that evening and found seats in the tent.

By that time, this meeting had really "broken out." God had blessed the meeting, huge crowds were attending, and souls were being saved. God's spirit of conviction was present, and I thought this was one of our best revivals.

I do not remember what I preached on that night, but God gave me power, and fifty people came to the altar, lining it from side to side. In the group, I noticed a frail-looking girl who wore a brown and yellow two-piece dress. Some way, to me at least, she stood out from all the rest. I was attracted to her. She gave her testimony and said she was glad that God had saved her.

Jacque said later that she had never heard singing like the singing at that meeting. She came forward when the choir sang, "Oh, why not tonight? Oh Sinner, harden not your heart. . . . Oh, why not tonight?"

"I had never seen freedom in a service like that," she said. "In my church I had been involved in church work and teaching since I was fifteen. I had worked in every aspect of the church even at that early age, but I knew that night that the Lord was moving on my heart."

She realized she was under deep conviction when she stepped into the sawdust aisle and walked to the altar to pray.

After the service, Jacque lingered and I went to her.

"I know you have all that soldier's mail going," she said, rather shyly, I thought. "I can type, and I would love to be able to help. I've been sick and not able to do much, but this is something I could do."

"I appreciate that," I said. "I thank you, and I will bring some envelopes and addresses to your house so you can type the addresses on the envelopes. Then I will return and pick them up."

A few days later I took a box of envelopes to her. We lived on Washington Road, ten or twelve blocks from where she lived, and after talking to her a few minutes, I left with the strangest feeling.

"This is strange," I told myself. "I have never felt like this in my life." All I had done was hand her the envelopes. "Why do I feel like this?" I asked.

I couldn't figure at first what was going on within me. But every time I took envelopes, or went to pick them up, whatever it was increased.

One day it dawned on me that I was falling in love. I hurried to my room and prayed, "Lord, if that young lady is the one God has appointed to be my wife and helpmate, if she is your choice, if you want us to serve God, win the lost, and do your will, Lord, if she's really the one—give me a green light."

I prayed in a big way. While I was praying I realized I was in love. God knew it, too, for before I said "Amen" he gave me the green light—and I floorboarded it!

Dr. Smith had told me the love bug could bite pretty hard, and when it bit me I couldn't get loose. When I realized she was really the one, I didn't want loose.

I went straight to her and told her I loved her and asked her to marry me. Much to my delight, she said yes, she would marry me. That was September. We were married in December, on Christmas Eve.

When I tell people now that I prayed seven years for a wife, they ask me why I prayed so long, and I tell them, "Some of you wish you were still praying." I also told them I didn't want to marry an orange blossom that when unwrapped at home would turn out to be a lemon.

We set the date for Christmas Eve and arranged to be married in the Gospel Tabernacle on French Broad Avenue where I had first started going to church. I telephoned Dr. J. Harold Smith and asked him to marry us, and you should have heard him laughing over the phone!

He said, "I told you the love bug would bite you," and he agreed to marry us. But he had to preach in Greenville, South Carolina, at three in the afternoon on Christmas Eve, so we set the wedding for six that evening.

I did not remember that I had ever seen Jacque before that night in the tent at Biltmore, but she remembered me. At one time, for a short while, we lived two doors down the street from her family. That was about the time I got saved, and she was eleven or twelve years old. We lived there when Lee and I bought that pair of speakers and painted up the LaSalle.

Jacque's daddy told her one day, "There's a bunch of boys moved in down the street and I'd better not catch any of them down here." There were eight girls and two boys in Jacque's family and six boys and two girls in ours. My younger brother and her younger sister were in the same grade at school, and they swapped comic books. Rather than go to her house to swap, he would shove his book in a hole in their hedge and later go back and find his gone and her's sticking in the hedge. Jacque's father always wondered how those holes came to be in his hedge.

After we had the date and time of the wedding established, and had the church and preacher lined up, I thought of something I had neglected. I had not asked Jacque's daddy for her hand in marriage! I decided to rectify that oversight immediately.

He was at work when I found him. He was at Wachovia Bank. I anticipated no problem with him because he was a friendly, thoroughly likable man. I walked with him as he made his rounds, telling him that Jacque and I loved each other and wanted to marry. I sensed that he was afraid to say either yes or no for fear of making Jacque unhappy either way.

In the basement of Wachovia was a target-shooting range, and when Mr. Buckner passed by he usually shot a few rounds, just to keep his shooting eye fit. When we reached that area, he pulled his revolver and as we talked he fired a few rounds. One of the bullets ricocheted and zipped through my hair, missing my head by a fraction of an inch. Some people wonder why I part my hair in the middle. Well, that bullet is not the reason. I simply like it parted in the middle.

That shot scared Mr. Buckner so badly that he had a heart attack the next day and was still incapacitated and unable to give Jacque away on Christmas Eve.

Some of the women at the Mission in West End decided Jacque wasn't the girl for me, mostly because she had been reared in a different social and religious environment and in a church they considered to be modernistic. Those mission women thought she didn't have enough spiritual understanding and would not make the kind of wife I needed. So they took it upon themselves to fast and pray that I wouldn't marry her. They even conducted a letter-writing campaign to Jacque and her family, and included clippings from the newspaper about the times I had been arrested for preaching on the streets. The clippings were accompanied by notes to the Buckners that read, "Do you know what your daughter is getting into?" They tried to build friction. But Jacque's dad, through his association with the sheriff's department as a security guard, already knew about my record with the police. And he understood the circumstances and never held it against me.

Christmas Eve dawned bright and sunny. When I went to the radio station to preach that morning, I was so overjoyed that I invited the radio audience to attend. I had announced the wedding before on the air, but this time I blurted, "I want everybody to come." I was overjoyed, but I did not realize what a long way WWNC reached. Once I had offered a Bible to the person who heard the program the longest distance away and wrote in, and a man wrote from Michigan said he had picked it up loud and clear.

That afternoon I dressed in a six-dollar suit my daddy had brought to me from the used clothing store he ran uptown, and went to the Mission to preach at three. At the same time, Dr. Smith began to preach in Greenville. He later said he drove to Asheville in fifty-two minutes, sixty miles up that narrow, winding mountain road.

I went back home and nervously waited a while, and then went on downtown to the church. I was amazed at the number of cars and at all the people standing around who couldn't get in the church. Jacque's brother-in-law, a city policeman, told me they had turned cars and people away for more than an hour, but the people found other places to park and walked to the church.

The building was filled, people sat in all the windows, they stood in every available inch of space—and I was so proud that they would come out of the mountains in such numbers to see a preacher boy get married. They wore every kind of garb imaginable from sharp dress suits to overalls, sweaters, and toboggans. They formed a perfect picture of mountain folk.

Homer Ward, who barbered at Paramount Barber Shop, said to me, "Preacher, after this wedding, it'll take them two weeks to get back home."

I was overjoyed. But when Jacque arrived, her reception was something less than mine. When she stepped out of the car, the enormous crowd parted and made a way for her to get to the church, and some of the women who had resisted our decision to get married came to her and said, "We want you to know that we prayed through last night, and we have the assurance that you'll never make it to the altar." What a way to greet a young woman at her wedding!

As Jacque walked down the aisle during the ceremony she saw a whole row of them, heads bowed, praying hard: "God, do what you have to do to stop her."

They did all they could to take the joy out of the day for her—but they couldn't, for this wedding, unknown to them, was ordained of God.

"I had never experienced anything like that," Jacque said later. "I didn't know how spiritual I was supposed to be, nor how much knowledge of God or the Bible I was supposed to have. I knew the Lord had saved me and I loved him, and I felt that was enough."

I remember the wedding vows well, but the thing I remember most about the wedding was that when we knelt, I thought, "Oh, my goodness, I've got a hole in the bottom of one of my shoes." I wore a two-dollar pair of shoes.

When we left the church, the crush of the crowd was so great that a soldier picked Jacque up and carried her over the crowd.

I am sure those women who prayed so hard for the wedding to collapse must have been disappointed when it was finished. Some of them later came to Jacque and apologized, but others never did. Jacque once fixed a meal for some of the women of our church, and one said, "I'm sorry but I can't eat your cooking."

Jacque was stunned. "Why not?" she asked.

"Because," the woman said, "I did too much to hurt you before your wedding."

"That's behind us now," Jacque said.

"I want to apologize anyway."

"Apology accepted," Jacque said, and the woman ate as much as anybody.

We both realized that the opposition of those women

was just one of the things we had to face in the ministry. We have faced jealousy and criticism, especially through the television ministry. We often get rebuked, but we just have to let God fight the battle.

After our wedding ceremony we went by her mother and dad's house where Jacque changed from her wedding dress to traveling clothes, and we left for Greenville. I had a 1938 Buick which we were going to drive to Florida on our honeymoon. I had borrowed five-hundred dollars to finance the trip.

First, though, we intended to spend our wedding night in Greenville after going on the radio for an eleven o'clock broadcast that evening with Dr. Smith. He had left Asheville as soon as the wedding was over and, judging by the way he drove up the mountain, I was sure he was back in Greenville before we left Asheville.

Darkness had fallen before we left Asheville. When we started down that curvy road through the mountains to Greenville, the hills seemed to close in on us.

Halfway down the mountain, I heard a BANG! and a PHEW! and one of the tires began thumping. I pulled off the road and with a flashlight surveyed a flat tire. I had an old jack in the car but had never been able to get it to work.

Jacque sat on the running board eating from a box of chocolates while I struggled with that jack, and even though in difficulty, we were as happy as could be, joking back and forth. She wore a cute little pillbox hat and appeared to have not a worry in the world. The only worry I had was with that jack.

I simply could not get the jack to work; so I bowed my head and prayed to God that if he wanted us to get to Greenville in time to go on the radio to please send someone to help us. Not a car had passed since we had the flat, but I had no more than finished the prayer when we saw headlights coming down the mountain from the north. A car, moving slowly, rounded a bend and came toward us.

It was barely moving and weaving from side to side and I was sure the driver was drunk.

I flagged the car anyway and the driver pulled off the road with his headlights shining on our car. He was a soldier, and he was not drunk but dead tired.

"Man, I'm glad to see you," he said.

"Well, you're not half as glad as we are," I said.

"I've driven from California," he said, "and I'm trying to make it home to Greenville to spend Christmas with my mom. I haven't had a lot of sleep the last two days."

A strange feeling came over me, the feeling that God had caused our tire to puncture so we would be there to help that boy get home for Christmas. Somewhere in Greenville that mother was praying for her boy to get home safely, and had he not stopped when he did he surely would have gone off that mountain and probably been killed.

By the time he helped me change the tire, he was wide awake. He followed us on into Greenville and we kept our eyes on his driving, making sure he didn't begin to bobble. Just before we got to the Greenville city limits, he passed us and blew his horn. He was home for Christmas.

We had missed the broadcast with Dr. Smith, so we drove to the Greenville Hotel where two weeks before I had reserved the bridal suite for this night. We got to the hotel about one in the morning.

"I reserved the bridal suite for tonight," I told the clerk.

He looked in the book. "Sorry. There's no reservation for you here," he said.

"But I made it two weeks ago."

"Well, I don't have it," he said. "All I've got is a room with twin beds."

"We'll take it," I said without hesitation. The hotel was filled with servicemen celebrating Christmas.

We were so tired by that time all we wanted was a room.

The next morning we met with Dr. Smith for a while, then headed for Florida on our honeymoon. At that time, you could stay in Florida a week for just a little money. Meals were about sixty-five cents with dessert. We could get nice rooms for three-fifty.

We went through Florida bit by bit, staying here and there, and reached Miami in about a week. One of the big thrills we got there was eating at the China Clipper Waterport and watching those big seaplanes come and go.

We left Miami and crossed the Everglades to the West Coast and worked our way back home. In the Everglades we found an abandoned Indian village. We had a frying pan and some food in the car and I built a fire and Jacque cooked lunch in that abandoned village. What fun we had! And we were as happy as two fat pigs in the sunshine.

We worked up through Fort Myers and cut back over to Winter Haven and noticed when we got there that Jacque had worn a shoe of a kind all that day and we were so excited we hadn't even noticed.

We drove back through Georgia and South Carolina and as we came up the mountain toward Asheville from Greenville, Jacque said, "Ralph, where are we going to live?"

The question threw me. I had been so excited about getting married and so busy with my preaching that I had not given one thought to a place to live.

Jacque thought I had a surprise place, perhaps a quaint little cottage in the country. She had been sitting there envisioning me carrying her over the threshold, and when I didn't say anything, she guessed what was wrong.

All I could say was, "I guess we'll go home to Mama and Papa."

I am sure she was stunned, but she tried not to show it.

I said, "Jacque, I honestly had not given that a thought. We'll find our own place quickly."

Mom and Dad put us up for two weeks, and every day we looked for a place of our own. Living with our family was a real experience for Jacque. Mom was an old mountaineer woman who got up at four in the morning—every morning. We went to meeting at night and sometimes didn't get home till midnight, but at the stroke of four Mom thought everybody ought to be up and about and getting ready for a new day.

She cooked breakfast as soon as she got up, and if you ate you got up when she did.

We found an apartment near the Municipal Golf Course in a building that later became a Carmelite Monastery. Places were hard to find because of the number of servicemen and their families stationed in Asheville. There were several military hospitals here, plus the Weather Wing, the Redistribution Station, and several POW camps.

Ours was a small place, one bedroom, a living room, a bath, and a kitchen. We hadn't been there long when I noticed that Jacque had a few things to learn about cooking. I bought a chicken at the store and brought it home for her to cook. I didn't think to have it cut up, so she said, "I'll cut it up," and when she finished she had so many pieces we couldn't even identify some of them—but we ate it and it was good.

From there, we moved to an upstairs apartment on Cumberland Avenue, nearer to downtown Asheville. This apartment was heated by a fireplace and we had to carry coal upstairs to heat our place. We had no refrigeration so we used a window box. Finally, we were able to afford a little ice box that held a twenty-five-pound block of ice. We had no stove until the people at the mission took up money and bought a gas stove for us for thirty-five dollars.

We didn't notice the hardships or the lack of conveniences. We were so in love with each other and with Jesus that we were carried away. One day Jacque was cleaning the table and she put the food scraps in the ice box and threw the butter in the garbage can.

Some couples today start married life with what we have accumulated in forty-one years of marriage, but we never tried to gather in a lot of material things.

I had no salary the first ten years of our married life. I preached at the mission, or wherever I could pitch my tent, and passed the offering plates and trusted God that we could pay the light bill and have a little left over. Sometimes there was nothing left. We had to make it on very little, but God provided the necessities, and we were satisfied.

We basked in the glory of God, and we had each other's love. What else mattered?

Mother Sexton holds baby Ralph in her arms on porch of cabin in which Ralph was born in 1919 in Sassafras Gap.

Leroy Sexton, about 2½, watches over his baby brother, Ralph, on porch of Sassafras Gap home in 1919.

Ralph, left, and Lee at their open air pulpit in Asheville's West End, 1939.

Ralph, left photo, at Nyack, N.Y., in 1939. Lee, at right in right photo, wrestles stone from quarry with friends to build the Jesus Saves Mission, pictured below.

Youthful preacher Ralph Sexton, at left, about 1940. Above, left to right, Lee Sexton, Pop, Mom, and Ralph at baptizing near Asheville sand drag on French Broad River in 1943.

Left, huge crowd lined banks of French Broad to see Ralph, below right, and Carroll Fowler conduct 1943 baptizing.

Ralph Sexton's first tent, a two-poler, pitched in Canton, N.C., in 1940. Truck, below, in which they hauled the tent, attracted attention with its locomotive nose.

Crowds filled gospel tent in West Asheville in 1944, above, and Ralph Sexton expanded his ministry by preaching in York Chapel, built by Sergeant York, in Pall Mall, Tenn., right photo.

The Sexton tent in Hendersonville, N.C., above, in which Ralph preached four months and three weeks. Left, Ralph at left, and Leroy just starting out as preachers. Below left, Believing Thomas, an itinerant evangelist who passed through occasionally. Below right, driving wasn't all pleasure in the good old days.

A beautiful girl named Jacque, left, came into Ralph's life in 1944. She was saved in his tent and he baptized her, above, in the Balfour Mill Pond near Hendersonville.

Below, Jacque loved the tent meetings from the start. Right, Ralph, center, and Lee, right, enjoy a trip to Florida with Troy Israel in 1945.

Wedding bells rang for Ralph and Jacque on Christmas Eve, 1944.

Below left, newly-weds Lee and Dolores on left and Ralph and Jacque with 1941 Dodge truck used for hauling tent in 1945. Below right, Jacque sews curtains in apartment soon after wedding.

Above, left and right, Ralph and Jacque play with Ralph Jr. in trailer Ralph bought in Miami in 1949. Left, Jacque and Ralph Jr. in the 1939 Plymouth Ralph bought to pull the trailer. Below left, Ralph Jr. plays with little sister Rebecca in 1951. Below right, Ralph with Ralph Jr. and Becky in 1957.

Left, Ralph, on left, and Lee in 1987 look at the "Jesus Saves Mission" they built with their hands in 1939-40. It is still used as a church.

Ralph and Jacque stand at the door of the Gospel Tabernacle of the Missionary Alliance where Ralph started going to church in 1937 and where they were married in 1944.

\bove is the "Send The Light
Iissionary Church" on State
Street in West Asheville which
Ralph pastored from 1954 till
970 when Trinity Baptist
Church, right, was founded.

Ralph poses behind bars in Asheville City Jail where he was locked up twice for disturbing the peace while preaching. Below left, he examines the springs of the bunk on which he slept, and right, he points to the very cell in which he was locked up the Fourth of July, 1940.

Ralph poses in front of the Buncombe County Courthouse in Asheville where he and Lee were jailed on an upper floor. Below, he points toward cellblock where hardened prisoners threatened to make them run the gantlet.

Photos on Pages 10-11
By Maurice Plemmons

Above, Ralph and Trinity Baptist Church members watch Jerry Payne break ground in 1983 for fellowship hall and gymnasium building. Below left, Jacque cries as Ralph says a few words at ground-breaking. Below right, Jacque and Ralph in 1987 photos.

# — 10 —

# Sergeant York

Those who didn't live through World War II might find it odd to think that one of the great heroes at that time was Alvin C. York of Pall Mall, Tennessee, who did his fighting twenty-five years earlier in World War I.

The reason was a movie entitled "Sergeant York," in which Gary Cooper starred as the Tennessee mountaineer who reluctantly went to war and became the most decorated and most heralded soldier of World War I. The movie was adapted from a book entitled *Sergeant York, Last of the Long Hunters* by Tom Skeyhill. It was published by the John C. Winston Company in 1930 and gave York's own account of his heroism in the Argonne Forest of France.

Sergeant York was a deeply religious man who went to war only after God told him through his written word that it was the thing he should do. After the war, York settled back in his native hills and became a country preacher of some note. I met him through a young man from Ashland, Kentucky, named Sammy Sparks, who had attended a Bible school in Cincinnati with Alvin C. York, Jr. Sammy Sparks, who was my friend, had been invited to Pall Mall to preach in a little church called York's Chapel, and he arranged for me to preach there, too.

When I met Sergeant York he autographed a copy of his book and gave it to me. I treasured it, but carelessly loaned it to someone years ago and haven't seen it since.

From the book, I learned the incredible story of Sergeant York.

Alvin C. York received only a modicum of education when he was a lad. He went to school ten weeks of the year for five years and finished with the equivalent of a second-grade education. Actually, it was doubtful that he could have passed the second grade. This was no fault of his own. Those were the educational standards of the time in the hills of Tennessee. His brothers and sisters and companions from surrounding hills received the same education. Because of this absence of educational facilities, York had to go through life handicapped by near illiteracy and a meager education.

Early in life he became a drunkard and hell-raiser. He shot up the community, drank barrels of whiskey over the years, palled around with scoundrels, and generally kept himself in hot water, both with his parents and with the law.

On the first of January, 1915, York gained one of the greatest victories any man can hope for. He conquered himself. He came home that morning half drunk as usual and found his mother waiting up for him. He asked why she hadn't gone to bed and she cried that she could not, since she knew he was out drinking and fighting. She said she knew how wild he was, and how big and strong and daring, and she worried that something would happen to him.

He was shaken to the extent that everything that was fine and manly in his character surfaced, and he took his mother in his arms and solemnly promised that he would never drink, gamble, fight, smoke, use a single "cuss" word, lose his temper, or raise his voice in anger again as long as he lived.

His little, old God-fearing mother had brought him to his knees, and he completely abandoned the old life. To his dying day, he never backslid. He became a religious man and often preached fiery sermons in his later days.

His struggle was hard, especially on Saturdays when his former companions rode by his house and begged him to come with them to Kentucky for a night of whooping things up. But he won out. He later said he had changed his ways because of three things: (1) the incident with his mother; (2) a fire-and-brimstone evangelist who "scared the devil out of me," and (3) because of a beautiful mountain girl named Gracie Williams whom he truly loved. She would have nothing to do with a wild man.

The dominating factor, in his own words, was, "I abandoned the old life completely and forever because I jes' kinder realized I was missing the finer things of life, and when you miss the finer things of life, you might jes' as well be a razorback hog grubbing for acorns on the mountainside."

When World War I came, York could not force himself to think of going into the army to kill other people. He abhorred that thought as much as he disliked strong drink. Official records in Washington show that when York was examined at Jamestown, he weighed more than one-eighty, stood over six feet, and was a perfect specimen of physical manhood. He carried his suitcase and walked out of the mountains alone.

He was taken into the army as a conscientious objector, which was about like the mark of Cain. In February, 1918, he was attached as a private to Company G of the 328th Battalion of the 82nd Division—the All-American Division. His company commander was Capt. E. C. B. Danforth, Jr., of Augusta, Georgia, and his battalion commander was Major George Edward Buxton, a friend of Theodore Roosevelt and a blue-blood from Providence, Rhode Island.

In the mountaineer's company were Greeks, Poles, Italians, Irishmen, East Side Jews, and some American-born boys. Almost half were unable to read or write, and a number couldn't even speak the American language. They were rough and tough, and they did their share of boozing, gambling, leave-breaking, and whooping up Ned. But they were good soldiers, loyal companions, and they later proved at Saint-Mihiel and in the Argonne Forest that they were as recklessly brave and fearless a company as ever crossed the seas.

At first York felt out of his element. He no longer drank, fought, or gambled, and he had never met foreign-born people. His knowledge of human beings was limited to the pure Anglo-Saxon type on the mountains of East Tennessee and Western North Carolina. He referred to everybody outside the mountains as "furiners," and he once wrote in his dairy, "I am the homesickest boy you ever seed."

York had been the best shot in the hills with a squirrel rifle, and with such a background in firearms, he felt at home with some aspects of the service. He was intelligent despite his lack of formal education, and he was conscientious and amenable to discipline. His captain wanted to promote him to corporal but he could not because of the cloud of conscientious objector hanging over York's head.

A few days after he entered camp, York wrote home: "They done give me a dirty, greasy old army rifle, and tomorrow they are agoin' to take me out on the rifle range and teach me how to shoot. Ho! Ho!"

York wrestled daily with his problem. He felt deeply that war and fighting were wrong, and the more he studied the Bible the more he was convinced of it. Finally, he went to Capt. Danforth and told him: "Captain, sir, I'm a-tellin' you, and I hain't afoolin', I have done obeyed every order right smart and I am agoin' to. If you order me overseas, I'm agoin'. If you put a rifle-gun in my hands and tell me to kill Germans, I'm agoin' to kill them, but I'm awarnin' you, Captain Danforth, that if you force me to kill any of my fellowmen, I'm agoin' to hold you responsible for their lives before God in Heaven on Jedgment Day."

The captain handled this problem in the army way: He passed the buck from company level to Major Buxton on the battalion level. The major gave York two weeks leave to think things over and York "lit out fer home." Near the end of his leave, York went alone into the mountains and spent days reading his Bible and praying. At the end of thirty-six hours of constant prayer, he said something happened to him. He got off his knees and walked home, explaining later that he felt "like the waters of a lake when the master said, 'Peace, be still.'"

He told his mother, "I'm a-goin' to war with the sword of the Lord and of Gideon." He took her in his arms. "I'm agoin' and I'm acomin' back because I have received my assurance from God himself that it's all right for me to go to war, and that as long as I believe in him, not one hair of my head will be harmed."

Armed with such faith, he felt invulnerable. He had that simple, total faith of the mountaineer, and I am sure scoffers and cynics laughed and sneered at him, but he went overseas and in one of the greatest individual fights in the history of modern warfare, he single-handedly whipped an entire machine-gun battalion.

Of all the millions of brave men who fought in World War I, Marshall Foch picked him as the outstanding hero.

Armed with the sword of the Lord and of Gideon, with the purest Anglo-Saxon blood in the world flowing in his veins, speaking the Old English of Chaucer and Shakespeare, the greatest shot and mightiest hunter in the mountains went forth to battle, a soldier in the 328th Battalion of the 82nd Division.

During the battle of the Argonne Forest, Corporal York's company was ordered to charge into the teeth of a machine-gun battalion's withering fire. Pinned down in no-man's land, the company cast about for ways to overcome the enemy's superior fire and a squad was sent around the flank to try to relive the pressure of the German machine guns. York's squad was chosen.

The squad found its way around the flank, up the backside of a hill, and suddenly it was face to face with the machine-gun battalion's headquarters. The Americans had the drop, and the German officers surrendered. But one of the captured officers tricked the Americans. He barked a command in German, his fellow officers hit the ground, and machine guns mowed down half of the American squad. Only seven privates and Cpl. York were unhurt.

The privates took cover and York stood his ground. Shooting offhand, he fired eighteen times and shot eighteen German soldiers in the head. The others were driven to cover. He had remembered the favorite motto of his mother: "When in danger, slow up and think fast."

Later, when questioned by General Pershing, he explained how he shot up the German battalion: "Easy, sir, every time I seed a German I jes' teched him off."

York's eyes swept the field. His doughboys held the prisoners. He glanced swiftly to both sides, and barely in time. Six German soldiers and an officer crouching in a gun pit only twenty yards away summed up the situation and realized they faced only one fighting man. They came to their feet and rushed York down a trail in single file, baring naked steel.

York dropped his empty rifle and flipped out his pistol—and accomplished what was perhaps the greatest individual shooting feat of the war. He shot the seventh German first, then the sixth, then the fifth, and so on, killing the officer last. The bodies of the seven dead were arranged in a straight line, the officer's head lying at York's feet.

When asked later why he shot the rear ones first, York said when turkey hunting in Tennessee he always shot the rear one first so the ones in front, thinking he missed, kept a-comin'. "If I'd a-shot the front ones first," he said, "the rear ones would have abandoned the rush and took cover."

Cautiously, another German head appeared over the nearby parapet and York "teched him off," too. That made twenty-six dead Germans with twenty-six shots.

The American privates and captured German officers

watched the incredible spectacle before them with mouths hanging open.

In English, the German commander asked York, "What are you?"

Before York could reply another head appeared over the parapet and York made it twenty-seven in a row.

"Are you English?" the German asked.

"No. American."

"If you will permit me," the German commander said, "I will make the battalion surrender."

"Can you?" asked the suspicious York.

His vanity stung, the German leaped to his feet, clicked his Prussian heels together, and answered, "I am the commanding officer. If I blow this whistle, they will surrender."

York sprang to the officer's side and pushed his pistol into the man's face. "Blow that whistle," he said slowly, "and blow it right smart."

The officer blew the whistle, and from the trenches the machine gunners rose with hands in the air.

On their own ground, in broad daylight, and in a fair fight, Corporal York had outshot a German battalion, killed twenty-seven men with twenty-seven shots, and captured 129 men, three officers, and thirty-five machine guns. He did it single-handedly.

I had seen the film, "Sergeant York," and admired the character greatly that Gary Cooper played, never realizing I would get to meet him.

When Sammy Sparks called me and said he wanted Bly Jackson, who worked with me as a wonderful singer, and me to come to Pall Mall, Tennessee, and preach in York's Chapel, I was thrilled to death.

In appreciation for what he had done in the war, Sgt. York's friends had built him a home on the bottomland he so admired. This was the home we went into. It was a comfortable home. Sgt. York, being a mountain man, lived plain and simple. It was a joy to be able to stay in his home. At mealtime, Mrs. York, the former Gracie Williams, spread every kind of food imaginable on a long country table.

Sgt. York walked tall among his people, but he was not a proud man. He was humble, and one thing he demanded was reverence to God's house. He also demanded attention to the preacher.

We went to the chapel and I preached on "Hell." God honored that meeting, and when we went back to Sgt. York's house, he said, "Preacher, when you preached that message on hell, I could smell the smoke."

I felt honored.

During our conversation, he said to me, "I wouldn't give a dime for a preacher who wouldn't preach holiness, the separated life for a Christian." When it came to things of God, I found him to be the same as he had been in the military: There was no compromise in him. I liked him very much.

On his property were underground caverns which he permitted us to go in. He cautioned us to the danger. He gave us a long rope and we tied it to a tree and let ourselves into the caverns, perhaps twenty-five or thirty feet down. Then with flashlights to light our way, we went deep into the caverns. The pathway was slippery wet, and the way was gloomy. Stalactites hung in eerie formations. We discussed what total darkness would be like, as depicted in the Bible, and we turned off the lights and stood in stygian darkness for several minutes. I thought what it would be like to be in Eternity in total darkness. That darkness reached out and wrapped us in its arms, and the strangest feeling overcame us. People wonder how hell could be total darkness and still be in flames. Scientists have learned that ether burns with a roar but you can't see the flames, and if man can do that in a laboratory, what can God do? I was glad to get back into daylight when we came out of the caverns.

While there, we invited the Sergeant to come to Asheville and preach in the West End mission. He said he was booked to come to Asheville and participate in a War Bond Rally, and perhaps he could work out the time on that trip. He said several movie stars were coming for the rally.

Before the rally, he was forced by illness or something to cancel his participation, but we contacted him and he agreed to preach for us at another time if we came to Pall Mall and drove him to Asheville.

We set a date, and Lee, Sam, and I drove to Tennessee and got him. We came back through Knoxville and called ahead to the Andrew Johnson Hotel to reserve a table for lunch. Word spread through the hotel that Sgt. York was coming for lunch.

I drove a Pontiac Silver Fleet and when we pulled up to the hotel, dozens of people standing there came to attention. They rushed to open doors for him, and we were escorted into that beautiful hotel's enormous dining room. The other tables were mostly filled with diners who had come to see Sgt. York, but the center table, a huge round table set to perfection, had a signboard on it: "Reserved For Sergeant York."

Those people didn't know Lee and Sammy and me from Adam's house cats, but they knew Sergeant York, and because we were with him, we were treated like kings that day.

As we prayed over lunch, I thought about the table being reserved for Sgt. York, but what will the inheritance be in heaven, the inheritance paid for by Christ's blood and reserved for him and the church, which, of course, is us.

We came on into Asheville and Sergeant preached at the mission that night. The tabernacle was filled and people stood all around it. People from the Veterans Administration were there, a lot of servicemen came, and veterans of World War I proudly wore their uniforms to the service.

For him to come to that little mission shows what kind of a man he was. He could have come to Asheville and hobnobbed with movie stars, but he came instead to rub elbows with the simple folk and to preach to them. He preached a good gospel message and when he finished he made an altar call, inviting those who did not know Christ to come forward. Six people were saved that night. Some of those saved are still living and still going for God. What a wonderful service we had!

We put him up in one of the downtown hotels, probably the George Vanderbilt or Battery Park, and the next day we drove him on to Statesville where he had a meeting that night.

God honored Sgt. York. His very presence in a city was a blessing. He stood tall and manly with a red tint to his hair. He dressed in a simple suit and tie, and he enjoyed living. But most of all Sgt. York enjoyed being a Christian. He helped his mountain neighbors in the Tennessee woods. He built a school for them and built the little church where I preached. He used a lot of the proceeds from the movie about his life to help the people he loved.

What a man was Sergeant York!

# — 11 —

# "God Will Take Care of You"

Early in 1945 while the war in Europe wound down and American forces advanced on the Japanese through the South Pacific, Sammy Sparks contacted me and said some businessmen in Huntington, West Virginia, wanted to hold a citywide campaign and needed a tent. I agreed to rent them my tent and told Sammy we would deliver it to Huntington.

We had a worn-out Dodge tractor-trailer that might make it to Huntington—and might not.

One day Lee and I walked up Lexington Avenue and saw a beautiful tractor-trailer parked on the street. The place was booming with produce stands. The truck was a Dodge and had been owned by Champion Paper and Fiber Company in Canton but was too small for the heavy hauling Champion needed. E. C. Burleson, who owned a produce market on Lexington, had bought the truck from Champion.

I remember saying to Lee, "Look, Lee, there's our truck." Somehow, God impressed on me that this truck could be ours. We asked who owned it and were directed to Burleson.

"Mr. Burleson," I said, shaking his hand, "I am Ralph Sexton and this is my brother Lee. We are preachers of the gospel and have been praying for a tractor-trailer truck to haul our tent equipment on. We saw yours outside and wondered if you might sell it."

Burleson indicated that he knew who we were because we had preached so much on Lexington, and after studying a few moments, he said, "I might sell it to you."

I am sure God spoke to his heart, because he said, "Yes, I'll sell it to you, but I have to have twenty-seven hundred dollars."

Well, that was a lot of money then, but can you imagine buying an almost new tractor-trailer rig for that price?

"God willing," I said, "we'll take it," and we shook hands on the deal.

We went straight to First Union Bank on Church Street and explained to the bank manager who we were and what we wanted.

"We don't have any money," I said. "We need the whole amount."

"What collateral can you give me?" he asked.

"We don't have anything for collateral," we said, honestly.

He thought a minute, and to show how God's hand was in that, he finally said, "I'll tell you what I'll do. I will give you the loan and use the truck itself for collateral. When would you like the money?"

"We'd like it right now if we can get it," I said.

He wrote us a check for twenty-seven hundred dollars and we went straight back to Lexington and purchased the truck from E. C. Burleson.

We drove it home, and for years we used that truck to haul our tents in.

We loaded the tent on the truck and Lee drove it to Huntington. I rode up in a car with my younger brother, Frank. Frank had never been saved, but on the way to Huntington he found the Lord. What a glorious trip that was!

We erected the tent for the businessmen. This was a heavy tent, strung with airplane cable. We spread it out on the ground and I crawled under it to get the block and tackle to raise the canvas, and halfway there the tent was so heavy on me I thought I would smother to death. But I made it and gulped in fresh air, and we got the tent up all right.

Jacque came up for the meeting, and it was a good one. When it closed we dropped the tent, loaded it on the truck, and I drove it back to Asheville. Jacque rode with me on one of the wildest rides of our lives.

Coming through those hairpin curves in the mountains of West Virginia, we topped a hill and started down the other side. I hit the air brakes and they were gone. The truck rolled faster, building speed down the long grade.

Wildly I tried to think of what to do, and there was nothing to do but hold the truck in the road. I knew if God didn't help us we would wreck; so I started to pray, and when I did God spoke to me and said, "Sing."

"Sing?" I said aloud, and Jacque glanced quickly at me.

I have never been able to carry a tune, and I thought here I am in a runaway truck and God is telling me to sing.

But God had made me do strange things before.

"What should I sing?" I asked.

God said, "Sing that old song, 'God Will Take Care of You.'"

I began to sing, "Be not dismayed what e're betide, God will take care of you." Jacque joined me, and we sang loudly as the truck gained more speed down the mountain and I had to fight the wheel to hold it in the road. Fortunately, we met no other vehicles.

Suddenly I saw the hood of the truck begin to quiver. I yelled to Jacque to look at it. Then the truck lost speed. The curves went by slower, and we came to a level place and rolled to a stop.

We sat there looking at each other, and two verses of Scripture came to my mind: "He shall give his angels charge over thee and they shall keep thee in all thy ways. They shall bear thee up in their hands, lest thou dash thy foot against a stone," that from Psalms, and from Matthew: "The guardian angels of the saints do always behold thy face."

The Scripture teaches the ministry of angels, and we

both knew that an angel had stopped that truck and spared our lives because God wasn't finished with us yet. What an experience!

Many Christians, unfortunately, never hear about nor know anything about the ministry of the angels to the saints.

We sat there a long time, and when the air built back in the brakes I drove on to Asheville with no further difficulty.

The war ended and the nation celebrated secularly and never really came back to its knees. Our work continued unabated. Actually we stepped it up because we saw the nation's need.

We continued to hold three services every Sunday at the mission; I continued my radio ministry; and we conducted tent meetings wherever we got the opportunity.

Sammy Sparks, who had been preaching in Indiana, wrote to us that the city of Hammond, Indiana, would like us to come up and preach a revival. We could pitch the tent on the shores of Lake Michigan in a beautiful spot, Sammy said.

We accepted, and Lee drove the tent to Indiana and put it up. Jacque and I drove up later and stayed in a small trailer. Tom Beam, the pastor of the Nazarene Church in Hammond, had set up the meeting with other Nazarene pastors and with the blessing of the district superintendent. Jacque was pregnant but in sound health. Several preachers from the Asheville vicinity went up for the meetings, including J. Bly Hill, Ed Kuykendall, and Bly Jackson.

Our tent was a sixty-by-one-hundred-twenty with three poles, a good-sized tent that seated a lot of people.

The revival began at a good pace. Crowds overflowed the tent and a lot of souls were saved. Each evening we had a young people's service and then a preaching service for all.

God honored that meeting in many ways. He also allowed for a bit of levity. Robert E. Stone, pastor of the Nazarene Church in Dayton, Ohio, addressed the crowd one evening. He was a huge man, probably six-feet-six. He was so heavy he had to go to the coal yard to weigh.

He was also a very emphatic man who, helped by his size, could score his points well with any audience.

"Lean on Jesus," he shouted that evening. "Lean on Jesus; you'll never go down!"

He said that over and over while backing away from the podium, and when he reached his chair at the rear of the platform, he shouted once more: "Lean on Jesus! You'll never go down!" Sitting down, he pushed his chair just a few inches to the edge of the platform, and when he put his full weight in the chair, he flipped over and went head over heels off the back of the platform.

One afternoon I walked down to the tent to check on things. The sun shone beautifully, not a breath of wind stirred the waters of Lake Michigan, and the day was as serene as anyone could have wanted.

I saw Lee standing by the water down the shore, and I walked over to him. He didn't look at me, but apparently sensed my presence. He was staring out over the lake, rather glassy-eyed, I thought.

I started to speak to him, but before I could, he said, "Ralph, this tent is going to blow away tonight."

"What?" I said. "Lee, what are you talking about?"

"Tonight it's going," he said.

I looked around and thought I had never seen a more beautiful day.

"I've been praying," Lee said. "But it's still going to blow away tonight."

We went on with the service that evening. Lee led the singing. The crowd gathered, the platform was filled with preachers, and the music was beautiful.

Lee led "Is Not This The Land of Beulah?" and in the middle of the song I heard something roaring in the distance. It sounded like a train coming—the same sound I heard in Hazelwood the night our tent blew down there six years earlier.

I looked to the top of the tent for the first signs of disaster, and I saw the canvas begin to quiver. Then the tent starting breathing, and Lee turned to look at me, still singing. The top of the tent raised up and came back down, slowly, then at a faster pace—and the roaring grew louder.

I went to the microphone and Lee stopped the song. The crowd quieted.

"Ladies and gentlemen," I said, "I want you to stand and march into the church—right now!"

The tent was pitched beside Tom Bean's church. As the crowd stood, I said, "Go quickly, but don't run. Don't panic. Just walk."

One young man began to wave his arms. "Stop!" he shouted. "Stop! Have faith in God!"

Over the loudspeaker, I said, "Young man, when God says to run, have faith enough to run. Now get gone!"

He left with the others.

Lee leaped from the platform and rushed to the back of the tent. He sat on the side wall, trying to hold it down, but the wind hurled him through the air as if he were a cock. When he landed unharmed, he was still singing, "Is not this the land of Beulah?" I saw that everybody was out of the tent except a man and his wife and daughter. I ran to them and helped them out. Just as they reached the church, the wind struck with a fury. The mast poles bent like wire. The wiring ripped loose and sparks flew before darkness enveloped the tent. It collapsed with a roar and the storm ripped it to shreds and carried parts of it into the air.

When the storm abated, we returned to look at the tent. Someone brought lights and as we poked through the canvas, we heard a groan and saw a man's head rise through a rip in the tent. When he stood we saw that he weighed three hundred pounds or more. He grinned sheepishly, shook his head, and laughed, "Boy, that was something!" He said he had tried to run and when he saw he couldn't move fast enough, he simply lay down between the rows of seats. He wasn't even scratched.

The morning after the storm, Lee and I went back to the tent and our worst fears were realized. The canvas was shredded and bits of it hung on telephone poles and in trees all around.

Our loss was great. We had no insurance. But we swallowed the defeat and continued the meeting in the church for three more weeks.

The people of Hammond were generous, however, and within two weeks they chipped in enough money to replace the tent with a new one, also a sixty by one-hundred-twenty supported by airplane cable. This one was stronger than the one we lost.

This tent and the one in Hazelwood were the only two we ever had blow down. We were in a lot of bad storms and sometimes had to station men at each pole line to hold the tent down until the storm passed, and except for those two we always succeeded in keeping the canvas in place.

When we returned to Asheville from Indiana, we moved from our apartment on Cumberland Avenue into a basement apartment on Starnes Avenue. This one had a woodstove for Jacque to cook on. It had electricity, of course, but no electric range.

I kept calling Jacque my Rebecca and she told me one of these days she was going to have me a Rebecca. But what we got that time was another Ralph.

Ralph Junior was born January 17, 1947. The doctor had told us when we were married that we should never try to have children, but we had prayed and prayed over the subject, and we prayed, "God, if it is your will for us to have a child, we pray first for a man child, and we pray that you will call him and use him in a mighty way to win souls to Christ." That was the gist of many of our prayers.

When we learned we had a baby growing inside of Jacque, the devil told us she would die because the doctor had said she was not able to bear children. Our parents were worried over Jacque's health, but she walked on clouds, so thrilled was she that she was going to be a mother. Dr. Harmon Bailey was her physician.

When Ralph Junior was born, I was so excited I didn't know what to do. We were both thrilled to death, and convinced that God had answered our prayers in giving us a man child first. We raised that little boy on love, careful all his life never to talk to him about preaching. If God wanted to use him, we wanted God to do the calling, but we kept our fingers crossed. He grew to manhood, went to college and then into business, and one evening when he was thirty he telephoned us that God had filled him with the spirit and called him to preach.

"Daddy," he said, "I know I must preach."

"I know it, too, Son," I said, "I've known it all along."

Then I told him how we had promised God before he was born that if God gave us a man child we wanted him to be used by God to preach the Word.

Oddly enough, Ralph Junior was in Hammond, Indiana, at the Holiday Inn when he telephoned us with the news that night.

# — 12 —

# No Beds of Roses

If I have left the impression that all we had to do to hold a tent meeting was go into a community and set up the tent and open the flaps, then I need to do some straightening out. We encountered opposition—stiff opposition—in many places. Some towns didn't want tent meetings.

In 1949 we wanted to hold a meeting in Hendersonville. The Brookshire Brothers had a horse barn around First Avenue, and in that area was a vacant lot that would be perfect for a meeting. It had room for the tent and space for a lot of parking.

I went to see the mayor, and he welcomed me with open arms. "We would love to have you run a revival here," he said, "but first, how about checking with the people in that area and see if they have any objections."

His suggestion was sound; so I went down to First Avenue and knocked on a couple of doors and asked if they had any objections to my putting up a gospel tent and holding a meeting. I showed where I wanted to pitch the tent. Both homeowners said flatly, "No, sir, I don't want a tent meeting there." They didn't if, and, or but around—they came right out and said they didn't want me.

There was an old grist mill across the road from the lot on which we planned to pitch the tent. The mill was beside the horse barn in which riding horses were kept.

"Sir," I introduced myself to the mill owner, "would you object if I put a tent over there and held a revival meeting?"

"Yes," he said unequivocally, "I would object."

"Why?"

"I don't want a meeting like that here."

"But why not?"

"This is a food establishment," he said, "We grind corn into meal that people eat. I want this area kept clean."

A horse fly buzzed by his nose and when he said that, I looked around and the flies were swarming, attracted by that horse barn. They were all around his head.

I wondered how many flies he bagged up with his meal, but I didn't say anything. I thanked him and left.

We would have to make a different approach to this area. I told Lee that I felt the people there needed a revival, but we would have to walk carefully.

We had the mayor's permission, and we had rented the lot. Lee and I called what we were about to do "gangstering for God." It was a plan we had designed to work around circumstances such as we faced in Hendersonville.

We rounded up a crew, waiting till everybody went home from the horse barn and the grist mill, and pulled the truck onto the lot. In the dark, we rolled the canvas off and stretched it. We used steel axle rods for pegs, and we wrapped burlap bags and old quilts over them to keep them from sounding when we hammered them into the ground.

We worked all night and when daylight approached, we had the mast poles up, the tent laced up and ready to raise—and here came the law!

The police pulled onto the lot and an officer stepped out of the car, holding out his hand. "Fellows," he said, "don't hit another lick."

"How come?" Lee asked.

"Not till you go see the mayor," he said.

"I'll go see the mayor," I said so the officer could hear me, and as I walked past Lee I said in a subdued voice, "I may go by way of Spartanburg."

He got the message. He knew I would kill enough time on the way to the mayor's office for him to get the tent up.

I drove around town several times, and figured Lee had had enough time to get the tent raised and tied off, then I went to the mayor's office.

The mayor said, "I'm sorry to have go back on my promise, but I can't let you put your tent up."

"But, mayor," I protested, "the tent is already up."

"What?" he was startled. "Already up?"

"We put it up last night," I said, "after you gave us permission."

"Then you'll have to take it down."

"I'm sorry, but we can't do that," I said, "We've gone to a lot of time and expense to get that tent up. And besides—you promised!"

Those who opposed us went to the elderly man who owned the lot. He told them that we had legally rented the lot and paid for it, but they coerced him into telling us we couldn't use the land.

He lived within walking distance, but he didn't walk over to see us. He wrote a letter to us and walked to the post office to mail it. He sent it registered and special delivery and it cost him sixty cents to mail it instead of the three cents an ordinary letter cost. To this day, I think he was playing to give us more time. When we got the letter, everything was ready for the meeting to start.

In the letter he gave us twenty-four hours to tear down and move off his land. Lee and I prayed in the tent, and God told us to go see a lawyer. We went to a Lawyer Jackson whose office was upstairs across the street from the Post Office.

When we walked in, I said, "Mr. Jackson, we're the Sexton . . . ."

"I know who you are," he said.

"We want to . . . ."

"I know, I know," he said. God was really working for us.

"You know why we're here?" I asked.

"Of course, I know," he said. "Everybody in town knows."

"Well, what can we do?"

"Tell 'em to go to hell," he said flatly. "My mother was an old-time praying mother. I'm not a Christian, but I'm for what you're doing. So tell 'em . . . ."

"I know," I said. "I heard you the first time. But we don't want them to go to hell. That's exactly why we're here—to try to save them from going to hell."

"Well, you boys are on safe ground," he said. "The only thing they can do is get an injunction and that'll take thirty days."

"Glory to God!" I shouted. "We can have a good tent meeting in thirty days."

We walked on air out of that office, and we could hear Lawyer Jackson laughing behind us.

We started the meeting that night and the crowds came in droves. That meeting developed into one of the greatest we ever held. More than a thousand souls were saved or gloriously reclaimed, and we stayed there one week less than five months—the longest tent meeting I ever held.

But keeping the meeting going was not without difficulty.

We hadn't been in the meeting many days when officials from the health department came to the tent and told us we would have to vacate.

"Why?" I asked.

"You're a health hazard," the man said.

"How is that?" I asked.

"Come with me and I will show you," he said, and he went straight to some human excrement someone had planted under the tent.

"You came straight to this spot," I accused. "How did you know where it was?"

The man was startled, and he didn't answer me. But I pressed him.

"How did you know?" I asked.

He left and didn't come back.

Another night someone came to the platform after the service began and whispered to me, "The law is outside. They want you to come out."

"Go back and tell them," I said, "that we are in service, and if they want to see me they'll have to come in."

They wouldn't come in; they just drove away.

We started that meeting in May and finally closed it in October. On three different occasions I closed the revival, but each time God said, "You closed it. I didn't."

Each time I announced, "God isn't through here. We'll keep the meeting open." The crowds didn't slack off at all until cold weather came.

One of the funniest incidents I remember occurred during that Hendersonville meeting. We hired a mountain boy named William Justice to watch the tent for us. He loved the job. He stayed in the tent at night, sleeping in quarters he arranged for himself under the platform. He had a hot plate and a cot and he told us he had all the comforts of home.

On a Sunday afternoon, when I got halfway though my sermon, the crowd on the front benches suddenly began to squirm in a restless sort of way. I continued to preach, wondering all the while what was going on.

Suddenly, I saw whiffs of smoke coming out from beneath the platform. Jacque, seated near the front, kept getting my eye and nodding her head toward the smoke.

I was about ready to tell the crowd to make its way orderly out of the tent, when I got an unmistakable whiff of bacon frying. Mingled with that odor was that of coffee perking.

William Justice was fixing his lunch in his quarters under the platform!

Out of that Hendersonville meeting rose the First Church of the Nazarene in Hendersonville, and a lot of other good things. A lot of people were saved, and many are still alive and living Christian lives.

All of our opposition in 1949 didn't come from tent meetings. We also decided to try evangelizing on the road in a different way.

Ralph Jr. was about two and a half years old, and I thought we should get a little house trailer and evangelize in faraway places. I had a 1940 Ford that Harry Burrell had rebuilt. He put a truck motor in it, and it was a strong car. I paid Harry nine hundred dollars for the car and used it for some time traveling to meetings and back. I advertised the car and sold it for nine hundred, and God told me to take that money and buy a car and trailer. I was so sure that was what God wanted me to do that I didn't question it. It also seemed that God was telling me to go to Miami and buy the vehicles.

Jacque didn't question my faith; so I caught the bus for Miami. The devil kept telling me I was out of my mind, but when God tells you something, you go forward with boldness. I didn't know how, but I was sure I would find a car and trailer for nine hundred dollars in Miami.

I looked Miami from stem to stern, and the only thing I found that looked good was a 1941 Nash. I telephoned Jacque and told her I was tired. I said, "I may just buy that Nash and drive it home, but I'm going to stay one more day."

I prayed, and the next day God told me to catch the bus and ride till he told me to get off. On that bus, the devil had a field day with me, but God waited patiently and after I warded off the devil, God said, "Get off at the next corner."

I had not the slightest idea where I was except that I was still in Miami. When I got off the bus, I looked at the maze of streets. God said, "Go up that one," and I went up that street. I topped a hill and saw some cars ahead. They looked like used cars. God said, "Go there."

As soon as I stepped on the car lot, a 1939 Plymouth attracted my eye.

A man came over.

"How much?" I asked.

"Four hundred dollars," he said.

On the back side of the lot I saw a house trailer, a popular little nineteen-foot model called a "Covered Wagon."

"How much is that little trailer?" I asked.

We walked to the trailer and the man said, "It doesn't belong to me. I'm selling it on consignment for a lady. I think she wants something over five hundred dollars for it."

Very quickly I noted that the two figures added to a little over nine hundred dollars. "This is it," I thought, and God affirmed my thought. "This *is* it," he said.

When we figured up, I lacked a little more than a hundred dollars having enough money to buy the '39 Plymouth and the house trailer. "Let me call my brother Paul in Asheville," I said. "Maybe he can let me have the money."

The man and his wife let me call on their telephone, and Paul wired the money to me. They drove me to Western Union and I got the money, and when we got back to the lot we completed the transaction.

When I started to hitch up, I saw the car didn't have a trailer hitch, and when I mentioned it the man put one on for me.

I hit the road and didn't want to stop. I was so excited that I drove until I was about to fall asleep, and I pulled off the road and slept a while. When I awakened, I couldn't get the vehicles out of the sand; but a truck stopped, and the driver hauled me out and put me on my way. Without further incident, I motored into Asheville as happy as a lark.

One of my brothers bought what little furniture we had and we closed our apartment, packed up what we had left, and headed for Muskogee, Oklahoma, where we had a meeting scheduled. Lewis Brown of Covington, Kentucky, traveled with us. He was my singer, and a good one. He had played and sung for Red Foley on the Grand Ole Opry. He had a wonderful testimony.

In Muskogee, we had a great meeting at a Nazarene church. We lived in that little trailer. After that, I had a call to go to Texas for a meeting, then one in California, and finally one in the state of Washington.

Not wanting to pull the trailer all the way to California, I left it in Texas. We had to pawn Jacque's rings to get enough money to make it to California. If we made a hundred dollars in one of those meetings, we were lucky.

I remember how amazed I was the first time I saw the Rocky Mountains. I didn't realize how high they were, but that little Plymouth climbed right into the mountains and just kept purring along.

No one had cautioned me not to try to drive through those mountains at night. Darkness came and we climbed higher, and it's a miracle we got as far as we did. The temperature drops so low in those mountains in the winter and sometimes in the spring or fall that if a car stalled you could freeze to death.

About two in the morning, the Plymouth seemed to explode. The lid blew off the radiator, and we slowed and stopped in a cloud of steam.

Jacque was in the back seat, lying under several blankets, cuddling Ralph Jr. to keep him warm. Very little traffic came along, but after a while a man and his wife driving a Kaiser stopped.

The man noted our condition and took pity on us. "I can't take all of you," he said. "I wish I could, but I can only take one."

"I'll go," Lewis said. "You stay here and try to keep them warm, and maybe I can find some help to bring back."

They drove down the mountain until they came to a little motel. The man let Lewis out there and drove on. Lewis saw one small light burning, and he told himself, "I may as well get shot as freeze to death." He knocked loudly on the door.

"Get away from here," a male voice inside shouted.

Lewis moved on to another door and banged on it. A man answered and Lewis told him about our plight. It was then about five o'clock in the morning.

Lewis and the man he awakened arrived at our car a little later with vessels filled with water. We repaired the car, filled the radiator, and were soon on our way.

God had wrought another miracle. If that man in the Kaiser hadn't come along, we might have frozen to death. We passed through Flagstaff, Arizona, that morning, and came to the Colorado River later in the day. When we crossed the river, it was springtime. The sun was shining, birds singing, flowers blooming. We were excited and thrilled and very glad to be off the mountains.

We talked about our plight that night in the mountains and agreed it was typical of how God in his mercy spares us when we are in sin, when we're lost and can't take care of ourselves. God brings us from darkness to light, from cold to warmth . . . .

We made it to California and up the coast through the giant redwood forests to Oregon and on into Kennewick, Washington, where we had a revival scheduled. Going through the redwood forests was a tremendous thrill, like driving through a gigantic cathedral. The feeling was unexplainable, but it made us want to fall down and worship the creator.

In Kennewick, we stayed in the pastor's home. His church was small, with seats for about a hundred fifty people, but the Sunday School board on the wall showed that only thirty-five came to service the previous Sunday. The devil whispered, "You're crazy. You've come three thousand miles to preach to thirty-five people!" He added, "You won't make gas money to get you back home."

But the church filled to overflowing the first night of the meeting, and crowds continued to come like that for several days. We had to set out chairs to accomodate those who didn't arrive in time to get seats. So many mourners came to the altar that we had to arrange for more altar space. God really blessed that meeting. Night after night, God sent people in, and he saved many souls.

One night, Lewis came to me and said, "Ralph, this pastor is not taking up an offering. How are we going to get back home?"

I told him to pray about it, and God then gave me boldness and I asked the preacher if we could take up an offering.

"I don't care," he said. Both the preacher and his wife worked on regular jobs.

We took an offering every night after that, and at the end of the meeting we had almost a thousand dollars to divide. On the last night of the meeting, one of the men who had attended regularly asked us to stop by his home on the way out of town the next day.

He lived in a mobile home and when we stopped to bid him goodbye, he gave us five hundred dollars more.

"Glory to God," I thought. "The devil is a liar!"

The pastor's wife, in whose home we stayed, had a big red cat which she kept in the house. One morning we came down to breakfast and her cat was on the table going from plate to plate. One Sunday morning Lewis became so aggravated with that cat that he grabbed it and flung it out in the yard. We couldn't go to church until we found that cat.

I spent two years evangelizing off and on, squeezing church revivals in between tent meetings. I held revivals in churches in South Carolina, Tennessee, Ohio, West Virginia, and other places. A Church of the Nazarene had been formed in Asheville and had rented the West End Mission from us; so we were free to evangelize wherever we wanted to.

I preached in Baptist, Methodist, Nazarene, Free Will Baptist, Churches of the Brethren, Christian Union churches and tabernacles, and many other denominational churches. As long as a church is not in error in its doctrine, denomination is not that important.

The year 1950 was significant to our ministry and to our lives, Jacque's and mine. We had to cross some of the toughest obstacles we ever faced: the birth of our daughter under difficult circumstances, a disputed tent meeting in Biltmore, and a fight with proponents of strong drink who were polluting our city with alcohol.

The three occurred simultaneously.

Jacque gave me my little Rebecca on March 3, 1950. Jacque was born in 1925, Rebecca in 1950, and Rebecca had a little daughter, Elizabeth, in 1975. We were quarter-century people.

We named our daughter Catherine Rebecca—Catherine for Jacque's older sister who could have no children.

During Jacque's pregnancy, I put out petitions trying to get beer and wine out of Buncombe County. While preaching in West End, I was confronted daily with the results of drinking. I knew that years ago God had used the evangelist to come in and stir a city or community against sin and vice. They used to preach a lot of temperance messages, and I felt it my bounden duty to cry out in Asheville against drink. I wanted to warn the people where we were headed. The results of alcoholic drink were everywhere, particularly in West End.

I felt if we could get enough people together we could vote wine, liquor, and beer out of the city. People used the argument that if someone wants to drink he will find it, and that's true, I suppose; but if it were hard to find, there certainly wouldn't be as many people killed from alcohol.

A lawyer drew up a petition for us and we set out to get fifteen percent of the city's registered voters to sign the petition to bring the matter to a vote. We needed 4,500 signatures. I took the petition to a ministerial association meeting at the First Baptist Church in Asheville, looking for help.

When I told the preachers what I had to present to them, those from smaller churches were eager to help fight alcohol. They wanted the group to band together and help get signers for the petition.

Then one of the pastors from a larger church cleared his throat and said, "Uh, do you think this is the proper time to present such a petition?"

"How many homes have to be broken," I asked, "how many wives abused, how many children beaten before it's time to fight? I say the time is now."

Another preacher said, "We are fixing to start a revival meeting, and we wouldn't want anything like this to hinder it."

More preachers began to back away. I could not believe my ears. Since when did fighting sin hinder a revival meeting? I knew I may as well leave.

I went out of the church and took a reporter from the *Citizen-Times* with me. I knew if he stayed in there among the religious compromisers they would load his wagon with the wrong stuff.

As I went home, I thought of all we had been through trying to get enough names on the petitions. I had come out strong on the radio in favor of banishing strong drink. I appealed for people to sign the petitions. About two months before Becky was born, we began getting threatening telephone calls. The callers said if we didn't drop the petitions something would happen to us. I was threatened first, then Ralph Jr. was threatened. My father became so upset that he went to the *Citizen-Times* building and sat in his car in front of it with a rifle, afraid someone would try to harm me as I came or went.

Becky was born on an ice-cold morning. A car parked outside our apartment followed us to the hospital, its occupants unknown to us. My mother kept Ralph Jr.

Jacque had a long, hard labor and Becky was born on a

Friday morning. I brought Jacque and Becky home the following Wednesday, and that night we went to church.

While we were in church, someone broke into our apartment, ransacked it, took the mattresses off the bed, emptied our medicine cabinet, and turned over every piece of furniture in the house, apparently looking for the petitions.

A public stenographer told me she had been hired by the beer companies to record for them the minutes of a meeting of beer distributors in the Langren Hotel, and that at the meeting they had voted to increase the price of beer by five cents a case to fight the petition.

For a while, I thought I might be forced to go off the radio, things got so hot, but God told me not to worry, if I were thrown off the air people would know the station was on the side of the beer companies. The station manager told me that beer distributors out of South Carolina had demanded that he put me off the air, but he didn't. Actually, the fight was good for his station. New listeners tuned in every day.

Asheville's chief of police, Charlie Dermid, told me not to leave my car unlocked. "They're mad now," he said, "and they could plant something illegal in your car and we would have to come if we got a call. They will try to frame you."

I appreciated his telling me that.

Tension mounted.

Someone knocked on our door one evening and I answered the door. "Come in," I said.

"No, I can't," he said. "I just wanted to tell you your driveway is full of wine and beer boxes."

Someone had dumped a truckload of empty boxes in the drive. I thought, "Praise God, they're on the run."

I telephoned a preacher I knew and asked him to help fight the issue, and he answered, "I'd like to help you, Preacher, the best in the world; but I've just taken over a new church, and they're paying me a good salary. If I start fighting that fight, they'll fire me, and I don't want to lose my church and salary."

I thanked him and hung up.

We pitched the tent in Biltmore that summer, near the place I had met Jacque at that earlier Biltmore revival. Ownership of the land on which we pitched the tent for the 1950 meeting was not clear but it appeared to belong to the man who owned an adjacent night club. He agreed to rent the lot to us, and we put the tent about where Wendy's is now.

We got the canvas spread and set the poles and when we raised the canvas it began to "walk." Sometimes if you don't criss-cross the outside ropes the weight of the tent will shift and the tent will actually move. That was what we called "walking." That happened here, but we finally got it under control, tied it down, put all the seats in, arranged the platform, and were ready to start the meeting.

During that revival, I continued to hammer away on drunkenness. A lot of people were saved and, indeed, gave up drinking. One of the points I concentrated on was, "If Christian people took a stand we could fight this thing through."

I looked for something dramatic to illustrate my sermons on drinking, and an idea occurred to me. I went to the Buncombe County Sheriff's Department and asked Bob Michael for a liquor still. The deputy peered at me and asked, "You want a what?"

"A still," I said. "A whiskey still."

"Aren't you making a living preaching?" Michael joked.

"That's funny," I said, "but I really need a liquor still. I know you have some that you've confiscated."

"Yes," he said, "we do. We've got two or three here, but you're gonna have to tell me what you want it for."

"I've been preaching against drinking," I said, "and I told the people I was going to have something unusual for them. I want to use it to illustrate my sermons."

"I don't see a thing wrong with that," he said. "I kinda like it."

"On a certain night," I said, "I want to have the still on the platform with me, covered with a tarpaulin, and at the most opportune time I will uncover it and display it as the thing that has broken more homes and done more evil than anything I can think of besides the devil."

"Sounds good."

"I'm going to invite people in the tent to help me destroy the awful thing," I said. "I'll tell them the night before to bring axes and hammers."

"You can have one if you don't destroy the copper," Michael said. "Copper's valuable."

We took the still, set it on the platform, and covered it with sheets. I told the people to bring axes and hammers the next night, that we were going to do something unusual.

The following evening, I preached on the curses of strong drink. I asked for testimonies from people in the audience whose lives had suffered because of drink. Anna McIntyre Davis, who was saved under the ministry of Lucius Compton, founder of Eliada Home, came to the front.

"My husband was a drinker," she said, "and when I got saved I always took the children and went to meeting—and when I got back home he had me locked out of the house. We slept outdoors on the porch a lot of nights." I knew she had been through a lot, and I had asked her to testify. Others came forward and told what strong drink had done to their families.

At the proper time, I told the crowd we were going to expose the evil of Asheville. "I want you to help me destroy this evil," I said, and when we ripped the sheets off that still the crowd went wild.

One old preacher from Swannanoa had brought a bush axe. He got in the first good lick. People tore onto the platform to take whacks at that still. They hammered it, cut it, beat it. One fellow didn't have anything to hit it with so he opened his pocket knife and tried to stab it to death.

The crowd shouted and screamed, and the noise we made attracted the people in the night club next door.

They came running to see what was going on. The nightwatchman from the club was saved that night.

We had a good time—and tore that still into small pieces, copper and all.

The next morning someone delivered a note to me from the owner of the night club. "Preacher," the note read, "I give you twenty-four hours to get this tent off my property."

He met us at the tent the next night. I walked on into the tent and as he came in, he pulled his knife, walked right up to me, and said, "I told you I'll only give you twenty-four hours to get out, or I will cut your head off."

I looked him in the eye. "Let me tell you something," I said. "I belong to God and before you start cutting, you'd better clear it with him, because he might not like it."

When we finished the meeting that night, Lee and I acted as if we were going to start carrying seats out of the tent preparatory to taking it down.

As the night club owner pulled away in his car, Lee said, "I know where a surveyor lives, an old retired Methodist minister."

"Let's go get him," I said.

Early the next morning the surveyor stepped off the lot, ran the lines with his transom, and said, "You're not even on the lot that man owns."

We had been paying him rent and were not even on his land.

God knew what he was doing when we put up the tent. When the tent walked, it walked right off that man's property.

That night we went to Biltmore prepared to go on with the meeting as usual. But before the crowd began gathering, the night club owner showed up with a couple of city surveyors. They laid their lines and went to work, and when the crowd began to arrive the people had to step over those lines.

One of the surveyors passed me. He appeared to be

mad, and when he was nearest me, he said, "Preacher, you don't have a damned thing to worry about."

When they finished surveying they determined that we had one tent stake on the fellow's property. We moved it a few inches and went ahead with the meeting.

We didn't know whose land we were on then. When we found out, he was very friendly and told us to go right ahead with the meeting and we didn't have to pay him a penny.

We finally got enough names on the petition to turn it in. In fact, we had about a thousand or fifteen hundred more names than we needed by the late winter of 1951. I was going to make my first journey to the Holy Land that year, and I decided to turn in the petitions so the names could be counted and checked while I was gone.

When I returned I went straight to the courthouse to check on the petitions and was told that we did not have the signatures of enough qualified voters.

"What do you mean, we don't have enough names?" I asked. "We had a thousand more than enough."

"Yes, but they're not qualified," the man said.

"What do you mean qualified?" I asked. "They were registered to vote."

"Take my word for it," he said.

"All right, then," I said, "give me back my petitions and I'll see that we don't make that mistake again."

"Can't do that," he said. "The petitions became property of the county the minute you turned them in."

I knew where he was coming from. If I had sniffed hard enough, I'm sure I could have smelled the smoke of those petitions burning.

# — 13 —

# The Holy Land

Whoever would have thought, watching me grow up, that at the age of thirty-one I would be riding the Queen Elizabeth? Nothing in my background prepared me for that experience. But here we were, Bly Jackson and me, looking out over the rail as that great steamship pulled away from New York and headed for the open sea. The year was 1951, and we were en route to the Holy Land!

For a long time I had felt that God wanted me to make a special trip to the Holy Land. When God saved me, one of the burdens he gave me in preaching the Word was Bible prophecy. I don't mean the far out stuff, but "thus saith the Lord." I have never prophesied dates for the end of time or anything else. God says no man can do that. Bible prophecy has always been one of my great loves, though. Dr. William McBirney, the Irishman who preached the revival in which I was saved, was a great prophetic teacher and preacher. I am sure that God had a hand in arranging whom I should be converted under, for one of the gifts he gave me was to preach prophecy.

The Scripture that quoted Jesus as saying, "Behold, I come quickly," has always been strong on my heart. I believe he is coming soon—and I believe in doing things quickly. When something comes to mind, when we feel God's hand guiding us toward doing something, we should do it quickly. If we think about it too long, we will start rationalizing, and after while the urge will go away.

The desire to go to the Holy Land, to see where Jesus

walked tall and preached to the people, to see where the prophets preached, to see where David ruled, kept burning within me, and I prayed constantly about it. If it is God's will for me to go, I thought, he will show me a way.

The money for such a trip certainly was not in my possession. If I made the trip, it would have to be by the grace of God. I felt I would be whole after I saw that land—that I would be able to preach the Word with greater insight. There were some obstacles. Ralph Jr. was about four and Becky going on two—and Jacque was unable to drive a car. But Jacque understood and encouraged me to go.

The jet age had not yet reached the airlines. Prop planes flew across the ocean—had been doing so since World War II—but I felt I should go by boat.

I was in revival in Orlando, Florida, in the Nazarene Church of the Rev. W. B. Horne when I suddenly blurted out that I had a burden to go to the Holy Land. I asked the people to pray, but they did more than that. They pitched nine hundred dollars into a fund to send me to Jerusalem. A ticket only cost about four hundred dollars, so that contribution put me a long way toward my goal.

Bly and I talked it over and were ready to go at the first opportunity. When we had the money in hand, we rode the train to New York, secured our visas, booked passage on the Queen Elizabeth, and before we knew it we were sailing on the open seas.

I was thrilled to death. I had never been anywhere. Oh, I had driven to California, and to Florida, Ohio, and places like that, but this was an experience! We were going to the Holy Land!

And Israel had only been a nation again for three years. The smoke from the War of Independence of 1948 had barely settled.

We had boarded ship about the third deck down and had an inside stateroom. There probably were three thousand people on the ship, which was a regular floating city. This was the thrill and excitement of answered prayer.

The food on board was fantastic. An old country boy like me had never seen some of the food available in the dining salons. Bly was bug-eyed, too. The menu was like that of the Waldorf Astoria. The beauty of the dining rooms was unbelievable. And we could order anything we wanted off the menu; the meals were prepaid in the ticket price.

Fifteen hundred miles out to sea, half the passengers were seasick, and most of them just had to sweat it out since there were not many good seasickness remedies available then. I had missed my smallpox vaccination, so after we got out of sight of land I went to the ship's hospital and took the shot.

Back in the dining room for dinner that evening, I thought the tables looked so nice, and suddenly I realized I was not feeling a hundred percent. I kept looking through those big glass doors wondering where the nearest bathroom was. Finally I located it and had to make a quick exit. Talk about sick! Every time the ship rolled, I heaved that much harder. There can be no more uncomfortable sickness than seasickness. It was terrible.

But after that bout with my stomach, I had no further problems.

We were at sea five days. Halfway through the voyage a storm struck us. We could see it coming a long way off, and as it drew nearer, the waves rolled higher and the wind blew harder. The crew quickly cleared the decks and battened down the hatches, and when the storm hit we were all inside. The sea became so rough that it felt every succeeding wave would overturn that great ship. One unthinking woman opened a door and stepped out on deck, and the wind flung her across the deck and into the railing. Luckily for her, one of the crew reached her before she was swept overboard.

We landed in Cherbourg, France, and went immediately by train to Wintertour, Switzerland, a beautiful ride. This was April and the land was just emerging from winter. The mountains of Switzerland were indescribable.

In Switzerland we met a missionary-businessman who had agreed to help us obtain tickets to Israel. We had come that far without full assurance that we could get on to Israel, but we had faith enough to believe we could.

I had told myself that we would be like Abraham. We would start and God would show us what to do along the way.

We had a Swiss meal in the home of that missionary, and his children were dressed in native costume with big, balloon sleeves. That was an unusual experience for us.

The American consulate had told us what primitive conditions we might expect if we got to Israel. Having been a nation only three years, the people still lived in lean-tos and food was scarce. The consul said passage might be hard to obtain because "every Jew in Europe is trying to get to Israel." He didn't tell us that Israel only had one ship—the S. S. Kedmah—sailing pilgrims into the Holy Land. We found that out for ourselves later.

At the tour agency in Wintertour we encountered no problems; the man sold us passage on the Kedmah which sailed out of Naples, Italy. Our tickets cost something under two hundred dollars.

We took the train to Naples, and the ride was spectacular. We had never seen scenery like that—those high, beautiful, snow-covered mountains. They appeared to go on and on forever.

Suddenly, after hours on the train, we went into a tunnel like none we had seen before. This one seemed endless. We went through the very bowels of that mountain.

When we shot out on the other side, the transformation was amazing. We were in Italy and it was springtime. The sun was shining, vineyards in bloom. The sights almost took our breath away. We got off the train in Milan.

I had never been to Italy, of course, and didn't know the do's and don'ts. In that enormous Milano railway station we found the men's room and went inside. It was a typical men's room, except for one thing: there was a woman in the room. Quickly I stepped into one of the stalls and closed the door and suddenly I could see the woman's feet standing in front of my stall. She began beating on the door and yelling. I had no idea what she was doing, or what she wanted, and Bly stood outside laughing his head off. Finally he said, "Ralph, she is the attendant for the restroom. She cleans the toilets and if you use one you have to pay her. She wants money."

I cracked the door a bit and stuck out a coin of Swiss money. She grabbed it and stomped off, still jabbering to herself.

All my life I had heard about real Italian spaghetti. We took a table in the dining room. "Praise God," I said, "we can finally get some real Italian spaghetti."

The waiter came and handed us menus, but we couldn't read them. I said, "We want spaghetti." He smiled and left, and returned in a few minutes with glasses of wine.

"No, no, no," I said. "We don't drink. No wine."

"Drink," he grinned. "Drink, drink."

"No, no, no!"

Finally he took the wine back and returned with two large plates of spaghetti. I had never seen such spaghetti! It was something to behold! We ate spaghetti until I thought it would run out our ears, then we leaned back and patted our bulging stomachs and talked about how good it was.

We couldn't have eaten another bite, but here came the waiter with two big plates of meat and vegetables. The spaghetti was an appetizer! And they call Americans gluttons!

From Milan we rode the train to Florence and met a missionary friend who was working with Gospel Projects of which Dr. James Stewart of Asheville was the head. Dr. Stewart had missionaries in different locations in Europe. I remembered Dr. Stewart as a man who walked along Shelburne road in West Asheville, praying that God would put a church on that street. Today, our church—Trinity Baptist—sits on the street, on land Dr. Stewart claimed for God. Dr. Stewart was converted in Scotland when he was fourteen, and God burdened him for Europe. He had to come to America to realize his life's work, founding the European Evangelistic Crusade, which was later called Gospel Projects.

Dr. Stewart's missionary gave us a personally guided tour of Florence. I couldn't believe the greatness of Michelangelo's work. I stood in awe and amazement. To see those sculptures and know that that beauty came from solid blocks of marble almost staggers the imagination. To produce something that beautiful from marble, something that lifelike, has to be a gift from God.

Naples was our next and last stop in Italy. There we would board the boat for Israel. We got a room in a Naples hotel that overlooked the bay, and from there we could look out to sea and view islands. What a beautiful sight!

We stayed in Naples a day or two and enjoyed sitting on the balcony of our room watching the fishermen net-fishing in the bay. They would go out and spread the net and come back to shore, and then wade out to grasp each end of the tent and draw it in. They drew and drew and when the net got close to them we could see the water boiling with fish. Their net would be full of fish. I had never seen fishing like that.

That evening as we sat on the balcony watching the action in the bay, we saw a little white ship sail in. We commented on what a pretty ship it was, little realizing that it was the ship we would ride to Israel.

We were to sail the next day, and we went to the dock early, found the Kedmah and boarded. As far as we could determine on that voyage, there were only three Gentiles on board: Bly Jackson, me, and a fellow from Texas. The rest were Jews coming out of Eastern Europe and heading for their homeland. They had never been to Palestine and were anxious to get home.

We went to the top deck to watch the boarding, and what a sight we beheld! They came down the streets and out of the alleys. Some wore the dress of the Hasidim, the orthodox Jew. Others were garbed in European clothing. Some had blankets over their shoulders, no doubt containing what was left of their life's possessions.

I had never seen anything like that in my life, and neither had Bly. Talk about the Scripture coming to life. This was an Exodus. I thought about God saying in Isaiah 11:11, "the Lord shall set his hand again the second time to recover the remnant of his people . . . ."

They streamed aboard the ship and filled every nook and corner on the boat. When loading was finished, and I was sure they couldn't have shoehorned another person onto the deck, I looked up and saw the blue and white Star of David flying from the mast. Goosebumps big enough to button my shirt on broke out all over me. This was a time of great excitement; Bible prophecy unfolded before our eyes.

Jesus said the Jews would go back, and here we were with a boat loaded with Jews going back to Palestine, fulfilling the Scriptures. In Isaiah, God said, "I will bring them from the east and the west, the north and the south." To think that we were in the midst of it, hearing, seeing, partaking of it made me want to fall to my knees. How great that God would let me, a mountain boy, stand in the midst of the unfolding of the Word of God and see it with my own eyes, and feel and sense it!

The whistle gave a long blast, and the captain backed the ship out and turned it around and headed out to sea. The Apostle Paul had sailed these seas when he came to Rome.

We departed Naples on Friday, and the Jewish sabbath began at sundown that day. When the sun went down, the ship went kosher. We ate kosher or we didn't eat, and we didn't mind because it was an experience.

Four of us shared a small stateroom—Bly and me, an orthodox Jew, and a younger Jewish man. They spoke enough English to converse.

In a little while, we heard a commotion outside and went out to see the Jews reading the Tablets of the Law. A rabbi conducted the service. I had never heard a Jew pray, and suddenly they were all wailing. It made the hair stand on end to hear them.

Early next morning—Saturday—I awakened and saw that the orthodox Jew's bunk was empty. I dressed and went on deck and saw him pacing back and forth as if something terrible rested on his mind.

We were the only two on deck. He walked by me a couple of times, then stopped and looked me in the face. He appeared to be so sad. He smote his breast and said, "My soul is like the sea."

I looked into his face and it was like looking through a window. I said, "Your soul doesn't have to be that way. The Lord Jesus came to save you and bring calm and peace into your soul."

He did not comprehend. "I know," he said, "that when Messiah comes it will be over, and the calm will come."

At dinner that evening, when regular food was again the fare, we sat with a Jewish professor and his wife from Mount Scopus University in Jerusalem. They had fled Palestine when war broke out and were now returning.

The professor appeared to be thrilled. With a gleam in his eye, he said, "For the first time in two thousand years, we are going to reap a wheat harvest in the Negev."

"That's wonderful," I said, interested.

"The army engineers sank shafts and struck water," he said, "and we are going to reap wheat."

He was so excited, but he really didn't know what his words meant to me. There was a prophetic meaning to what he said. He did not realize that he was telling me what the Word of God said in Isaiah 35:1, "The wilderness and the solitary place shall be glad for them; and the desert shall rejoice, and blossom as the rose." That's millennial Scripture, but coming events cast a shadow, and here was sunlight streaming into shadow. Talk about a mountain preacher wanting to leap for joy! It was all I could do to contain myself.

Early Monday morning we were awakened by shouts of "Land! Land!" Columbus did not look forward with more enthusiasm to the sight of land than did those Jews, and indeed, than I.

We leaped into our clothes and rushed on deck. Hundreds of Jews lined the rails; the deck was crowded with them. They laughed and talked, clapped their hands, and rejoiced. We found someone who spoke English and asked what was going on?

"Don't you see it?" he asked. "Don't you see it?"

"See what?" I asked, peering into the fog, trying to sight land. "It's so foggy I can't see anything."

He grasped me by the arms and laughed. "Don't look into the fog," he shouted. "Look above it. Look at the mountain!"

I looked above the fog and a great, blue mountain peaked out of the haze.

"That," the man said, "is Mount Carmel! We are home!"

He had never been to Palestine. He had lived all his life in the persecuting cauldron of Eastern Europe, and here he was saying, "We are home!" His joy was unspeakable.

In a little while as the sun burned the fog away, beauty unfolded before us. The bay of Haifa was a jewel in the sun, sparkling and shimmering. The bay lay in a three-sided bowl and houses dotted the mountainsides above the bay to our right.

But the sight that captivated me was that of the people of Israel. Hundreds, even thousands lined the shores of the bay, waving handkerchiefs, welcoming home the Jews.

Tugs pushed us into a berth in the harbor, and when the gangplank went down, the Jews on board rushed down and fell into the arms of those waiting, crying, hugging. Praise God, we got right in the middle of them.

"Thank God," I shouted. "You're shouting because you

are at your earthly home, and I shout because I will soon be in my heavenly home." Jesus said, "When you see this, I will be nigh, even at the door." I could hear him knocking!

Finally, Bly and I made our way to an information booth where we found a young woman who spoke English.

"Young lady," I said, "will you give us information about rooms?"

"No rooms," she said. "No rooms."

I thought, God has sent me over here and he has a room for me somewhere.

"Let me see your directory," I said.

"No rooms," she said again.

But she handed me a directory that listed all the hotels in Haifa.

I bowed my head and prayed, "God, you told us to come, and we have come all this way. If there is a room anywhere in this city, Lord, as I go down this list, show it to me."

Starting with the A's, I ran my finger down the list, and I prayed, "Lord, we're in your will, and you sent us. You promised to be with us."

I passed the B's and the C's, and everything looked so dead in that directory.

The devil kept interfering. "You are crazy this time," he said. "You've come all this way and he doesn't even have a room for you. What are you going to do?"

God said, "Keep looking. Seek and ye shall find." I heard him clearly.

I went through that list almost to the end. The W's came under my finger and still everything looked empty. But when the word "Weiss" came, it leaped right out of the book at me. It was as if someone had turned on a light.

God said, "There is a room there."

Turning to the girl in the information booth, I said, "Please call this hotel for me."

She said, "No rooms."

I looked her squarely in the eye. "Young lady, I have prayed," I said, "and God said we would find a room there."

She called the hotel and spoke Israeli into the phone, and suddenly she looked as if she had dropped her teeth.

"They said yes," she said. "They have a room."

She said the hotel was on Mount Carmel, where we wanted to be, and she had asked them to hold the room for two Americans.

We visited the American consul in Haifa, and he told us the long story of the persecution of the Jews and how they were streaming back to the homeland. He helped us make the necessary arrangements to get to Jerusalem, and we boarded a train and departed Haifa.

On that ride, we saw how the deserts were blooming. As the little train chugged through the outskirts of the city, we passed orange groves and saw huge piles of oranges and then high stacks of boxes filled with oranges. The windows of the train were open, and the aroma from those orange trees filled the train. We basked in the glory of God, and we rejoiced.

For two thousand, five hundred years this had been a semidesert in which little or nothing grew. It was barren land, dead land. But here it was in full bloom.

As we rode along on that little train, with the rails clacking beneath us, I thought all those Jews returning home, and I thought of Daniel and the prophetic handwriting on the wall.

Belshazzar and his crowd were deep in a party—actually an orgy it should be called. Suddenly the handwriting appeared on the wall, "Mene . . . Mene . . . Tekel . . . Upharsin."

No one could decipher it and tell the king its meaning until Daniel was brought in. He translated for the king, "This night thy kingdom shall be taken from thee and divided. Thou hast been weighed in the balance and found wanting." And that night the kingdom fell to the Medes and Persians.

Mene . . . Mene . . . Tekel . . . Upharsin!

Mene is a Babylonian word that can mean a thousand. It is a weight measure. Mene . . . Mene . . . That would be one thousand and one thousand more, or two thousand.

Tekel means twenty, and Upharsin means to divide.

When God gave Belshazzar the message of judgment, he also gave Daniel a message. Daniel had prayed for deliverance for his people and had asked God when they would be delivered. So the handwriting on the wall spelled out, "A thousand, a thousand, twenty, and divide."

In the Bible, the number one thousand is the number of the glory of God. The number two is the number of witness. God always establishes everything in the mouths of at least two witnesses. So the message was "A thousand and a thousand"—that's two thousand—"twenty," which represents Belshazzar. God said, "You are weighed in the balance and found wanting." If you put two thousand on one side of a scale and twenty on the other side, which way will the scales go? Then the word "Upharsin," which means divide.

In Daniel 7:25, he gives the formula: "Until a time and times and the dividing of time." If you divide the time (singular), which is a thousand, you get five hundred. So adding all together, a thousand, a thousand, twenty, and five hundred, you get an answer of 2,520.

The figure 2,520 means years, so God told Daniel that 2,520 years from that night, his people would start back home.

The Israelites were taken into captivity in the year 606 B.C. Three years were required to prepare Daniel, Shadrach, Meshach, and Abednego to serve the king, so in 603 B.C. the handwriting appeared on the wall. Two thousand, five hundred, twenty years from 603 B.C. brings us to the year 1917, the year of the Balfour Treaty which allowed Israel to start back home.

The homecoming was still going on and we were in the midst of it. How could we help but shout and praise God?

Smelling the oranges riding down the coast from Haifa, and seeing all the bee hives around the town of Petah Tikva, I thought of Joshua and Caleb coming into Canaan where there was milk and honey, and I was filled with glory.

Approaching Jerusalem, I studied the barrenness of the land. Coming from the west into Jerusalem today is different. The Jews have irrigated the land and set out millions of trees, and the countryside is vastly different from its barrenness of 1951. Arriving at the train station, we made our way to the King David Hotel where Samuel Krykorin, the son of a missionary, was awaiting us.

The city was divided then into Jordanian and Israeli sections, and between the two was a no-man's land. Hostilities abounded, for this was just after the War of Independence.

The Jews could not get into the Old City, and that was the location of the Western Wall of King Solomon's Temple—actually King Herod's Temple—which the Jews called the "Wailing Wall," the most sacred place in Judaism. Jews would go to the roof of the King David Hotel and look toward the Wailing Wall and pray.

Sand bags and barbed wire were everywhere, especially around no-man's land.

Samuel Krykorin took us to the Scottish Rite Mission outside the Old City where we spent the night.

We awakened the next morning to look out upon a fresh Jerusalem day, and no one who has not visited the Holy City can know what I mean by those words. We were going to cross the border that day, and early in the morning we were taken down to the no-man's land. An Israeli soldier pointed to a trail through no-man's land and indicated that we should walk the trail.

Luggage in hand, we started across that fortified strip of land, walking slowly. We knew the Arabs were watching us from the far side. When we were fairly close to the Jordanian side, a young Arab boy came toward us. He didn't say a word, but took our luggage and walked back the way he had come.

We passed through the Jordanian wire, through a heavily-sandbagged area, and were taken into a little room. Soldiers in the room were snappily dressed.

"My friends," I said, "I hope you speak English. We are preachers of the Gospel and have come here to see the land, not to become involved in anything political."

"Yes, yes," said one of the officers. "You are welcome. You are most welcome."

"What beautiful uniforms," I said, and Bly and I both bragged on their dress. Through an interpreter we told them we would like to have our pictures made with them. That pleased them and we all went outside and made a round of photographs.

We rode a taxi, driven by an Arab, to Jericho, passing through Bethany on the southeast side of Jerusalem and riding down through the wilderness of Judea. In those twenty-five short miles we passed from Jerusalem's altitude of 2,500 feet above sea level to Jericho's 1,000 feet below. The wilderness was spectacular. Not a tree in sight, but it was wilderness just the same, barren, uninhabited except for wandering bedouin. Here and there we saw a sheep trail winding off into the wilderness. What a sight!

As we left Jerusalem, another Arab man and his son opened the door and leaped into the taxi, apparently looking for a free ride to Jericho.

The road was one hairpin curve after another, and the driver sped along, shouting and arguing with that man and his son in Arabic, gesticulating, threatening, scowling. They screamed at each other all the way down the mountain, and we sat in the back seat praying. We prayed all the way to Jericho—and what a relief it was to arrive alive!

We made our way across the Jordan River beyond Jericho and up the mountain to Amman, the capital of

Jordan. Amman is now a modern city of more than one million people, but in 1951 it was just a town, and a primitive one at that. It was very small.

The women were still veiled, the men all had thin mustaches, and everywhere we looked we saw camels. Coming into town were men riding little donkeys, their feet dragging the ground and their women walking behind them carrying loads on their heads.

All roads leading to Amman were dirt roads, and the only airport was a little dirt strip for small planes. Later we flew out of that airport, and that was an experience.

A missionary friend, the Rev. Samuel Krykorin, whose son had met us in Jerusalem, awaited us in Amman. We stayed in his home. At four o'clock in the morning, the cry of the *muezzin* woke us, calling the Moslems to prayer. The Arabs started their day of commerce then. In the heat of the day they shut everything down and went to sleep, reopening late in the afternoon and remaining open into the night.

We didn't stay in Amman long. Krykorin took us back to Jerusalem and from the Plains of Jericho, which we explored with him, he pointed into the mountains and we could see little trees growing there. That was a fulfillment of Ezekiel 36:8, "But ye, O mountains of Israel, ye shall shoot forth your branches, and yield your fruit to my people of Israel; for they are at hand to come."

God knew they couldn't come unless there was something for them to eat; so he commanded the mountains to start bearing fruit. We were seeing all that begin to happen.

I still use these truths and prophecies fulfilled in preaching. They were so thrilling then and they are just as thrilling today. We saw it firsthand; we saw the restoration when the land was still barren.

Rev. Krykorin took us to an English inn on Mount Zion for the night. He told us we would arise early the next morning and be on the Mount of Olives when the sun came up.

"That is quite a spectacular sight," he said.

We were escorted by our hosts into the inn. Bly was given a huge room with stone floors and three beds, but I was taken to a smaller room with a little window high on the wall. I wondered why they didn't let us stay together in the big room. I bolted the door well, and about two or three in the morning something awakened me and I saw the door handle moving. Someone was trying to slip into the room, but the door was barred so heavily he couldn't get in. Right then, I realized everyone in the Holy Land wasn't holy.

The next morning we went to the top of the Mount of Olives and saw the sun rise over Jerusalem. The sun broke over the ancient hills behind us and flooded the city across the Kidron Valley with light. It was a glorious sight.

The streets were filled with veiled women, for we were in East Jerusalem, still in Jordan. Burros and camels stood about.

Krykorin took us to a little Armenian Mission Church on Mount Zion and those in attendance asked me to preach. Brother Jackson sang "Amazing Grace," and I preached. Krykorin told me to go ahead and preach and later he would interpret what I said. I prayed, and the Lord laid it upon my heart to preach on the Second Coming of Christ.

God moved on the service in that little church and filled it with his presence. Suddenly, while I preached, the people began leaving their seats and kneeling at the altar praying. More than a dozen people came to the altar to pray and rejoice.

I asked Krykorin what they were saying.

"They are rejoicing," he said, "that God sent the missionary to preach to them, and they are getting saved and getting right with God."

He never did have to interpret my message. God let those people understand what I was saying. I thought of the Scripture in Acts where the people spoke in foreign languages and others understood. Seventeen precious souls made things right with Jesus at that meeting. Seventeen is the number of Victory in the Bible!

Afterward, one of the young men came to me and said God had saved him. I received a letter from him later in which he wrote that God had called him to preach to his own people in Jerusalem. What a miracle that was! And what a blessing!

After that, we went to Calvary. In 1951 they let us go to the top of the hill, which is a Moslem cemetery. No one is permitted to enter that cemetery now, so Christians are restricted from going onto Calvary. I had always thought if I ever get on Calvary, I will shout and leap for joy, but being there was different. I felt exactly the opposite; I wanted to fall down and thank God that he so loved us that he took upon himself flesh and died for us.

We came off Calvary and entered the Garden Tomb, and it was such a great thrill to see the empty tomb. I still have pictures I made there that day.

The Israelis were beginning to rebuild Jerusalem then. They were building all over the side of the mountain. The law in Jerusalem is that you can't build with anything but stone, and they don't know it but they are building for the millennium.

We finished our tour of the Holy Land by riding a car over dirt roads to Galilee. We drove up through Samaria and all along the way we saw women carrying heavy loads and huge buckets of water on their heads, still living basically as they had two thousand years ago. Some still lived in caves.

We came to the town of Tiberias on the west side of the Sea of Galilee, and what a beautiful, peaceful area it seemed from afar. Closer inspection revealed as much or more barbed wire and sandbags than we had seen in Jerusalem.

At a little restaurant by the sea we ate St. Peter's fish, and they were extremely tasty. While we ate, a young Jewish man came and talked with us. He had a wife and baby, and I remember him saying, "We know Russia is coming, but I will never live under Russia. First I will die."

We walked up and down the seashore where Jesus had called his disciples together, and we were unable to walk on a straight line because of the barbed wire on the beach.

I have returned to the Holy Land many times since 1951, but that '51 trip is the one I will remember best. I have never gone to Israel that it wasn't a thrill to me, and the most exciting thing I find there is Bible prophecy unfolding before my eyes. Every time I go, I see more and more. I have watched Jerusalem expand, growing over hill after hill, stretching out beyond Bethany on the east and down toward Tel Aviv on the west. It is growing steadily to the north, too. I have seen modern roads come in to that great city.

Across the Jordan River in the country of Jordan, it is a thrill to see a super road being built down toward Egypt, for this is also fulfillment of prophecy. The 19th chapter of Isaiah talks about the day when Egypt and Assyria (present day Syria) and Israel will be allies, and how roads will bind them together. All of those things are of great interest to me, as they should be to any serious Bible student.

In 1969, my brother Lee, the Rev. Jerry Payne, our associate pastor, and I went to the Holy Land with the Rev. Howard Estep of California. This trip was bound for Petra, the "Rose Red City half as old as time." I had never been to Petra, and I had long wanted to go.

Petra is a city carved out of solid sandstone by a tribe of people known as the Nabateans, who ruled that part of the world from a hundred years before Christ till a hundred years after. Petra is found in the Book of Obadiah. It is located in the land of Edom.

In Amman we loaded up to go to Petra. We were making the trip in automobiles. We took packed lunches for the four-hour drive. There were fifteen or twenty cars for our group of people.

On the way down, we swung out to Mount Nebo and got

the same view of the land of milk and honey that Moses saw in his last days on earth, and then we came back by Madaba, where one of the oldest mosaic maps of the Holy Land is located in a church. At Madaba we were taken to a place and seated at tables and served salads. I had been warned about eating salads there. These looked so appetizing, and we were hungry, but most of us resisted. One fellow from Kansas, however, said, "God said to eat whatever is set before you, and I'm going to do that." He ate the salad, and it wasn't long before he wished he had never seen a salad. He was sick as a dog. Those people knew nothing of sanitation. Pilgrims in the Holy Land have to be careful about food and water or they will spend most of their time lying in a motel room with a bug.

As we approached the entrance to Petra, we saw scores of wild horsemen galloping toward us, and I thought the Arab army was attacking. But it was only horsemen who wanted to rent us their horses for the mile-long ride down the "siq" to Petra. The siq is simply a deep gash in the sandstone that permits entry to Petra. It is the only entrance. Riding down to Petra was a great thrill. Petra is one of the places referred to in Revelation Chapter 12, a place where the woman will fly to the place that has been prepared for her in the wilderness. Daniel 11 tells us the three places that will escape the Anti-Christ are Ammon, Moab, and Edom. Petra is in Edom. This will be one of the places of fulfillment of Bible prophecy when Israel flees from the Anti-Christ and hides in the rocks of Petra and in Ammon and in Moab. Israel will hide during the tribulation right under the nose of the Anti-Christ.

What a thrill it was, then, to ride out of that siq and see the facade of the treasury building of Petra, a facade reaching almost a hundred feet into the air and carved out of solid rock. The whole city of Petra is carved, nothing was "built." All the homes, the places of commerce, the ampitheater, even the cemetery, were carved into the great, towering sandstone walls. Some of the rooms in the walls of the mountains had been carved out before Christ was born.

We spent two nights in Petra, sleeping in the caves and in tents. There were few tourist rooms in Petra. How exciting it was to sleep in that Rose Red City, realizing what a great part it played in the history of Israel and how it will figure in Bible prophecy.

The next morning we explored all of Petra. We climbed to the "high place" and saw the rooms of judgment and others. The great sandstone mountains shone all around us, looking like dumplings piled in a pan. On the high place, they worshipped the god of the rock and sacrificed the virgin girls. So much has already happened there.

On the following day we went through the south end of the valley of Petra. We walked to the area where Moses' brother Aaron was buried.

Near Aaron's burial site was an enormous building carved out of stone. I stepped off the room and it measured sixty-six feet in every direction, the mark of the Anti-Christ. Those people in Petra may have been cave dwellers, but there was an abundance of brawn and brainpower among them. They built a remarkable city at Petra. It should have been one of the wonders of the ancient world. I am sure it surpassed by far the Hanging Gardens of Babylon and the Lighthouse at Alexandria.

It is the most spectacular thing I have ever seen besides the Grand Canyon.

I have returned to Amman. Once in the 1970s when I made the trip with the Rev. Estus Pirkle, we spent a night in the caves of Petra. We slept on cots and our water was brought in on muleback. In darkness I stepped out of the cave and the stars were so big and bright it looked like I could reach up and touch them. The Book of Obadiah speaks of how the Edomites dwelt among the stars. Staying in Petra shows you the meaning of that verse.

To me, the things that make Holy Land travel most interesting are: the Bible prophecy being fulfilled, and the continual rebuilding of the land, the reforesting in particular with the millions of trees they have planted.

We have had some great experiences in the Holy Land. The day that Egyptian President Anwar Sadat was assassinated in Cairo, I was in Jerusalem. We were walking around one of the holy sites when the news was flashed over Israeli radio that Sadat had been killed, and when we returned to our bus the driver told us of the assassination. By the time we returned to the Intercontinental Hotel on top of the Mount of Olives everyone was gathered around television sets watching the news. I was called to the telephone, and the television station in Asheville was calling to ask me about the situation in Jerusalem. I remember saying, "Sadat was a bridge over troubled waters." He really was. He played a part in Bible prophecy. Israel, Syria, and Egypt will come together, and Sadat was seeking just that. He was almost like a man born out of time, for later that prophecy will be fulfilled.

Once Jacque and I went to the Holy Land alone and toured Israel by car with George Kort as our guide. George was one of the most famous and best informed of the Holy Land guides. He took us to his parents' home in Jerusalem, and they treated us wonderfully. We saw the Holy Land with him in a private car.

One of the places special to me is Masada. I went there first in 1969 before the cable car was installed to carry people to the top of that huge rock butte. We drove to the town of Asad on the back side of Masada, walked in, and climbed a pathway to the top of Masada. It was quite a vigorous climb. Masada is a special place, a place where around 70 A.D. more than nine hundred Zealots held off the Roman army until the Romans, using Jewish slave labor, carried enough dirt to fill in a valley and build a ramp to the top of the mountain, and then rather than capitulate to the slavery of Rome, the Zealots committed mass suicide. The dirt ramp is still there on the west side of Masada; it is hard to imagine that anyone would take the time to pile up that much dirt to capture nine hundred people. The Romans couldn't starve them out, however, unless they were prepared to keep the mountain under siege several years.

When Jacque and I went there, it was thrilling to hear George Kort tell how the Israelis now bring their soldiers, after basic training, and have a ceremony on top of Masada. That rock has become Israel's Alamo, and the soldier's cry of "Never Again!" refers to Masada. The Israelis are filled with such desire and determination never again to capitulate to anyone that the world's strongest military force would have to make an exaggerated effort to whip them.

The first problem in the Arab world is not oil, not the Palestinian situation, not the occupied West Bank of the Jordan River, but Jerusalem. Jerusalem is a holy city to the Jew, to the Christian, and to the Moslem. It is the holiest city in the world to the Jew, and the third holiest, behind Mecca and Medina, to the Moslem.

The vow of the Moslem is to recapture Jerusalem, and toward that end they work.

# — 14 —

# Tomorrow Will Be Better

Jacque and I have never lived in a mansion, but our home has always been comfortable. That's because of her; she is such a fine homemaker she can make do with what I have been able to provide. We have never tried to accumulate worldly things, especially money. Money in the bank isn't doing any good. I believe that money given to a preacher for God's work should be used; so we use it. As it comes in, we put it to work for God. We don't let it lie idle. God has blessed us for this. He has provided for us what we need, and we have never once asked for more.

God has given us enough food to eat; a comfortable, though not extravagant shelter; and he has allowed us to travel to see much of the world. That has been educational and has been of tremendous help in our ministry. I have heard people say, "Save your money and one day you can make a trip." Well, when we didn't have the money to save, God sent us where he wanted us to go. If I had waited till I saved up the money to go to the Holy Land, I still wouldn't have been there. By honoring God, we have been able to do what we needed to do—not always what we wanted to do, but always what we needed to do. Thank God, what we needed to do was usually what we wanted to do. God said, "Seek ye first the kingdom of God and his righteousness and all these things will be added unto you." How God has blessed us! How he blesses others who honor his name!

Jacque once said, "We had it so hard starting out that I just thought everybody had it that way. We simply faced each day by thinking tomorrow would be better."

Her words make sound philosophy. That attitude always worked for us.

Too many of today's young married couples have had so much done for them that they have little or nothing left to work for. Parents provide everything they need; so they have nothing they really need to save for, and little to look forward to. They don't really know what it means to work by the sweat of their brows for something they really want, and they don't know the joy of attaining it. We had to struggle for everything we got, and we appreciated it. We were motivated.

And what fun we have had along the way!

At the conclusion of a meeting one night, as the crowd filed out of the tent, a man asked Jacque, "Sister Sexton, do you know what faith is?"

"I think I do," Jacque answered, "but what do you think it is?"

"Well," the fellow said, "I've got faith enough to believe my wife has got a tumor instead of a baby in her."

Jacque was dumbfounded. "You crazy critter," she said, "you'd better pray to God that it's a baby and not a tumor. You could lose your wife if it is a tumor."

A few days later, the man telephoned our home and asked for Jacque.

"Sister Sexton . . . ."

"What's the matter?" she interrupted.

"Can you come?"

"Is that tumor bothering her?"

"Yassum—bad."

Jacque knew a midwife and she hurried to the midwife's house. "I think we've got a baby to deliver," she said, and the two drove quickly to the woman's home.

That man and his wife had nothing, no sheets, no pillow cases, not a clean rag in the house. While the midwife attended the woman—and it was a baby coming, not a tumor—Jacque came back to our house and gathered up linen, a gown, some clean towels, and took them back.

The only medication the woman had was two aspirins, but without delay a bouncing baby boy arrived. Jacque and the midwife cleaned up the baby and gave it to the mother, and Jacque fixed the mother some soup.

She called for the father. "Come on up here," she yelled downstairs. "I want to show you your tumor."

Instead, he slammed the door on his way out. Jacque stayed till dark and the man did not return.

We had a lot of fun with our children, as most parents do. Ours were a blessing to us, and we relished them. In some trying times, there was laughter.

When Ralph Jr. was six and Becky four, we lived on Pearson Drive. I had a set of old-fashioned loudspeakers and I kept them in the house. Ralph Jr. learned to turn them on. He made Becky sit as the congregation, and he preached. He turned on the speakers and said, "First, we will sing." And he and Becky sang, "Hang down your head, Tom Dooley—hang down your head and cry."

Then Ralph Jr. preached.

"Becky," he boomed through the loudspeakers, "you are doomed!"

She didn't know what doomed meant, and it made her mad. She screamed and cried.

"I'm not doomded," she screamed. "I'm not doomded."

Ralph Jr. was quite a little evangelist.

We were invited once to the home of the Keenan family in Greenville, South Carolina. They were a wonderful family, very talented, and unusually good singers. We took Ralph Jr. and Becky who played with the two daughters of the Keenans. The girls were growing up and had received their last dolls. One was an ice-skating doll and the other a ballerina. Both wore satin clothes. The mother confided that the dolls cost forty-five dollars each. "They are the girls' last dolls," she said, "so we splurged and bought them the best we could find."

When we were called to the table, the daughters came in with tears streaming. Ralph Jr. strolled behind them. "I just bap-sized their dolls," he said. He had baptized the dolls, which were now dripping wet, in the toilet.

We didn't have the money to replace the dolls, but the father of the girls did. He was a contractor of some means. We regretted the incident and tried to teach Ralph Jr. who to baptize and who not.

God helped us not to become depressed when we had no money. We learned to laugh at circumstances. Had we not been able to see the hand of God at work, we would have had nothing a lot of times. At times we had to dip into the children's penny banks to get money for supper. At other times God sent us money in various ways.

When I preached at the old mission, the offering sometimes was twelve dollars, sometimes fifteen. That was our grocery money, our rent, and all.

Once I remember Jacque saying, "Ralph, we have to have grocery money," and I dug into my pocket and gave her what I had. I said, "Can you make it on eight dollars?"

Jacque washed our clothes on a rub board, and if she thought one of our families was coming over, she would hang the wet clothes in the closet between dry clothing.

The morning I gave Jacque the eight dollars, which was every dollar I had to my name, I went out and came back at noon, and I remember I was walking on air.

"Guess what?" I said to her. "I just went in debt fifteen hundred dollars for a tent."

She asked, "Do you really think you are supposed to do that?"

"Yes," I said, and I could see hostility in her eyes, "I feel most definitely I was supposed to do it."

The next morning I mentioned on the radio that I had purchased a new tent by faith, and Mrs. Junie Frady, who ran the Frady nursing homes in Asheville for twenty-five years, came by the house on Pearson Drive later that morning and asked, "How much did you say that tent was?"

"Fifteen hundred dollars," I told her, and while Jacque and I watched aghast, she wrote a check and paid for the tent right there!

Glory! That was God's hand at work.

When I went to the Holy Land that first time in 1951, all the money I could leave for Jacque was thirty-five dollars, which would see her through until I returned, provided nothing unusual happened.

Unfortunately, just after I left, Jacque's mother was diagnosed as having malignant cancer and was given only a few months to live, and right after that the children took chicken pox and measles back to back. The thirty-five dollars was gone within two weeks.

But Jacque knew what to do in an emergency. She telephoned Mr. Hensley at the produce stand and told him what was wrong. "I need some groceries," she said.

"Tell me what you want," he said.

When she told him, he sent the groceries and ten dollars in cash by his delivery man.

God has always provided for us.

One morning Jacque thought how nice it would be if she had something sweet to offer the children, but she had no sweets and no money in the house. A while later, one of the women from our church knocked at the door and said to Jacque, "Your face was before me when I woke up this morning and I decided I would make you and the kids a couple of pies and a cake." She brought in two lemon pies and a pound cake.

In the early days of the mission we didn't have a salary and usually didn't have money to do with. But we did what we could to help the people who came to church. Some of them had less than we had.

One family had a beautiful little girl with big brown eyes and naturally curly hair. She was a doll, but was always dirty and unkempt. One Sunday Jacque asked the girl's mother if she could take the little girl home for the afternoon.

Jacque had saved up enough money to buy the little girl a dress. She gave the girl a bath and scrubbed her head till her hair shone and fell in ringlets. She made a slip for the girl out of one of my undershirts.

She dressed the little girl in the new dress, shoes and socks, and put a ribbon in her hair—and she was beautiful.

That evening Jacque took the little girl back to her parents at church—and the girl's mother didn't know her.

Years later we were in a restaurant and a beautiful woman and her husband walked over to our table.

"Do you know me?" the woman asked Jacque.

"No, I don't," Jacque said, "but I would love to meet such a beautiful lady."

The woman laughed. "I'm the dirty little girl you took home and scrubbed and dressed up that Sunday so many years ago," she said, "and I want to hug your neck and thank you for what you did."

We tried to help some of the little boys, too. We took them home and cleaned them up. We loved them and they knew it. They waited turns for Jacque to hold them and love them. Children know when they're loved. They also know when they're not.

We used to give some of the kids a little money, just a few cents to have in their pockets. Or if a boy really needed a haircut, I gave him the price of a haircut so he wouldn't be embarrassed at school.

God is the bookkeeper. He keeps good, accurate records.

On another Sunday Jacque brought a wretched woman home from church. She was ragged and dirty and her life had been one of deep abuse. Jacque had never heard grace preached until she came to the tent meeting when we met, and she had never understood that a person is what he is only by the grace of God. But she was filled with compassion.

I know Jacque thought this woman was so pitiful she brought her home, gave her clothing from the skin out, and let her take a bath. Then they sat down to talk.

The woman often slept in the old rock quarry down by the river. She had never been in a bathtub before that day. She had never seen a refrigerator and was amazed at ice cubes in water.

The woman had never had anyone to be kind to her; she could not remember anyone ever doing anything but using her, from childhood on. She was beaten and abused as a child and used by men for immoral purposes later on.

"There's no place for me," she said.

Jacque talked to her about her soul. She told her that the Lord could forgive and cleanse her as surely as she had cleansed her body in the bathtub.

She told the woman that God could give her a new beginning and a new life. And new motivation.

But the woman could not grasp what Jacque was saying. We intended to try to reach her again, but soon after that the woman was struck by a car and killed on the Smoky Mountain Bridge.

Soon after we were married, Jacque would pack our lunch and we would visit people who lived around the rock quarry where Westgate Shopping Center was later built. I remember going to see a woman there who had just had a baby. She had pillows stuffed in broken windows to keep out the cold, and when Jacque looked for something to feed the woman, the only scrap of food in the house was a fried slice of potato.

It is a mystery to many people that poverty in this world of plenty is a world-wide problem. Through the ages, God's church has done more than any other institution, governments included, to care for the poor. The church addresses universal poverty. When we went to Haiti to preach, women tried to give us their babies to keep them from starving.

After we established Trinity Baptist Church on Shelburne Road in West Asheville and it grew and became successful, I thought something should be done to help senior citizens of the church. It was not right for them to have to live in fear. We built a few efficiency apartment units on the church property and made them available to some of the widows in need.

One of the widows was a woman who invited Lee and me into her home many times when we were teenage boys. What an encouragement she was to us. Now we're trying to help her keep the wolf from her door. Going through her scrapbook, Jacque found cards sent by this woman when Jacque was given a bridal shower, when Ralph Jr. was born, and again when Rebecca was born.

Another woman who lives in Hebron Haven, the name we gave to these apartment units, is Mrs. Noah Radford, widow of the West End bootlegger who gave his life to Christ. Still another is the woman who lived on Hominy Creek and walked her children over a long distance to church every Sunday. She telephoned me one morning and said, "I can't wake my husband." I rushed to her home and her husband had died in his sleep.

Both Jacque and I have walked businessmen all night to sober them up and get them to their jobs the next morning.

Our world has too little compassion. We need all of it we can get.

We are grateful that the Lord kept us in good health until our children were grown, and we are still grateful for the health we have.

Jacque made me proud when she confided in a friend, "Ralph has been a good husband." That is a compliment most husbands seek. She also said, "I couldn't help but love a husband who led me to Jesus. He has helped me understand the Bible so much. I have always studied and read and I love to teach, but Ralph has always had an answer from the Word of God for me when problems came up. That is a strength that so many women don't have and don't understand. I feel I have something few women have had the privilege to have. I don't know how to thank the Lord for it and I don't know how to love Ralph for it."

That last statement could be contested in a court of law. Jacque has petted me till she spoiled me. Once when Jacque started to the hospital for surgery, she told the girls who wait tables at Holiday Inn West in Asheville, where I often eat, not to let me have French toast and syrup for breakfast.

When the doctor told me I had low blood sugar, Jacque said, "That's the worst insult I've ever had. I've been hugging and kissing him all these years and you tell me he has low blood sugar!"

Anyway, the first morning I went for breakfast while Jacque was in the hospital, I ordered French toast and syrup, and the girl said, "Sorry, Preacher, you can't have that. Wife's orders. You have to eat protein."

We have laughed a lot over incidents like that.

In a recent sermon on why homes break up, I preached that if families lived according to Biblical principles couples would get along. We don't really have to have riches in our homes; all we have to do is honor God, have grace at the table, pray together—and music in the home is important. Jacque has always played the piano in our home. Becky said that some of the happy memories of her childhood were lying in bed at night after Mother had tucked her in and drifting off to sleep to the tune of old hymns Jacque played on the piano downstairs.

Isn't that better than little children going to bed with television's satanic horror programs on their minds?

Through all our trials in making ends meet while our children grew up, Jacque and I are proud of the way both Ralph Junior and Becky turned out.

Ralph Junior resisted the call to preach for several years but finally accepted it at the age of thirty. He has been preaching ten years and has become an outstanding evangelist, actually more of a revivalist, for he feels his calling lies in reviving churches and pastors. In the summer of 1986 he pitched a huge, five-pole tent on the National Mall beside the Washington Monument in Washington, D.C., and conducted a four-day revival to the absolute glory of God, right in view of the White House.

His future as a revivalist appears to be bright, because he has both feet on the ground, and he is an astute fellow in recognizing the problems of the church and moving to meet them.

Ralph Junior married Muzette Thaxton more than twenty years ago. Her father is D. W. Thaxton, superintendent of the Houston, Texas, district of the Church of the Nazarene. Ralph Junior and Muzette have three fine children, Beverly, Mark, and Kent.

Becky married James Templeton, a number one musician who is our pianist at Trinity Baptist Church. He is a building contractor.

They have two children, Matthew and Elizabeth.

Ralph Junior and Becky live within a shout of each other in the community of Leicester, outside of Asheville.

## — 15 —

# My Churches

By the 1950s I began to get the itch to settle down more than I had been in years past. I felt the need of an anchor in my preaching life—a home church perhaps. A Church of the Nazarene had been formed in the old "Jesus Saves Mission" we ran for so many years in the West End, and I missed not having a church like that to come back to.

I had enjoyed evangelizing in other churches for a couple of years, and I loved tent preaching—still do—but I really missed that affiliation.

The Church of the Nazarene was ready to move out of the mission and build a church of its own. The congregation needed six hundred dollars to buy a lot on Ann Street on the outskirts of downtown Asheville, and I asked the Lord to help me help them raise the money.

When that congregation began meeting in a tent on Ann Street, the Lord spoke to me and said, "When people want to send a message in a hurry, they send a telegram." We decided to send God a telegram and spell out what we needed. We wrote it out: "Dear Jesus, we need $600 to purchase the lot for the new church." We signed the telegram from the church.

We called the woman who owned the lot down to the mission and called an "altar of prayer." Placing the telegram on a table, we gathered round, laid lands on the telegram and asked God to send it in. After praying for a few minutes, we went to our seats and sat in silence, letting God work among us.

In just a few minutes, a little boy slipped up beside me and whispered, "My daddy says he has the money."

That is one of the thrilling parts of the ministry, when God answers prayer. The Church of the Nazarene was able to buy the lot and worship in the tent until it could build its church building, which it did before long.

With that church established, God told me to go back and start having services in the old mission again. But the Nazarene Church was drawing most of its congregation from the West End and I told God I didn't want to interfere with its operation and growth. He assured me that I would not; he said he would give me another crowd of people and not touch the Nazarene's attendance. And that's exactly what he did.

The Church of the Nazarene continued to grow, and the roots of the church that later became Trinity Baptist Church took hold.

I preached in the mission until 1954 when a small Church of God on State Street in West Asheville came up for sale. We bought it, moved from the West End mission and organized a church we called the "Send The Light Missionary Church." We affiliated with the Church of the Nazarene, feeling God's guidance in that.

Not long after that, a conflict arose across the nation with the National Council of Churches and the World Council of Churches. I felt the conflict deeply. New versions of the Bible were coming out and confusing the people. Much of our church literature followed the teachings of the International Sunday School outlines, which had been great in the beginning many years before. Then the World and National councils took over the International outlines and began injecting liberalism and modernism into Sunday School literature.

The Church of the Nazarene used this literature, and also had found it all right to use the modern translations of the Bible. I have always used and will always use the King James Version of the Holy Bible. I felt strongly that the National Council had compromised the Word of God that I had been preaching all my life. People came to me on several occasions and said, "Preacher, you preach against the National Council but use their literature in your church."

Too, a lot of little churches didn't realize what happened to the Sunday School money they sent to the National Council in New York. From there it went to the World Council which used part of it to help back communism in Africa, knowingly or unknowingly. A lot of people didn't know that and I felt burdened to tell it. I gathered material exposing the World and National Councils and used it every way I could.

This was not the first brush I had with the councils. In 1943 God had given some of us the courage to stand and fight.

Lee and Bly Jackson and I were just young preachers then, but when we learned that the Federal Council of Churches, which later became the National Council, planned a huge meeting in Asheville to take all churches into the Federal Council and affiliate all denominations, we decided to oppose the issue. God told us the council was wrong. We did not think we should have to be fellow members with churches that harbored all sorts of beliefs. We looked upon the movement as a hodgepodge of modernism and liberalism.

Further, we felt burdened of God to warn the people against the movement.

We began to pray, and the Lord helped us get information from the Navy Intelligence Department and the American Women Against Communism and other organizations that stood strong for America. As that information rolled in, we had no good way to get it out to the people. We were preaching in the old mission and couldn't afford to buy ads. We prayed for help and God helped us buy a little "Speed-O-Printer" for thirty dollars.

We had a lady type up warnings for us. At the top of the

page we put a picture of a skull and crossbones and the word "WARNING" in large letters, or something of that order. Then she would type our message below and run off copies on the printer. These we handed out to expose the council.

The ministerial association didn't pay much attention to us, sluffing us off in their heavy preparations for the coming meeting.

We printed a paper which we entitled "Wolves In Sheep's Clothing," put the familiar skull and crossbones on it, and printed documented proof of our charges against the council.

We folded the papers and stationed boys outside City Auditorium to hand them to all delegates entering the building for the council's meeting. The people thought the boys were handing out programs and grabbed up the papers.

When they got inside and unfolded the papers . . . . Do you believe they were mad?

The president of the council arranged a meeting with us in the old YMCA building. Lee and Bly and I went. The council president opened the meeting by saying, "Gentlemen, we need your support to put this thing over." But we told him in no uncertain terms that he could never have our support.

Their approach to us was definitely "soft glove." But the door burst open and an imposing man entered, and as he came through the door he blurted, "Where are those . . . mealy-mouthed . . . two-faced . . . compromisers? I don't like this a bit."

Some of his friends calmed him but he had let their cat out of the bag. He wanted to hang us from the nearest yardarm, and he was really mad.

To quiet things down, the president of the ministerial association suggested we pray. He called on the man who had burst in, and while this man stood the others bowed their heads like they'd swallowed crow bars. The man prayed, "Let the words of my mouth and the meditation of my heart be acceptable in thy sight, O God."

They stood when they prayed, and when they finally asked us to pray, we got on our knees. I thought of Elijah when he faced the prophets of Baal, when he prayed down fire from heaven . . . but I decided not to try to burn the auditorium down.

We prayed old-fashioned prayers, and we prayed long and hard—and when we finally finished the other preachers hustled out of there in a hurry.

I made up my mind then that I would never compromise the Word of God. People who sell out God miss something, but those who sell out *to* God wind up in the thick of the battle, and on the right side.

I remembered all of this when I wrestled with the problem of the new revised versions of the Bible coming out and the wide use of them in the Nazarene church. I warned the people against the *Living Bible* and *Good News for Modern Man,* and against all the other paraphrases. To paraphrase means to change.

A truly disturbing thing was preaching against the National Council and using the International Sunday School outlines.

At that time I had a tent revival going in Arden, and the Rev. Fred Toms of Kissimmee, Florida, was here helping with the meeting.

I told him, "Fred, I either have to move forward or back down—and I have never backed down against the devil."

The Nazarenes went into convention in Florida during that tent meeting and Fred and I went to Florida and talked with the general superintendent of the Nazarene Church. He was a good man who heard me out. I spelled out my fears and told him how I felt about the literature and the new translations of the Bible.

He studied me closely, and at last he said, "Are you thinking of leaving the denomination?"

"Yes, sir," I answered honestly. "We are."

"You cannot leave the mainstream of religion," he said.

"If it concerns the truth we can," I answered. "We will have to leave it."

Back home, I discussed the problem with our church.

"We may lose everything we have," I said, "but some things in life are so valuable they are worth taking a stand for." I explained that we would never leave the church over non-essentials, but this concerned the Truth. I told them that their children needed to know that somewhere in their lives they loved God and the Truth enough that they were willing to take a stand.

I met with Dr. James Stewart in the S&W Cafeteria on Patton Avenue, and among the things we discussed was the universal attack on the Trinity—the Father, the Son, and the Holy Ghost. And we talked at length about the deity of Christ. We thoroughly discussed the situation within my church. We talked of all the pros and cons.

As I left there, God seemed to be saying to me, "Name your church Trinity Baptist Church in honor of the Trinity."

Our congregation was attentive the night I told it God had spoken and we had to make a stand.

"Remember," I said, "sometimes when you take a stand over the truth, you may lose everything. I warn you that we could lose this building and our property, and we may have to start over again in a tent."

God seemed to be whispering to me, "That's all right. You've got a tent."

We took a standing vote so the people could clearly state their support or their opposition—or their indifference, if there was any of that. All but three families voted to take the stand, leave the Nazarene Church, and cast out on our own as Independent Baptists.

God honored our withdrawal, and we didn't lose the church and property. The Nazarene Church settled for payment of the funds it had invested in our church when it took us in. We paid the Nazarenes twenty-seven hundred dollars and were on our own.

We quickly reorganized as Trinity Baptist Church with about sixty members.

I was ordained in the Southern Baptist Church in 1944, and my credentials are still with the Southern Baptist Convention, but when we considered affiliation with a Baptist organization we felt that liberalism had gotten into their colleges and seminaries, and within the convention there was an attack on the Genesis account of Creation. We could not support that; so we felt we could not affiliate with the Southern Baptists.

We affiliated with the Independent Baptist Association of America. If the conservatives and liberals in the Southern Baptist Church had made their split, there never would have been a need for an independent Baptist Church.

We did not alienate ourselves from anyone or any organization. I love the Nazarenes and still preach in a lot of Nazarene churches. And I have preached in many Southern Baptist churches and count such men as J. Harold Smith and Estus Pirkle, both good Southern Baptists, among my dearest friends. They certainly love God and have a burden for souls.

Many other churches have pulled out of the Southern Baptist Convention and become independent Baptists, and some of the largest Sunday Schools in the country are in the independent church.

Our little church grew so rapidly in the late 1950s and through the 1960s that we bulged at the seams of our building. We knew we must soon make a move.

A plumber, A. W. Jones, came to the church one morning and said, "There is some land for sale on Shelburne Road and I think we ought to look at it."

Jerry Payne, our church treasurer, Mr. Jones, and I drove down Shelburne and found the tract, seven acres, mostly landscaped, with huge white pines and a gentle roll to the land. The old Zephyr Hills Sanitarium stood on the grounds, a one-time recuperation place for the tubercular, but the building had been empty for several years and was run down.

This was the land Dr. James Stewart passed on his daily walks and constantly prayed that someone would somehow obtain it for the glory of God.

We did not know of Dr. Stewart's burden at the time, but we liked the property and saw that it would fit our needs.

We made overtures to the people who owned the land and found their asking price to be forty thousand dollars. We only had one thousand dollars that we had borrowed. As we negotiated with the owners, the price was reduced to thirty-eight thousand, and they wanted eight thousand down.

Ours was not a wealthy church. My salary was thirty-five dollars a week and the church's operating budget for a year did not exceed five or six thousand dollars.

We didn't have the kind of money we needed, but we knew if we didn't get the land a builder would buy it for development.

We searched for ways to buy the land. I had bought a plot of land outside of Asheville, nine acres for six thousand dollars. I had paid five hundred dollars down and agreed to pay fifty a month until the land was mine.

I offered this land—the equity I had in it—as a start toward raising the eight thousand we needed for a down payment, and others began to sacrifice. Money came in dribbles, but the dribbles were not spaced far apart, and from one Sunday to the next, we raised the eight thousand dollars and bought the land.

Soon after that, Maze Jackson came to town. He is an old-time gospel preacher. He and Bobby Buchanan and I went to see the land we had purchased. The old sanitarium still stood and around it I heard doves cooing. I told Brother Maze, "Listen to the doves. They are a type of the

Spirit. I believe God has breathed on this transaction."

"So do I, Brother Ralph," he said. "It is of God."

We rejoiced over this.

Our first job was to tear down the old sanitarium and the men of the church decided to do it on Saturdays. Every Saturday morning we met at the place and worked all day, ripping apart, hauling away. The women cooked at home and brought lunch. Those were joyful times. We were working for the Lord, and I have found that one of the blessings in the Lord's work is when people come together in a time of crisis, or great need, and the fellowship and binding together is cement to hold the church together. Some churches get so well off they lose the closeness and contact with each other, and fellowship drains away. Pressure binds people together.

That's the way we were, working together and fellowshipping. We tore that building down piece by piece. When finally we got enough torn down to get a bulldozer inside to do some real damage, the man who drove the dozer in yelled as his machine began sinking in the ground. That's when we realized there was a huge cistern under the sanitarium. It must have held thousands of gallons of water, maybe millions.

We had decided to build the church on the same spot where the sanitarium had been, and that cistern was that much land we didn't have to dig out for a basement. By building in that exact place, we could take advantage of the landscaping for the sanitarium.

After a few Saturdays we had the sanitarium cleared away. Dr. Stewart came by the day we finished and was so overjoyed that he ran to about where our church's pulpit would be and began quoting Scripture. He was truly thrilled over what God had allowed us to do.

The devil told us it would be three years before we could start the foundation of the church, but what a miracle God performed! He moved, and money began coming in to pour the foundation. The work progressed so quickly we almost had to run to keep out of the way.

We broke ground August 6, 1970, and began to work. When the floor was poured, we put up block walls, covered the basement and put black tar paper on it for a roof. Then we began meeting for services in it. When it rained we only used one side of the basement. The other side leaked like a sieve and when we met on a rainy day we had to set buckets all over the floor to catch the drips.

A spirit of joy was on the people. They watched the work progress step by step, slowly but surely, and they realized the hand of God was in it. Some of our most blessed services occurred during those times.

We always ran close on money. Jerry Payne wrote checks on Friday to pay the workers and to pay for materials used that week, and then on Sunday morning we prayed and I passed up and down the aisles to gather in the money to cover the checks. We rushed to the bank Monday morning to make the deposit before the checks came through.

Some people thought we were foolish, but we weren't. Ours was a reckless faith, and it was a joy to behold because it covered the entire congregation.

A lot of times when you see a beautiful little church out in the country, you have no idea how much sacrifice and back-breaking labor went into building it.

We were not like a church with building funds and bank accounts; we had to build a little at a time. God said to the church in Laodicea in Revelation, "Ye are rich and have need of nothing." There is a danger when a church reaches the point that it no longer has needs. First it will lose its feeling of fellowship, then the need to pray, then the people will lose each other, and finally they will lose God. That's when the congregation should build a golf course around the church. It becomes a social club.

We kept praying and buying a little more material and building a little more.

I had no idea how big the church would be until they got the columns poured to set the arches on. When they brought those arches in from the factory and began to set them in place with a giant crane, I was amazed. I thought that God certainly has to be in this. I had not dreamed the church would be that big.

Then I knew what God said is true: "Except God build a house, they that build, build in vain."

We had more trouble getting the roof on than any other thing. The roofing delivered to us was the wrong kind and it sat for days waiting to be picked up and exchanged for the right roofing. Sometimes we had to battle with the companies furnishing materials to us, but we did not permit ourselves to become discouraged. God encouraged us, and we prayed and kept on building.

The men of the church met at the site, stood on the incompleted church and prayed, and all the time we knew that the women were gathered somewhere and were praying, too.

Finally we got the right roofing and got the entire building roofed. Then we moved services from the basement to the upstairs, and what a joyous time that was. For pews we used old tent seats, old-fashioned benches with metal ends.

Our main emphasis was on preaching the Word of God under the anointing of the Holy Spirit. God told us we could not build a church on singing, personality, or on anything human; it must be built on the Word of God and if that isn't pre-eminent, the building will be in vain.

That is just as true today as when it was written two thousand years ago, and we all felt it and adherred to it.

God talked to me. "Just preach the Word," he said. "Don't go in for a lot of programs." I would hear him say: "If I be lifted up I will draw all men unto me. Just preach the Word. Preach Christ and depend on the Holy Ghost to draw the people." God sent the people in.

I remember what Dr. Stewart told me before we bought this property. "Ralph," he said, "you must build a church in Asheville. The day will come when they will drive many, many miles to get where they can hear the Word of God preached without compromise. Liberalism and modernism are rampant within the church. There must be a place where people can come . . . ."

Indeed, they began to come—from Brevard, from Hendersonville, from Canton, from all around Asheville. And during our Jubilee each year, they come from all over the nation.

When we finished building the church, we must have been the proudest congregation in town. We had heard "You'll never get it done" so many times that it would have been easy to believe, but God kept telling us, "You *can* do it." And we did.

Adjoining the church was a twelve and a half acre tract of beautiful land with a house on it that had been built by the father of former Asheville City Manager J. Weldon Weir in 1905. A Fleming family owned that land and had a greenhouse and nursery. The woods were filled with azaleas and all kinds of flowers, and in the springtime people marveled at the beauty of the place. People came from all around to buy plants and flowers from Mr. Fleming.

He was a gracious man. When he reached the point in age and health that he could no longer care for the place, he wanted the church to buy it. But we didn't have the money.

When Fleming died, Mrs. Fleming made it known that she would like to sell the property to the church. One day Jacque and several other women from the church marched around the house and claimed the land for the Lord. They didn't know how we would manage to buy it, but they knew we had to.

The first asking price was in the neighborhood of one hundred eighty thousand dollars, but we finally made the purchase for a little more than eighty thousand.

A strange thing happened after the women claimed the property. We needed twenty-three thousand dollars for a down payment, and we didn't have nearly that much. So we prayed. When my church was in doubt about anything, we prayed, and God usually worked things out. This time we prayed hard because we felt we needed the property to develop the church like it should be developed.

In Jerry Payne's Sunday School class was a man named Norman Pinkston, who lived on Sugar Loaf Mountain beyond Hendersonville. Jerry and the class prayed on Sunday morning that we might be able to find twenty-three thousand dollars to purchase that property, and at the end of the class as the other members filed out, Pinkston came to Jerry and said, "I have the money for the down payment."

What a surprise—and what a blessing! Little did we know we had to purchase the land so soon. Pinkston let us have the money on a loan, but not a pressure loan. We had no deadline to pay it back.

The day after we closed the deal and made the down payment, a real estate woman stopped her car on the property and began walking around, looking the place over.

Someone from the church went over and met her.

"I'm just looking around," the real estate woman said. "We have bought this property."

"You have bought this property?"

"Yes. A doctor is buying it. He is going to put an adult school on it."

"Have you signed the papers and paid for the property?" the church member asked.

"No, not yet," the woman said. "But the doctor has decided, and he is ready to close the deal."

"Then you'd better check further," the church member said. "We closed on this property yesterday for the church."

We came that close to missing the property. And we would have if God hadn't impressed on Norman Pinkston that Sunday morning to let us have the money for the down payment.

God answered the prayers of those praying women. If

we honor God, we may run close, but he will never be late.

The church designated the house on the adjoining property as a parsonage, and Jacque and I moved in. Later, the church did some remodeling of the house and added a large study and a "Send The Light" office beneath the study.

Lee lived in Florida at that time. He moved to Florida in the late 1940s after he married. He pastored the First Baptist Church of Hudson, Florida, and also built a successful home remodeling business. One day when he was visiting, I told him we were going to change some of the walls inside the house. He went out and returned in a few minutes with a sledge hammer.

"Which walls are you going to take out?" he asked.

"That one for one," I pointed to a wall.

Lee swung the sledge and knocked a sizeable hole in the wall. A few more swings produced a hole large enough to walk through.

"Ralph," he said, "if you don't start, it won't ever get done."

Same old Lee. Always a doer. When Lee wanted to do something, he did it then.

Talk about a mess! Lee made the old plaster and dust fly everywhere, and when he all but had the wall down, he wiped his brow and said, "There! Now you have to fix it!"

Around 1975, Jacque had surgery on her legs and came home with both legs in full casts. She was in bed and could hear crews building the study and working on some of the walls Lee had knocked out.

Lee came to see her. "Jacque," he said, "they want to knock out this bedroom wall to make one big room out of the two bedrooms. Can you lie in the study a while?"

"I can," she said, "if you can carry me in there."

We carried her into the study and Lee grabbed the sledge hammer and in a few minutes there was no more wall between the bedrooms.

Dust boiled out of that wall and covered everything.

Lee was suddenly a demon with a sledge hammer. We sat eating breakfast one morning and saw marks of a chimney above a mantle in one wall. However, there was no fireplace.

"Lee, do you think there was a fireplace in this dining room?" I asked casually.

"Well, we can certainly find out," he said, grabbing the hammer. WHAMMO! He found the fireplace. It seemed that tons of soot fell out of that chimney and covered everything in the room, including Lee and me and our breakfast.

An inspector who came to inspect the wiring in the parsonage said he had lived here when he was a boy.

"I worked for Weldon Weir's daddy," he said. "I got a dollar a day and my bed.

"I remember when they wired this house," he said. "They wired it free because Mr. Weir agreed to let the electric company bring potential customers to see that they could have electricity and that it was safe to use."

After we moved in, the thought occurred to me that the Weir family must have had well water. Somewhere on the place there must be a well. One day as I came through the woods on the north side of the house, I saw under the laurels an old iron well pump. It was rusty and hadn't been used in decades. I peered closely under the laurels and saw some pieces of board sticking out. Scratching away the leaves and debris, I found an open well about fifty feet deep. It had been dug by hand many years before. I tied a string to a rock and let it slowly descend into the well. A long way down the rock struck water.

The well is still there, but we had it closed and topped with cement so no child could ever wander over there and fall in the well.

My brothers and sisters often visit us in the parsonage. I am proud of them. Paul has been in the dry cleaning business all his life. He bought Superior Cleaners in Asheville and operated it until he retired. Perry also has been a dry cleaner and worked with Paul a good part of the time. Raymond stayed in the army for years after World War II and wound up working in the aircraft industry in California. He later moved to Denver. Frank, who served in the Marines during the war, has been in the cleaning business in Asheville for years. He was in charge of the laundry at Memorial Mission Hospital for some time, and later was in charge of the laundry at Grove Park Inn.

Evelyn lives in Maryville, Tennessee. Her husband has been dead a long while. Ethel married Roy Hyatt, a golfer of some note in Asheville. They live here and he works with General Electric.

My mother passed away December 27, 1959, and my father died January 13, 1969. Jacque's parents died four years apart; her father on February 3, 1947, and her mother on February 1, 1951.

But they all still live within us.

# — 16 —

# Seeing Is Believing

Probably the most effective illustrated sermon I have preached was in that Biltmore tent meeting in 1950 when I had the congregation beat up the whiskey still with hammers and clubs. The still served as the illustration of Satanism.

Over the years I found that illustrations were appreciated by congregations.

I used one that might be called a "gimmick." That was during the fight against alcohol, too.

In those days, preachers thundered from the pulpits against the use of strong drink. They preached against the evils of alcohol. Now its hard to find a preacher who'll even mention whisky in the pulpit, but in those days of temperance, you could hear it preached all over town.

I have seen the fruits of drink. Years ago I remember going to my sister's apartment on Montford Avenue, and once one of her neighbors got drunk and walked up and down the halls of the apartment house with a German Luger, threatening to kill everyone he saw. Men do things when drinking they would never do sober. Having seen many things that alcohol had done, how it had broken homes, destroyed lives, made children suffer, I rarely missed a chance to get in my licks against it.

One day I was uptown window shopping and noticing all the mannequins in the store windows, I got the idea for "Old Man Booze."

Someone in one of the department stores gave me a male mannequin and I dressed him like a drunk.

At the start of my next sermon against alcohol, I read different Scriptures in which God told of the evils of liquor. Then I read from the Bible what drink did to Noah, to Lot, and to other men. I told what drink did today in the lives of parents and of teen-agers especially, and of little boys and girls.

Sometimes I had people from the congregation testify what alcohol had done to wreck their lives.

Then, just as I reached the climax of the message, I had someone bring out "Old Man Booze" and put him in a chair.

I asked him questions and someone hidden behind him answered for him so the congregation could hear. He had answers for all the questions, but his answers could not defend him against the Word, which convicted him every time.

"This man," I said finally, "represents the wine, liquor, and beer industry, and all that strong drink stands for. What will we do with him?"

And the crowd responded, "Hang him! Hang him!"

Quickly, someone wheeled a gallows onto the platform, put a rope around Old Man Booze's neck, and hung him. Then he swung back and forth, back and forth, out over the audience, and the crowd rejoiced. The point of the message was that the only way to deal with drink was to put it away permanently.

Once I used that message in Hendersonville in a tent meeting, and the crowd really responded. When we strung up Old Man Booze and swung him out over the audience, a young fellow got so carried away he leaped onto the far side of the platform, raced across it, and made a flying tackle of Old Man Booze.

When the young man came to himself, he and Old Man Booze were swinging out over the audience. He really wanted to see Old Man Booze destroyed.

I wish people would get that stirred up over drink again.

I give God the glory for the sermons he has given me.

Every man has to abide in his calling, and when God called me to preach, he didn't tell me to go to school and become a little June-apple boy preacher. I could never have done that. He said, "Son, you will have to follow the leadership of the Spirit." Many times God gave me the ideas for illustrations for sermons. Illustrations make the sermons so simple that children understand. The illustrations show what the Word says. I believe they help fill people with the Spirit. I do not mean that God will lead you to do something fanatical that will bring reproach to the name of Christ. If something doesn't honor Jesus and lift him up, then leave it alone.

I have dressed young people like angels and Death to illustrate the twenty-third Psalm; I once used an old-timey pressure cooker with the handles you have to pull up into notches in the lid and screw down tight to seal it, to illustrate a sermon on a nationwide Christian Broadcast Network telecast. I called the sermon, "Israel—God's Pressure Cooker." I put dry ice in the cooker to make it look like it was really steaming and let the cooker represent the plight of the Jew under persecution. I used pieces of wood, each with words written on it—"Anti-Christ," "Anti-Semitism," "Auschwitz"—to fuel the fire under the pressure cooker and said they were the things that made the pot boil.

These are prophetic truths. When God nudges me in the direction of illustrating my sermons, I usually lean into Biblical prophecy. The average church seldom hears anything about the second coming of Christ. God burdened me when he saved me to preach on that subject. The Bible strongly teaches the return of Christ.

I have always believed that the Jew is the great miracle of the world and I preach a lot on that. It is a miracle how he existed all those centuries without a homeland, under severe persecution. He couldn't have come through without God.

When God gives me an illustrated sermon I always enjoy preaching it. They are fun to do, they let others participate in the sermon, and people remember what they learn from them.

In January of 1986 two major occurrences in the United States were the Chicago Bears' victory over the New England Patriots in the Super Bowl, and the explosion of the space shuttle. Around the country, people did the "Super Bowl Shuffle" as done prior to the game by the Bears.

Then when the shuttle exploded the nation was pulled from ecstasy into shock and sorrow. That space shot was built up to gigantic proportions by the government and the press because it carried the first school teacher into space. Millions of school children watched the launch on television and saw the explosion.

Everyone was concerned about what should be said to children about death. Counselors and psychiatrists had a field day, discussing what should be explained to children. I thought some of them panicked because they didn't know how to talk to children about death. In all their counselling, few counselors even mentioned God or his Word, and certainly few if any said anything about the answer being found in God's Word.

God spoke to me and said I should do an illustrated message the following Sunday, one about understanding and accepting death.

I called the message, "From the Super Bowl Shuffle to the Space Shuttle Sorrow," or "Explaining Death to a Child." I announced that I would preach the message on Sunday and would direct it to children.

My son, Ralph Jr., and his wife Muzette had a sheep that had given birth to triplets not long before this. My daughter, Becky, and her husband, Jim Templeton, had two little lambs that were born to their sheep. One was solid white and the other solid black. I am sure those sheep were there because God was getting things ready. He told me to use the lambs because children would understand better. Before I preached the sermon, another of Becky's sheep gave birth to another lamb—making six I could use in the sermon.

They brought the sheep on Sunday morning and we had everything ready to fix a place with straw for them on the front of the platform. Several men who knew sheep stood by to help.

My sermon began with something about how exciting the week before the Super Bowl had been, with the nation looking forward with great anticipation to both the game and the space shot. I talked of the excitement of the game and of the lift-off of the shuttle, and when tragedy struck, the nation didn't know how to handle it. There were no answers. I heard on television during that time that there were no "absolutes." I could not believe my ears. I knew there were absolutes, for God's Word is true. Heaven and hell, right and wrong, light and darkness, life and death are absolutes. We were dealing with an absolute in the space disaster.

To help illustrate the sermon, I dressed in a bath robe to represent a shepherd's robe, and I wore a *kefeyah,* a shepherd's headdress I had bought in Jerusalem.

Working down in the message to the place where I talked about death, I read the twenty-third Psalm. That was the cue for the men to bring out the lambs and straw, make a fold on the front of the platform, and put the lambs in the fold.

What an immediate hit those lambs were! They didn't try to run away, and occasionally one would cry a little. I wish everyone could have seen the audience's eyes.

But there were only five lambs. I said, "Children, something is wrong. One lamb is missing." I read the Scripture about the ninety and nine sheep being safe and one missing, and the shepherd went after the one.

"He's somewhere lost out there," I said, "and I must go and hunt him." I had the cordless microphone, so I came off the platform and told the children, "I'll go look for the little lamb."

While I went up the aisle looking, the Burns Trio sang "Jesus Loves the Little Children."

I said, "He is out here somewhere. He is supposed to be in the fold, but he is lost."

In the vestibule, Becky waited with the little black sheep. I draped the lamb across my shoulders and said, "I have found him; I have found the little lost sheep." When I went back through the door into the aisle, I could feel God's presence. A hush fell over that auditorium, even though the people were excited and thrilled. The trio began to sing "The Ninety and Nine."

As I came down the aisle, I said, "I found him, but he is a little black sheep. Sin will make your heart black, but Jesus loves this little sheep and died for him."

At that point I reached the fold, and said, "Now we have rescued him and brought him back. He is black but he belongs to the fold with the rest. Even though he is black, Jesus still loves him."

The kids were so excited.

I said, "God said, it is appointed unto men once to die, and after this the judgment. This little lamb that is back in the fold represents you and me, and he represents all the little children. The Bible says we all have to die. This little black sheep is a type of you, and one day he will have to die."

On the platform was a big box with the letters D-E-A-T-H on its side. I said, "This sheep has to die," and we opened the box and put the little black sheep inside. The children seemed to understand.

I quoted First Thessalonians 4:13 where Paul says, "I would not have you to be ignorant, brethren, concerning them which are asleep, that ye sorrow not, even as others which have no hope . . ." Then I quoted verse 16 in which Paul said, "the dead in Christ shall rise first," and verse 17, "Then we which are alive and remain shall be caught up together with them in the clouds, to meet the Lord in the air." I finished that part of the drama with Scripture from Corinthians, "The trumpet will sound and Christ will return."

I said, "Children, one day the Lord is coming. When you die, if you die in the Lord, your body has to go into the ground and go back to dust. But the moment you die, the real you, the redeemed spirit in you is with Christ." Children can understand that.

"One day, the trumpet will sound," I said, and as the words came out, a woman in the vestibule, out of sight of the congregation, began playing "Taps" on a trumpet. Then she immediately went into "Up From The Grave He Arose." It was like God had charged the atmosphere in the church. Brother Eddie Evans, our music director, sang "Up From The Grave He Arose."

Someone turned that big box around and on the side then showing was written "R-E-S-U-R-R-E-C-T-I-O-N." In that box with the little black lamb was its white twin.

"Now, children," I said, "the Lord has come and the old black nature has gone forever," and I pulled that little white lamb out of the box. Do you believe those children's eyes got big? They were the size of saucers.

"When Jesus comes," I said, "your body will come forth and be glorified and be united with that spirit that has already gone to be with the Lord. Then you'll be with the Lord forever."

And, last of all, to show the children that we hadn't killed that little black lamb—for kids will wonder and worry about something like that—we took him out of the box and put him in the fold with the others.

The children then knew the sermon was an illustration—and parents told me later that it had effectively helped their children deal with death and with the explosion of the space shuttle.

You see, if we listen to God, he knows how to handle life's problems.

## — 17 —

# Spreading the Word

My work—my job, really—has always been simply to get the gospel to the people through the best means available. Francis Asbury got it there by horseback. The Apostle Paul took it mostly on foot, or sometimes by donkey, I suspect. Billy Sunday conducted mass evangelism by holding great crusades in metropolitan areas. Billy Graham pioneered the gospel on television and thereby opened a new era of evangelism.

The way to reach the most people today is by means of television. In Asheville our station was WLOS-TV, Channel 13. Its transmitter was located on a tower on Mount Pisgah, the highest hill in the vicinity of Asheville, and was so powerful the station's signal beamed strongly into seven states: North and South Carolina, Georgia, Tennessee, Alabama, Virginia, and Kentucky.

I had preached a lot on radio and felt I could make the transition to television rather easily, but my problem was twofold: first was getting on the air, or convincing the station I had a program worth watching, and the second problem, of course—What Else?—was money.

I knew if God didn't give me favor with the station, I stood no chance of getting on. Those things God has to work out, and that challenge became such a burden deep inside of me that I felt God's hand at work. When I felt that old familiar surge within and knew God was at work, I simply turned my attention to raising the necessary money. I prayed constantly that God would help me raise the finances and that he would give me the ability to conduct an appealing and informative program, one that would win souls for the kingdom.

In the summer of 1960 I accepted an invitation from a church in Amelia, Ohio, to do a revival, and while in meeting there I mentioned to the folks that I was burdened about going on television. I told them our station back home had such a powerful transmitter strategically located that it could reach much of the Appalachian area. There were about six million people in the area, and while I knew I couldn't reach all of them I wanted to reach as many as I could. I also explained the need of money to finance the program.

In that meeting was a young couple named Bill and Mary Arnett. Bill worked in the steel industry, and they were a kind and gentle pair. God had spoken to their hearts, and after the service one evening they told me they had been praying about the television ministry and that they were going to the loan company and borrow a thousand dollars to give me to start the TV program.

"What we're doing," he explained, "is giving you a gift. You use the money the way the Lord tells you to, and we will repay the loan."

"Praise God," I said. "He's answering prayer."

What those two precious people did that day has been a tremendous blessing to me and to thousands of others.

After I returned to Asheville at the conclusion of that meeting, their thousand dollars arrived by registered mail. Immediately, I went to Loyd Leonard, the television station's advertising director, and told him that God had worked it out for me to get started. We discussed details drinking coffee at the lunch counter in Eckerd's Drug Store on Patton Avenue in Asheville.

The devil was working on me again, even as I handed Loyd a check for one thousand dollars. Satan said, "You're really crazy now. You've jumped off the deep end. As soon as that thousand dollars runs out, that will be the end of this."

Loyd was very kind. "We'll sign you up for thirteen weeks," he said, and we agreed to a price of a little more than two hundred dollars per program. The thousand dollars would cover almost five weeks, and I knew I had to open up some avenues of revenue if I went past that point. We had to trust God for the money; we didn't have a church treasury to take it out of.

Our first program was in October 1960. Those were the days of black and white, and the station didn't have editing machines, which meant if we encountered an insurmountable problem at any time in the thirty-minute filming, we had to start all over from the top.

At times we started filming at eight o'clock in the evening and finished at midnight. Four hours under those bright, hot lights wore a man out. But what did I care? I was doing this for God.

From the first program, I always took my wife. I felt she should be on with me, and we arranged for her part to be reading the Scripture, giving a few words of encouragement, and praying. She is strong in her prayer life. There was no doubt in my mind that her ministry was needed to make this program a success. The audience was made up of many mothers and daughters, and they related to another wife and mother who shared in their problems and understood their heartaches. Even today, after so many years on television, we get letters every week from people who say how God has used Jacque and her prayer life to help them over the years.

For a while, at the start, I had to fight another battle with the devil. He told me if I wanted to do the thing right I would have to build props and stage scenes, and all of that. I thought, what will I do? But God intervened. He said, "Son, don't build any of them. I didn't call you to build props and stage scenes. You just go on television and preach the Word of God. That is what the people need. Preach the Word, Preacher—preach Jesus!"

God also nudged me to preach along prophetic lines on the air. Most of the people watching seldom got to hear about the Second Coming. They don't know what the Bible says about the end of the age, or how to prepare to meet God. They don't know the admonition: "Behold, I come quickly." I tailored many of my programs along those lines, balancing them with preaching the straight gospel. And God honored the broadcasts.

When that first thousand dollars ran out, the devil said, "You are finished." But money came in the mail for another week, and then another and another.

That's the way it has been for more than twenty-five years: We go from program to program, week to week, month to month. The whole thing has been a miracle, but the people who watch manage to scrape up enough to send in to keep the program on the air.

Soon I began to see the scope of the thing that God had had me do. He made me realize how many prisons there are in the reach of Channel 13. Mail streamed in from prisons, nursing homes, and other such institutions. Someone in a nursing home in Kentucky wrote to say that every person in the home who was mobile gathered in the sitting room every Sunday morning and watched the telecast. We reached hospitals, motels, and private homes where our program would be the only religious service the people were acquainted with. Some could not go to church; others would not go.

I received a letter from a man who worked in a fire tower deep in a forest on the North Carolina-Virginia border who said that his church service every Sunday morning was watching the telecast while keeping his eye peeled for forest fires.

As I had done on radio, I named the telecast "Send The Light." I have used the name constantly since 1940.

In the television ministry, no one will ever know until he gets to Eternity all that God has done through TV. We will never know how many sinners have been converted because of the program, or how many homes have been blessed. We have heard from some who were on the verge of suicide when the telecast brought hope into their lives. Many people told us how they have been encouraged, and preachers mentioned how they have been helped and how they have received thoughts and ideas from our telecasts that helped them with sermons. The outreach of the television ministry goes on and on.

Unusual things have happened because the television program is an unusual ministry.

How well I remember the sermon God told me to preach on the first Sunday of June, 1967. Had I not known it before, I would have been convinced by the sermon he gave me that he is a miracle-working God, and certainly a God of knowledge.

I made that Sunday's television program on Thursday morning, June 1, and preached from the nineteenth chapter of Isaiah. I used the title of *"The Sword of the Lord Over Egypt and the Thirteen Arab Nations."*

Some specific Scripture in that chapter reads like this: "Behold, the Lord rideth upon a swift cloud, and shall come into Egypt: and the idols of Egypt shall be moved at his presence, and the heart of Egypt shall melt in the midst of it."

And: "In that day shall Egypt be like unto women: and it shall be afraid and fear because of the shaking of the hand of the Lord of hosts, which he shaketh over it."

That was an unusual passage for God to impress on my heart, and I thought there must be more to it than meets the eye. For some reason unknown to me at the time, I went to the newspaper office of the *Asheville Citizen-Times* and took an ad in Saturday's paper announcing what the Sunday telecast would be about.

On Sunday morning as soon as the program aired, my telephone began to ring. Jewish people called me from all over town. Rabbi Friedman telephoned. "Our people were stirred by your message," he said.

God was moving. God was opening a door that man could not open by himself. Do you think an Orthodox Jew would listen to a mountain Gentile preacher? Not ordinarily, and that's why God directed me to place the ad in the paper.

I wondered all day, is that why God had me place the ad? Is that why he made me preach the sermon? What am I supposed to do among the Jews? Deep down, I felt that the drama had not yet been played out; it was unfinished.

The following day was Monday, June 5, and we were awakened to the news that war had broken out between Israel and its Arab neighbors, Egypt, Syria, and Jordan. This was the start of the Six-Day War in which tiny Israel whipped those Arab powers in six days.

My mouth fell open in shock. I knew then why God had me preach that sermon. It was a prophecy of the war!

God had known the war would start. I did not know it. But he had deliberately had me advertise the sermon so our Jewish friends would tune in.

They telephoned me all day Monday, all wanting to know what I knew about the war. Mail streamed in from Jews in other cities and areas. God had opened the door between me and the Jewish people, and to this day they still watch the program. They are hungry to know the Word. They ask good questions, and I take time in answering as accurately as I can from the Bible. I tell them that according to Daniel, Chapter eleven, God has promised to make Ammon, Moab, and Edom, which contains Petra, hiding places for the Jews in the Great Tribulation. They are interested and want to hear, and they are not resentful. God saw to that in 1967.

God blessed my ministry mightily during the Six-Day War and its aftermath. When Jewish forces broke through the Arab lines and made a bee line for the Wailing Wall, the chaplain of the Israeli forces went with them. They raced to that wall and for the first time in two thousand years realized that their most sacred place was back in Jewish hands. Tough soldiers wept openly and kissed the stones in the wall, some of them dating back to Herod's days—the time of Christ.

The rabbi took the *shofar,* the ram's horn, and blew it there for the first time in twenty centuries and proclaimed, "The Messianic Age has begun!" When I read about that in the newspaper, I realized that we are really in the "end" hours.

That's why God opened the door to get those things on television. Not only did the Jew hear them, but other preachers, mothers and dads, and all were able to see and know that the end times are near. We are the generation that has seen the fulfillment of this prophecy begin.

What a powerful weapon television can be in our fight with the devil!

Television also has its comical side.

In February of 1967 I had a heart attack. I was forty-seven years old when I was laid low, and I was in the hospital twenty-one days. I was helpless and really felt it. I was unable to do anything, and my wife was left with the television program to run.

The Reverend Brown Caldwell, of Greenville, South Carolina, came to our rescue. He was a dear friend of ours, originally from Waynesville, North Carolina. He was an old-time mountain preacher who preached the unadulterated Word of God.

When he offered to fill in for me, I jumped at the opportunity. He was accustomed to preaching on the air; he had been on the radio for years—but he had never been on television! And that made a difference. When that television camera's red light blinks on and you know you're on the air, it does something to you.

Jacque took him to the television station to cut the first program. He was positioned before the camera, and the director of the program explained the procedure. Brown nodded his head in understanding, cool as a cucumber, and the director went ahead with his business.

The cameramen began their countdown: "Ten, nine, eight, seven, six . . . ." As they counted, they displayed the fingers of their hands, folding one up as each second was counted away.

Suddenly, in horror, they saw that the Reverend Caldwell was not watching them at all. He was staring at his pocket watch, held firmly in his right hand.

The cameramen sought vainly to get his attention. One got on the floor, trying to distract him from his watch. Nothing worked. The reverend continued to stare at the watch!

Jacque was bent double with laughter.

As the red light went on on the camera, the reverend looked up, and the cameraman stabbed his finger frantically at the light.

The reverend opened his mouth and said, "How can I watch those lights, watch those men, read my notes and preach—and know when to start and when to quit without using my watch?"

Jacque laughed so hard tears streamed down her cheeks. The director pulled his hair.

Jacque heard Mr. Caldwell continue, "Just leave me alone and I will go by my watch. Let's get on with it, and let me use my watch!"

It was hilarious, and it continued, though toned down in subsequent weeks, until I returned to the program.

During these years, Jacque's legs began to weaken and surgery was required. She has had fifteen operations on her knees. Once when she was in the hospital recuperating, I bemoaned the fact that she could not be on the program. "She's vital to me—and to the program," I said.

"Don't worry about it, Preacher," said Ken Hensley, who was directing the program that week. He arranged it with the hospital, took Bill Banner to photograph her, and filmed Jacque reading Scripture, praying, and saying words of encouragement from her hospital bed.

That was one time God hadn't spoken to me—but he spoke to Ken Hensley, all right.

I always had excellent relations with Mort Cohn, station

manager and vice president of WLOS-TV. He was a good fellow who understood our ministry. He also realized that a lot of people watched the program each week, and as a station manager he was happy with that. But through my ignorance I got him in hot water once—scalding water, in fact.

A fellow named Kenneth Goff came to Asheville to preach. He was strong against communism, and I like that, but he was also a good preacher. He had been a member of the communist party and when God saved him he quit the party and began exposing it.

When he came to Asheville, I had him preach at our church. The people were so receptive, I asked him to preach on my television program. He jumped at the chance.

On the air, he didn't really preach. For thirty minutes he exposed communism like I had never heard it exposed.

The following week I received a letter from Mort Cohn in which he said the station was considering taking me off the air because of the predicament I had put the station in. He explained that what I had done was in violation of the "Fairness Act," and that the communist party could actually force WLOS-TV to give it thirty minutes of equal time. Furthermore, I would have to pay for their time, he said.

In the letter, he requested that I come in and discuss the matter with him and with several of the station's officials. God told me to inject a bit of comedy in the proceedings, to print on a three-by-five index card the words, "I PLEAD IGNORANCE," and take it with me to the meeting.

When I opened the door and walked into Mr. Cohn's office, he sat there with three or four others waiting for me, and you could have cut the tension with a knife.

The first thing I did, before speaking even, was to hold up that card for them to read, and suddenly they burst into laughter and the tension was relieved.

We discussed the matter seriously. They had already decided not to take me off the air—(I had prayed hard about that)—and Mr. Cohn said, "I hate communism as much as anybody, Mr. Sexton, but you have put me on the spot."

I really did not know all that was involved, but I learned valuable lessons that day that have probably kept me out of hot water since.

I have had a lot of guests on the air with me. Not all were cut out for television. Some froze like blocks of ice when the camera came on. Once a man was on with me whose beard was so black they had to stop the filming and dust his beard with white powder. And sometimes I would be preaching in Asheville and a quartet singing on my program would be in WLOS's studio in Greenville, South Carolina. They had to sing on cue, and when the camera caught them by surprise their expressions would be hilarious.

In the early 1980s, Mort Cohn was moved to Miami and put in charge of the Wometco television station there, and Dave D'Armond was made station manager in Asheville. He was a precious Christian man, friendly toward us and toward the gospel. It was a genuine pleasure working with him.

In 1984, halfway through our twenty-fourth year on television, Wometco sold WLOS-TV to a co-op group, and Dave D'Armond was replaced as station manager by a man named Charles Birdwell. He was sent in by the new owners from Oklahoma.

The first thing I heard about the new manager, even before I had time to meet him, was that he intended to drop all religious programming and devote all of Sunday morning to cartoons.

The news deeply disturbed me. For almost a quarter-century I had been on television, and we met young adults who said they grew up with the program and it became a part of their lives, and now their children watch it. To stop the program just like that would be a shock to people.

Soon I received a letter from Mr. Birdwell which stated

that the station would drop all religious programming, confirming our fears. That meant that not only my program would be dropped, but those of Brother Wesley Grant, E. J. Daniels, and Robert Schuler as well—and the Sunday morning services at First Baptist Church. Actually, the station made First Baptist a price for which it could stay on the air, but the price was so steep it was prohibitive.

After praying about the letter, I went to see Mr. Birdwell. He was gracious to me, but I felt immediately that his mind was made up. The die was cast and he was not going to change his mind.

I told him, "Mr. Birdwell, outsiders come into these mountains and buy up businesses and force changes on us. In your case, you will pipe in from outside what you want us to see and hear.

"But when you cut off religious programming, you are cutting off our heritage. Our forefathers came into these mountains in wagons, and the wilderness was so thick and the mountains so steep the first wagons had to be dismantled and slid over the mountains.

"The early people dug this place out of the wilderness, first to glorify and worship God as they pleased, and to build their homes and rear their children in the fear and admonition of Almighty God.

"Mountain folks love old-time gospel preaching and singing," I continued. "That is their culture, their life. When you cut that off, you deliberately cut off a part of their heritage. It's like cutting off their arms and legs."

But my reasoning bounced off the walls of his office as if I had never said the words.

"There is another station here," he said, "Channel twenty-one. Maybe it can carry some of the religious programs."

The station removed Wesley Grant, E. J. Daniels, and me from the air, and allowed Robert Schuler to stay, but moved his program to seven o'clock.

I went back to see Mr. Birdwell for one last try. "How

much money would it take to stay on?" I asked him, and soon I realized that money wasn't the object. He did not want religious programs on at any price.

Finally, perhaps to rid himself of me, he said I could remain on the air for an outlandish sum of money—at six o'clock in the morning.

"That," I said flatly, "is an insult to Almighty God. You know no one is up at that hour. The roosters still have laryngitis at that time of the morning."

I walked down the steps, opened the big door, and stepped out into the sun. When I closed the door behind me, I felt so strange and alone. I started to leave, and God said, "Wait a minute. Wipe off the dust of your feet against this station. It has rejected me—and now I will reject it."

A flood of mail came into my office, objecting to our removal from the air. Leading businessmen of Asheville complained to the station, but to no avail. Mr. Birdwell ignored all pleas.

Within twelve months, the station fell to last place in local ratings and red ink ran ankle deep in the studios.

I was off the air about a year, and everywhere I went people told me how much they missed the program. They always asked when I was going back on, and the only thing I could tell them was to pray. "It will take a miracle of God to get us back on," I said, "but pray."

And people prayed.

With so much interest expressed in the program, I knew that it hadn't died. God was not finished with it. People did not lose their burden for the work.

Then one day, Mr. Birdwell was gone from the station.

I met Wesley Grant on the street and he said, "Brother Ralph, I heard Mr. Birdwell was going back to Oklahoma." Wesley was then preaching on WFGW and WMIT-FM, the Billy Graham stations in Black Mountain, North Carolina.

"I got on the radio," Wesley said, "and prayed that God would give him safe travelling mercies."

He wanted to be sure Mr. Birdwell got back to Oklahoma.

When the new station manager, Mike Gehring, came to WLOS, one of my friends at the station said, "Give him a few days to get settled and then contact him."

I urged people to pray, and after a few days I telephoned the station and arranged an appointment with him.

He was a kind man, pleasant as he could be, and he seemed to be glad to see me.

"I know the station has made some mistakes," he said, "and we are going to try to correct them. We would like to have your program back on, and we would like to have First Baptist and the others back on, too."

The next week I received a letter from Mr. Gehring confirming that the station would be receptive to our returning to the air, and in the letter he quoted a price which was twice what we had been paying before. He offered the time slot of eight-thirty to nine on Sunday mornings, and he offered a one-year contract with an option for four more, equal to a five-year contract. Five in the Bible is the number of grace. "God is working," I told people. "His grace is coming through."

Mr. Gehring promised that in no year would the price be raised more than ten percent, if raised at all.

By faith, I signed the contract, and on the first Sunday in March, 1986, I returned to the air. People were excited and thrilled. Receiving mail from the listeners, hundreds each week, was a shot in the arm to me personally and a great help to my ministry. We still depend on gifts from the watchers to keep the program on.

When we arranged the date of the first Sunday in March for my return to television, I had a startling thought: I will have to get another theme song cut and all the slides made to use on the program. The first of March was only a couple of weeks away, and I knew I had to hurry. But I didn't know exactly how to go about it.

When in doubt, go to the source. I went to the station to ask Roger Melton to help. That was a cold day and I met

Roger coming out of the station to start his car and let it run a few minutes to warm up before he left.

"Roger, Praise God, we're going back on the air," I said.

"I heard, Preacher," he said, "and I'm glad. We're all glad up here."

"But how in the world will I get my theme song cut and the introduction and the slides and everything else ready in time?" I was genuinely concerned.

"Come in with me," he said, "and we'll see about it."

He took me in the Control Room, and a fellow named Burns came in. They opened a locker and began pulling out slides and tapes and things.

"We knew you were coming back, Preacher," Roger said, "so we didn't destroy anything."

Burns went over to another place. "Here's the music," he said.

They had hidden all my stuff away when I went off the air.

They had faith, and I thought that was wonderful.

God has used my television ministry in many ways over the years. It has been like a family thing. Churches and camp meetings have used it to keep up with what was going on in different places. I have announced camp meetings, revivals, special meetings, and other things for many churches. The program sometimes is like a miniature community religious calendar.

To God be the glory. He may use the program any way he wishes.

That was one reason so many people missed it when it was off, I am sure; they had to look elsewhere for information.

Through the years we have been blessed by people willing to help on the telecasts, by singers in particular. This mountain area has always been the home of great gospel singers, and we have been able to have the best of them on the telecast.

The original Kingsmen Quartet sang on my first telecast back in 1960. Reese and Raymond McKinney, Frank Cutshall, Jack Henderson, and Eldridge Fox. Eldridge built that quartet over the years into the number one quartet in the nation. They have appeared on the program many times since, and Eldridge and his family attend Trinity Baptist Church when he is home.

Then there were the Inspirations, from Bryson City. I met them in 1967 soon after they began singing together. I pitched my tent on the old airport east of Sylva and started a revival. I had strange feelings about it; I didn't know how the people would accept it.

When I opened the meeting, it was a battle from the first night. The crowds were small and the response was not great. But I kept plugging along the best I could and after a while the Lord answered prayer and people began to come.

One evening people from Victory Baptist Church in Bryson City came in a bunch. They had taken five hundred dollars they were saving to buy pews for their church and gave the money to me. "We know you're struggling financially, Preacher," they said, "and we want to help."

Then Martin Cook came in a little Greenbriar van. He had his quartet of high school boys with him. Archie Watkins was about fifteen, Troy Burns sang bass though he was only fourteen, and Jack Laws and Ronnie Hutchins were in their teens. Martin was their high school teacher, and they had begun to sing at churches and meetings. They called themselves the Inspirations.

"We've come to help you, Preacher," Martin said. He knew I was having spiritual warfare, trying to get that meeting going, and I knew if we broke through to the people, it would be God's doing. God used the Inspirations to get that meeting going.

They sang night after night and God came into the tent. People came from all over Jackson County and soon were filling the tent each night. One evening Archie sang "Little is much if God is in it," and God began to move. The meeting broke through that night and people began to get saved, and we had a glorious time.

One night a little boy about ten or eleven years old came to the altar and was saved. His mother was with him, and she found the Lord that night, too. Before the meeting ended that little boy came back one night lugging the biggest Bible I've ever seen. He said, "Preacher, God has called me to preach." The following Sunday the mother took the little boy and some other children to Maggie Valley. She stopped at the eastern foot of Soco Mountain and bought gasoline. When she went inside to pay, a man from Florida lost control of his Cadillac when the brakes gave way coming down the mountain. He ran through that gasoline station's pumps and smashed into the woman's car, killing the little boy and some others.

I have had the Inspirations in many meetings since that one in Sylva. They have sung on my television show and in my church. They are outstanding Christian men who are doing a tremendous job for the Lord.

The Primitive Quartet of Candler has sung on many programs for me. They are fine Christian people. When they help me on the television program, sometimes we use a video and sometimes they sing live on the program.

Singing is such an important part of my program. Sometimes I let the Inspirations have a whole program, and they always honor God.

When Squire Parsons came down from West Virginia to join the Kingsmen, I knew he was an outstanding Christian. What a ministry he has had through the years! The first Sunday the Parsons were here, Squire's wife came to our church and brought the children to Sunday School. The first Sunday Squire was home and not on the road singing, he came to church with her. They told me that morning they wanted to join the church, and they did.

I praised God when Squire told me he felt led of God to go out on his own preaching and singing. God honored his work, and now he travels the nation over preaching and singing in his beautiful baritone voice. He may have the best singing voice I have ever heard.

Squire has been on my television program many times, and the people love him. Sometimes I let him take the entire thirty minutes.

Once a year his family comes down from West Virginia and they have a singing family reunion at our church. We have a night of their singing and the people fill the church.

Evangelist Billy Kelly has helped me many times on television and in my church. The Burns Trio of Greenville, South Carolina, has been a great blessing to me. We used to have the Carolina Ladies Quartet from Greenville. They sang on my program for years until they disbanded when some of the members died.

People asked why I didn't try to expand my program to nationwide television, and I would have loved to do that, but God seemed to say, "Stay where I've put you."

This television ministry has a glorious history. For more than a quarter-century now it has been reaching people in these seven states.

Wonderful, wonderful things have happened because of it.

# — 18 —

# Philosophy

Not everyone has responded kindly to my preaching through the half-century I have been spreading the Word of the Lord. Not everyone responds kindly to any forceful preacher's preaching. There are always some who get upset, and I constantly receive letters, mostly unsigned, from people who want to rake me over the coals.

Criticism does not bother me. When I am criticized, it tells me that God is reaching the critic. But I think critics should have the courtesy to sign their names, especially if they are sincere in their criticism. I have learned that the best thing to do with such letters is to file them in the wastebasket.

I have received telephone calls from angry people who rant and rave and curse me roundly. Sometimes I just put the receiver on the desk and let them rave. Once when I did that, I passed by every little bit and they were still fussing. If a person can get his frustrations out of his system like that, okay. When they finish, I hang up and go about my business.

People have telephoned threats of bodily harm to me, and to my family, but God keeps us.

There are some major problems in the world today, and if people around the globe just realized it, the answers to those problems lie within the pages of the Bible. God can solve *any* problem.

First and above all, the root of every problem in the world—crime, violence, whatever—goes back to the fact that man is a fallen creature, totally depraved, totally unclean, and totally undone. If man is not brought into a saving knowledge of Christ, he will fulfill the lust of his body and his mind—and his greed.

We have seen a lot of terrorism these last few years. Much of it goes back to the Palestinian problem. The Palestinians feel they were uprooted from their homeland and now they are like the Jews were for two thousand years: They have no homeland. They are bitter. It does not bother them to kill. When they declare a holy war they feel it is their God-given duty, and if they kill that is just a part of duty.

In 1969 the leaders of the Moslem world met in Mecca, and *The Jordan Times,* an Arab newspaper printed in English in Amman, reported that the delegates to the summit vowed to take Jerusalem back at any cost.

Oil . . . the West Bank of the Jordan . . . the basic problem of the Palestinian . . . Those things mean nothing to the Moslem when compared to his foremost goal—the recapture of Jerusalem. And therein lies the root of most of the acts of terrorism we have seen around the world.

It does not bother the terrorists to blow up airplanes and airports. They think it is part of their Holy War against the infidel, and, of course, we are the infidels. They have declared war. We have been in World War III for some time now without really realizing it. It will continue to escalate, and one day it will blow . . . .

Greed is a great problem in our nation and in the world. The commandments tell us that we shall not covet our neighbor's wife, nor anything he has, but we are not teaching our children not to covet. We are bringing up generations without teaching them to deny themselves or to honor God. We teach them that whatever they want they can have. We teach them greed. They see acts of greed on television. Children have cars, money, credit cards. Everything feeds their greed. And if some of them don't have these things, they don't mind killing to get them.

Greed became a cursed Satanic spirit when Lucifer

rose up and said, "I will exalt my throne above the most high God." He became greedy—and that is the same spirit that is on the land today.

America is on the verge of destroying herself by greed. The government is greedy. Instead of taxing the people properly, the government has decreed oppressive taxation. The Book of Daniel tells us that in the last days there will rise up in his estate a raiser of taxes. When Christ came, the world was being taxed. God used that in his sovereignty to get Mary and Joseph to Bethlehem where Jesus was to be born. His birth there had been prophesied centuries before. Now, every way we turn, we are taxed. People live in fear of losing homes and fortunes to the government. Greed is a curse of the nation.

Divorce has become a millstone about our necks. The Bible teaches one man and one woman for each other, and till death do they part. When I was a child in the 1920s divorce was almost unheard of. Preachers came down hard on the subject.

Lenin said three things would bring America to her knees: destroying faith in God, destroying home life, and prostituting womanhood.

Dr. Harold Sightler, an expert on the subject, when asked what we should do with so many people who were divorced and remarried, said the only thing they can do to reconcile is to go forward and seek Christ with all their hearts.

"They need to ask God to guide them," he said, "and they need to serve God. They need a home church and they need to serve in it, as teachers or ushers, or in whatever capacity the church needs them.

"They can fill every capacity in the church," he said, "except that of being a deacon because the Bible qualification for a deacon is the husband of one wife."

If a divorced person is saved, his past is under the blood. I preach often on divorce, and I encourage the people to marry in the Lord and keep their homes. Many divorces happen because the people have not been taught. In my church, we teach them.

Schools teach humanism. Magazines and newspapers are filled with humanism. Television has become one of the worst enemies the nation has ever had—because of irresponsible programming by the networks. Homosexuality, Lesbianism, living together without marriage—our life styles help to bring all this on.

I have devoted my life to helping people strive for a better place than any we have on this earth. Heaven is more real than the breath you draw. It is a definite place. The Almighty God's throne is there. Christ is there. The Holy Ghost is there. I am living now to hurry and get home. Heaven is my home. Modern liberal preaching that all of these things are just myths is a bunch of tommyrot and hog wash.

If there was no real heaven, then my life—all that I stand for—would be a joke. A lot of people think that earth is "it." But earth is just a little speck in the great ocean of God's creation.

This creation was not a big explosion. That's the most ridiculous thing I ever heard—that something exploded, and everything came from that. The Big Bang! That would have been a popgun beside what God is capable of doing! From the word of the mouth of God the stars, the worlds, the planets, and the galaxies were formed.

When God created the earth, he created it perfect. Some say God created matter and then formed something from it. If God can create a ball of mass, he can create perfection. And Isaiah 45:18 reveals that God created the earth not in vain but to be inhabited. That was his purpose.

From the time God spoke the earth into existence, he put life on earth. There was life on earth before Adam. Adam was the first human, but before him there was angelic life. Lucifer's throne was on earth, and since he couldn't have a throne without a kingdom, there had to be inhabitants to form the kingdom. Lucifer had authority over the earth.

Some scholars believe that when Lucifer sinned against God he said, "I will exalt my throne above the most high God and above the stars," but what he said was that he would exalt himself above God. He said, "I am going to be worshipped. I am going to be in authority." He must have had a lot of influence or a third of the angels would not have come with him. They became the fallen angels. No doubt God created millions, even billions of angels, and one third came with Lucifer.

When he did that, Jesus said, "I saw Lucifer as lightning fall from heaven." That shows the eternalness of Christ because he was there when Lucifer was cast out of heaven. When you see lightning coming down in big bolts, it is extremely bright, so bright that it might hurt the eyes if it were prolonged. But as soon as it hits the earth, its brightness is gone. Lucifer was at one time the Prince of Morning—light—but when God cast him out into the earth he lost his light and became the Prince of Darkness.

He still wants to set up his kingdom on earth and overthrow the son of God so he can take the earth back and set up his evil domain. He is trying to do it now through human beings.

God became so angry at Satan that he turned the world upside down. That's in Isaiah 24:1. The earth is still upside down. When Jesus comes again, God will turn it back like it should be. He will lift the curse.

God was so angry at sin that his whole universe carries his curse. The moon and the planets are barren. Some of the planets are ice balls. But when Jesus returns and God restores everything, those planets will probably become like gardens of Eden.

These are my thoughts—the results of my long years of study. These are some of the things I preach and teach. These are the things my family has lived with all these years, and my family agrees with me. We are of one accord in the gospels.

I am a conservative in the religious world. Conservative is a broad term that some sneer at, but I believe it is the ideology that will eventually save the world.

Conservatism is born in a man. People are willing to die for it. That is why I believe a man is a true conservative if he is a true believer in Christ. That is first, the foundation of conservatism.

He also believes in his country and in his fellowman. He is willing to stand up for or die for his country. He believes it should be a Godly country free of the filth and hell that is in our land today.

A conservative as a true follower of Christ has been converted and regenerated. He is then one who with all of his heart and to the best of his knowledge and ability honors God and tries to obey the Word of God. By that, I mean he lives a godly life, a Spirit-filled life, a separated life. A conservative will not be half-world and half-God; he won't be a fence straddler.

A conservative stands for the Word of God without compromise.

Liberals say we are red-necked, ignorant fools, but to be a conservative you have to take God at his word without leaning to the left or to the right, and there is nothing foolish about that.

If God said it, I will stand on it.

That sums up my life in a nutshell.

Praise God!

Popie & Nana at their 50th wedding anniversary reception, with great-grandchildren, Winston and Savannah Parrish.

Ralph and Jacque
Sea of Galilee - 1996

Ralph with secretary of more than 30 years.
Mrs. Judy Proffitt - 2002

Ralph Sr. with son Ralph in Bethlehem - 1994.
Sharing their love for the land.

Feeding the seagulls,
Treasure Island, FL.
Jan. 1995

Communion Service at the
Garden Tomb.
Jerusalem, Israel - 1994

Ralph with Rev. Alan Woody assisting victims in the aftermath of Hurricane Andrew.
Homestead, Fl. - 1992
(Start of Hearts with Hands)

Father and son in the home study. Exploring the Word together.

Charles Harrison Sexton and Mary Elizabeth Shetley Sexton, with their oldest child, Evelyn. - 1908

The young evangelist in 1943

Ralph Sexton, early 1960's

Jacquline Sexton with her newborn, Ralph Hanes Sexton, Jr. 1947

Rev. & Mrs. Ralph Sexton Sr.
1945

Dr. & Mrs. Ralph Sexton Sr.
1995

Stick Drawing - 2002

# Epilogue

## II Corinthians 5:1-8

*For we know that if our earthly house of this tabernacle were dissolved, we have a building of God, an house not made with hands, eternal in the heavens.*

*For in this we groan, earnestly desiring to be clothed upon with our house which is from heaven:*

*If so be that being clothed we shall not be found naked.*

*For we that are in this tabernacle do groan, being burdened: not for that we would be unclothed, but clothed upon, that mortality might be swallowed up of life.*

*Now he that hath wrought us for the selfsame thing is God, who also hath given unto us the earnest of the Spirit.*

*Therefore we are always confident, knowing that, whilst we are at home in the body, we are absent from the Lord:*

*For we walk by faith, not by sight:*

*We are confident, I say, and willing rather to be absent from the body, and to be present with the Lord.*

On Tuesday, January 13, 2004, Dr. Ralph Hanes Sexton Sr., took his first breath of heavenly air. He passed gently from this life into eternal life with his Savior, surrounded by family and friends in his own home, just as he had prayed to do. The Bible tells us that he was instantly in the presence of the Lord, and healed from the infirmities and sorrow of this life. What a joyful homecoming that must have been!

Nearly 20 years have passed since Mr. Terrell first put highlights of Dr. Sexton's life in book form, and many changes have occurred.

The next few pages will serve to provide "the rest of the story".

The Sexton family has continued to grow.

Pastor Ralph, Jr. and Muzette's family includes Dwight and Beverly Sexton Parrish (son Winston and his wife Miranda Holcombe Parrish; daughters Savannah, Scarlett, and Sophia Parrish); Mark and Sheri Hollifield Sexton (daughters Alexis and Lola Grace); Kent and Leigh Parsons Sexton (children Preston, Ian & Jacqueline Juliet).

Becky and Jim Templeton's family now includes Matthew and Heather Tweed Templeton (children Alena, Titus, and Jocelyn) and Josh and Mary Elizabeth Templeton Ingle (children Irely Faith and Kaydon Ruth).

Ralph Sexton's son, Ralph Sexton, Jr., continues the work of Trinity Baptist Church in West Asheville, serving as Senior Pastor to the congregation since March 1988. The church now meets in a new, larger sanctuary, and though Dr. Sexton, Sr. saw the beginning of construction on this building, he was never able to preach in the pulpit. His love for his flock never wavered, and he remained a true and gentle shepherd until the end.

In all of his years of preaching, Dr. Sexton's message never changed. The fire and passion that was lit in the heart and soul of the young boy from Buzzard Rock back in 1937 to share the Gospel burned, and his legacy continues to have an impact on lives for the Kingdom of God.

While reprinting the story of Dr. Sexton's life, we decided to print the stories and testimonies of some of the people touched by this mountain preacher. His legacy lives on, and people who've written these words are the fruits of his labor.

Let them tell you their stories.

***Dick and Lorraine McKinney***

In 1968, we met Dr. Sexton while attending a Sunday service at Trinity Baptist Church on State Street. I was impressed with this man of God's preaching. He took the time to speak with us and made us feel so welcome, although I was young and unknown to him. God had us where he wanted us to attend, and years later I was honored to become one of his truest friends. God allowed me the opportunity to spend a lot of time with him, driving him to meetings, taking him places and fellowshipping.

There seemed to be a spiritual bond and a mountain cohesion that was knitted together in a real friendship like those you can count on one hand. Many times on the road Dr. Sexton would say, "Dick, I'm so glad I can talk with you; a preacher needs someone to talk with and it stays between us."

What a caring and devoted person he was; he showed nothing but pure kindness to everyone. Never did I hear a derogatory remark about anyone. His life was devoted to his God; while studying, writing, and preaching, his ministry was steered as the benefit to those of God's children.

Over a decade ago, the church lost a dynamic preacher, a zealous worker, a prayer warrior, capable writer, and father. I miss the encouragement, the phone calls, and the the untold prayers for me, our family, and business. I understand today to some extent of how John Mark and Timothy felt by being called a son; he was a father figure to me. I now realize what he meant when he said, "Dick, stay in there with Ralph and stand by him when I'm gone." He stood so strong in the things of the Lord, and in the defense of the precious inerrant words of God.

***Cliff and Shirley Taylor***

I first learned of Ralph Sexton, Sr. at the State Baptist church in Asheville, NC where he was the Pastor. I had just moved my family from Thomasville, NC to Asheville in April of 1970. My wife, Shirley, wanted to get our two children in church. Shirley, who was a mountain girl, grew up in church.

I grew up in eastern North Carolina in a very liberal Baptist church. I thought church membership was all you needed. Shirley's mother told us that she had heard Ralph Sexton preach and she thought we might enjoy hearing him also. I was not interested in church, nevertheless, I had my family to think of. The next Sunday we headed to State Street. The church was full, and we sat half way down on the right side. About half way through the service, I became very uncomfortable. I had never before been in a service like that one.

Ma Stewart cut loose and the preacher was all over the platform. I told Shirley we had to get out of there. Shirley told me just to sit back and enjoy it! I turned and looked behind me; the aisle was full. After the service, I decided that I would find a church to attend.

Meanwhile, Shirley talked to a friend and she invited us to her church, a fundamental Baptist church. After making a profession of faith, I couldn't quit thinking of the little church and the preacher. I began to pray about it and in a short time, I took my family to Trinity Baptist Church where Ralph Sexton, Sr. was now preaching. I learned a lot and began to grow in faith under his ministry.

When in the presence of Ralph Sexton, I learned that he was a man very in touch with God. He could teach you so much doctrine in just a conversation. He could teach you so much humility in just one gesture.

In my line of work as an insurance adjuster, traveling across Western North Carolina, I encountered so many people whose lives had been touched through Ralph Sexton, Sr.'s ministry.

Let me insert one in particular here. I do not recall the man's name, but he was running a body shop in Robinsville, NC. In the course of my work, we began to share religious experiences and the grace of God in our lives.

When I mentioned Dr. Sexton being my pastor, he shared with me the following story about Ralph Sexton, Sr. "Many years ago, Dr. Sexton was holding a tent revival and my wife had gotten saved. I was furious and decided that I would take my gun and go to meeting with her the following night. I planned to shoot Brother Sexton! When the invitation was given, I went forward, and instead of shooting this man of God, I was gloriously saved!"

At the time the man was telling me this story, he was pastoring a church in Robinsville..

I am so thankful that Bro. Ralph took time to lift me up in prayer at a time when I need an intercessor. I am thankful for his faithfulness to preach the Word to my family. ~

***Pastor Donald Jennings – Moody, Alabama***

Dr. Ralph Sexton was the most Christ-like man I have ever known. His love and grace continue to be some of the most influential things in my life.

***Alicia Pate James – Rutherfordton, NC***

As a little girl growing up under Popie's preaching, I remember how loving and genuine of a man he was. He always had a smile on his face and the ability to make you feel loved and special. He was an amazing example of God's love and how we, as Christians, are supposed to try to live our life here on earth. I am so thankful and blessed to have grown up under his example.

***Anne Payne***

Some of the sweetest memories Jerry and I have of Popie are when we had our first child, Amy. He assured us she was a gift perfectly fashioned and to place our trust for Amy's life in the Lord's hands. The times Popie would gently lay his hand on her head while saying a prayer for her and our family are innumerable. He epitomized Christ with his gentleness, compassion, and love, while his quiet and peaceful spirit brought such comfort to anyone who was blessed to be in his presence.

***Debbie Grooms Browning***

The one thing Popie always told me was, "no matter what, stay faithful." He would always encourage me and say when you can't do anything else stay faithful. His words ring loud in my mind when I feel like quitting or giving up.

***Sharon Stewart Wilkerson – Asheville, NC***

Uncle Ralph, as I called him, became a great friend to my missionary parents when they made Asheville their home base.

He became my friend after my early arrival into this world on January, 1951. My father was preaching away from home and could not drive to Asheville in time for my birth or in time to take me home from the hospital. Uncle Ralph and Aunt Jackie took Dad's place and made sure we were settled into my new home.

Uncle Ralph became part of my family and I loved him very much while I was growing up. I am thankful for the times he and Aunt Jackie allowed me to stay with them while my parents were in meetings. I am thankful for the love and friendship both he and Aunt Jacque extended to our family, especially during my Dad's long illness. A child needs godly men in their life, and I am thankful for the godly and loving influence of Uncle Ralph Sexton in my life.

***Tim Lee Evangelist – Garland, TX***

From the very first time that I met Pastor Ralph Sexton Sr., he treated like a son. He and Mrs. Sexton would welcome me in to their home and talk with me as though they had known me all of my life.

Their son, Ralph Jr., and I became friends from the moment we met. We had so much in common as far as being raised in Pastors homes and we both had gotten away from God in our teen years yet our parents never gave up on us.

I could sense the same love from Ralph Sexton Sr. as I had experienced from my own dad. I think another thing that drew me close to Pastor Sexton was his love for this great country. He loved America and was so burdened for real revival in this land.

He invited me to speak at Trinity Baptist Church on numerous occasions and would encourage me to preach my burden for America. He would openly weep and pray over America.

I could write more, however the last thing I want to mention here was Pastor Ralph Sexton's Spirit. He had a contagious laughter and a contagious spirit. If a person was discouraged he could sense it and within minutes bring encouragement. I loved and appreciated this giant of man. America needs some more men just like him.

***Hughes Family Sweetwater Youth Ranch – Asheville, NC***

I have enjoyed going back through my memory tracing the encounters we had with Popie. I believe with everything in me that he was genuine in his actions which I'm sure drew many to the Lord. As far as one thing standing out to us, it wouldn't be something he said necessarily; rather, it was the way he made you feel. It didn't seem to make difference what your background was, how educated you were, or how much money you had, he made you feel like part of a family.

He accepted everyone, and they didn't have to prove anything. To us that was Jesus!

I think we can safely say Popie's example was instrumental in the beginning seeds sown for the Sweetwater Youth Ranch we run now. That acceptance is the foundational attitude we hope children and families feel when they come here.

***Laura Frye Nygren – Asheville, NC***

I am honored to have grown up under the preaching of Popie. My sister and I were a part of the original Trinity Teens. Popie was there for all of the youth. He was Popie to everyone! I have many found memories of Popie getting "blessed". He would run the aisles of the church. Once he took the American flag for a go around the church waving it over the pews as he ran.

My most treasured memory was the day I asked him to sign my Bible. I had heard he had beautiful handwriting. He took out his pen and wrote, "In all thy way acknowledge him and he shall direct thy paths." Proverbs 3:6. He handed my Bible back to me and gave me this look like, "I'm watching you." I read the inscription and looked up at him and he smiled. Yes, Popie was watching me, but he was telling me that God was watching me; look to God and He will direct my paths. Not just one path, he said paths – ALL of them.

Even when I chose the wrong path, God was there; I just had to acknowledge him. That scripture became my favorite. Popie may have written that same verse in many Bibles, but to me he chose that verse just for me. It did and still does make a difference in my life. And yes, his handwriting was beautiful! I still have and cherish that Bible.

***Scott and Becky Matthews The Rochesters Blacksburg, SC***

One of the first things that come to my mind when I think of Popie Sexton is *GENUINE*! He was definitely one of the greatest men ever to walk on earth, and was a legend in my opinion! I'm so thankful for his stand for the Lord. We were always honored to be in meetings with Bro. Ralph Sr.

***Peggy Carson – Leicester, NC***

Preacher Ralph Sr. wanted a garden planted at his house, so Wayne took his tractor and plowed the ground, and I planted. We canned 298 quarts of beans out of that garden! I really enjoyed my time in his garden that summer. We sure loved our Preacher!

***Tim Cox – Panama City, FL***

One of my favorite things to do with Popie and Nana was to go to Lake Julian to fish and eat lots of Tootsie Rolls! (I'm talking the big bag from Adams) I still think about them every time I eat a Tootsie Roll! I will never forget how special they made everyone who came into contact with them feel! They truly embodied Christ like love and had a compassion for people that we were blessed to experience!

***Eileen Kelley Forster – Naalehu, Hawaii***

Three families from Florida heard Ralph Sexton Sr. preach in their home church, and then packed up and headed for Asheville to make Trinity Baptist their new church home. The Johnsons, Siedentopfs, and the Kelleys enjoyed a few meals with him and his dear Jacque, and they treated us like family.

One day, at church, Pastor Sexton dressed like a shepherd, walked with a shepherd's crook, and carried a lamb around his neck. The sight of the Shepherd of our church made us cry. It was as overwhelming as when he danced on the platform with the US flag draped around his shoulders. Both times, his actions told the whole story, teaching us to love Jesus, our country, and each other. When my husband and I fell seriously ill at the same time, he visited our home in Leicester, and shouted outside our door that he "felt God up on this mountain!" He knew how to give comfort and peace to our hearts, this gracious man after God's own heart; one of our treasured memories forever. He never missed an opportunity to reflect the love of God.

Frank Kelley has since gone to be where Bro. Ralph Sr. is...in heaven with their Jesus. I have remarried and live in Hawaii now. My grandchildren call me Nana and they call my husband Poppy in memory of this blessed couple.

***James H. Johnson Jr. (Jamie) Crossfire Ministries – Asheville, NC***

Years ago, Ralph Sexton, Jr. called me and asked me to come by to see him. Not longer after the call, I drove to Trinity Baptist to visit with Ralph Jr. After chatting for a few minutes, he pulled out a Bible and handed it to me, then said, "This is one of my dad's Bibles and I want you to have it." On the inside cover of the Bible a note was written by Ralph Sexton Jr. to me. The note was wonderful but I want to focus more on the man who owned the Bible that was given to me on August 1, 2009.

Brother Ralph Sexton, Sr. was an amazing husband, father, pastor, counselor, teacher, preacher, and friend. His influence was so strong that many within the church as well as those outside of the church had great respect for him. If I had needed a second father to step in I would have been thrilled if Ralph Sexton Sr. were the man. I am honored to have known him and to have been influenced by his example. He is forever remembered and a hero of the faith in the modern era.

Maybe the day will come when people will speak well of me just as they speak of him. Can't wait to see him again but until that time, may I carry the banner of Christ in the same way. To God be the glory!

***Pastor Daniel Buchannan – Connely Springs, NC***

Dr. Ralph Sexton was a great Man of God in the true Biblical sense of the word. He was godly, gracious, and good. He was a man of holiness, humility, and honor. He lived in the wonder in the glory of God's Son, God's salvation, and God's spirit. He laid down his life for his family, friends, and even his foes by being a living sacrifice, and counting it is privilege to represent his blessed Lord.

He loved the worship of God, the word of God, and the Work of God. He loved the glory, lived in the glory, and now he's beholding the glory of the living Son of God!

Praise God, Popie and his darling Jacque have met again at the feet of their wonderful Lord and Savior, to part no more. As John the Beloved penned, "He that doeth the will of God abideth forever." I pray someday I can be half the Christian that Bro. Ralph was. Thank you God for Bro. Ralph Sexton.

***Harold & Joyce Rochester The Rochesters – Blacksburg, SC***

The last visit we had with Brother Ralph Sr., we took him some fig preserves. He loved fig preserves! We were able to visit for a couple of hours, and we had a very sweet, special visit with them. Bro. Ralph, Sr. really encouraged us to keep on singing and traveling for the Lord. Often times, our memory goes back to that special day when we were privileged to visit with Bro. Ralph and his sweet wife, Jacque, and it still encourages today!

***Dr. Robert Jarvis Welcome Baptist Church – Union, S.C.***

As part of the first graduating class of Trinity Baptist Bible College, it was my honor and privilege to be around Bro. Sexton on many occasions. He put the hood upon me at our graduation. He preached for me at Welcome Baptist Church in Union, S.C. where I have been pastoring for almost 20 years.

One of my fondest memories of him occurred at a Bible College supper that we had in the Family Life Center. It occurred sometime after I graduated and started pastoring. I went back as an alumnus for this special occasion. It was very formal, and we were sitting and talking quietly until Bro. Sexton started telling us about being filled with the Holy Ghost. I am guessing there was a hundred people or more there, and most of them had no idea what was going on in our little spot at the table. As he talked, the Lord began to touch his heart (and ours) again. He suddenly slid his chair back from the table while blowing and crying. I would call it at least a bit of a scene that we caused as we rejoiced over the goodness of God, and were blessed by His touch and presence. With him, it was out with the formal and in with the Lord.

Words cannot describe the influence that Dr. Sexton has had upon my life and ministry. He has been special to me and my family ever since we have known him. His walk with the Lord, preaching, and ministry are still an example to us all. I thank God for the privilege to have known him.

***Pat Slingerland – Asheville, NC***

There are so many things I could say about the Sextons. I always told them if I put a sugar cube in their mouth, it would not melt because they were so sweet! One thing I will never forget, preaching on prayer. He urged us to never give up on praying, and he told about his brother that he had prayed for salvation for 40 years! He said one day his phone rang, and it was his brother calling from out west. He asked Popie to pick him up at the airport, so he went to the airport to get his brother. As they were coming back from the airport, Popie said he thought they were going to his house, but his brother said that he wanted to go up on the mountain where they were born. He told Popie that he was born there the first time, and he wanted to be born again there! That made me want to shout! There are so many wonderful stories about that man, that makes it hard to choose, but this one is one of my favorites. I thank God and count it joy just to know the Sexton family. I thank God for Pastor Ralph!

***Jessica Henson Allen – Candler, NC***

It was sometime in the 90's, I was maybe 10 or 12, and crazy colored finger nail polish was all the rage. I had painted my fingernails lime green. My parents and I ran in to Popie and Nana at the grocery store. After we exchanged pleasantries, he noticed my fingernails. He held my hand up and looked at them for a second. He said, "Child, we should we pray for you! Do you have a case of the gangrene?" I thought that was so funny! Every time I paint my nails a normal color, I think of that!

***Rudy & Ann Morrell – Fletcher, NC***

We came to Asheville in 1971. We were very young and it was the first time we had ever lived away from family and where we grew up. Immediately, we started looking for a church and visited several Baptist churches in the city, none of which felt right for us. On a weekend trip back to Bristol, a preacher from somewhere in N.C. was preaching at our home church. I asked if he knew of a church in the Asheville area and he said he had never been in the area, but he said he had just attended a preacher's Jubilee at Maze Jackson's church in Atlanta and heard a preacher there from Asheville named Ralph Sexton. We came home, looked up Ralph Sexton in the phone book, and called him.

He told us the name of the church and where it was located. The first Sunday we went we knew we had found our home. The rest, of course, is history.

As I said, we were young and away from family and friends for the first time. We knew two families here, but not well, and after the initial excitement wore off, we became kind of home sick and lonely. Popie and Nana took us under their wing as if we were their own kids and helped us make it through those early, lonely months.

The Sexton family and our church family at Trinity became our family and we have felt as close to all of them as our own families. Even more than the bond of friendship that has been such a blessing to us was how simply, yet profoundly Popie preached God's word. He used every day words and experiences to teach us spiritual lessons that were easy for us all to understand. He lived what he preached and so did Nana.

We still on occasion talk of something he said or preached. They had a great influence on our lives. We have wonderful memories of the times spent with them at our house or theirs. We remember also the tent meetings we went to or drove him to. We know that God lead us to Trinity and the friendship of the Sexton family.

***Larry Mitzi Riddle Primitive Quartet Candler, NC***

I remember the time that Bro. Ralph came to our Hominy Valley Singing Ground in the mid 1980's. He had loaned us his tent for our singing and was there helping us set it up for our July singing. At the time, the Primitives just owned a narrow strip of land big enough for our singings. Brother

Ralph saw the big field adjoining our singing ground and said "You boys need that field! Someone might buy it and give you trouble about having your singings here!" He then simply raised his hands to God and said, "These boys need this land, God and I plead the blood over it for them!" Wow! It was not long after that the property came available for sale and we purchased it! Praise the Lord! What a blessing it has been to our quartet for many years! I will never forget that day!

Bro. Ralph and Sister Jacque were a blessing an encouragement to The Primitive Quartet and we loved them dearly. What a joy to have known such Godly prayer warriors!

***Amy Morrell Schenimann***

Ralph Sexton, Sr. was my pastor from the time I was born until he retired when I was 15. I learned so much from him, and I am so thankful I was able to grow up under his preaching. The illustrated messages that he preached were so easy for a child to understand. How many pastors let a live bird go in the sanctuary, carry a lamb around, or throw out bread while preaching? Most of all I always knew that he cared for me and my family.

One evening when I was in the fifth grade, my parents left me with Popie and Nana while they were away. Popie wanted to take me out for dinner. He asked me if I had ever had a New York strip steak, and when I said no, he said, "Well, you will have one tonight!"

I have so many special memories of a great man. Now as an adult, I often find myself asking, when making decisions, what would Popie say about that? I am grateful for the Godly influence he had on my life, and I hope to pass that on to my own children.

***Dwight Parrish– Leicester, NC
Grandson-in-law***

What a privilege it was to be on the "list" to drive Popie to his next preaching engagement. Beverly and I hadn't lived in Asheville very long before I received the invitation to drive. I remember vividly the events in the car even though I can't remember much about where we were going. Everyone knew Popie prayed about everything, so before we backed out of the driveway he began to ask God to put His angels around us to protect and guide us to our meeting. He prayed about the church service and for the "little children" present, that God would prepare hearts to hear the message. This was all before we left the driveway. We had made it as far as the entrance ramp to 1-26 when he began to pray in earnest." Oh God, I plead the blood over this car, put extra angels in charge as Dwight drives!" I looked over for a quick glance only to see his eyes closed, clinching his fist and begging for traveling mercies! I was afraid and we had only been in the car about 3 minutes. I had grown up in church and understood that when you plead the blood of Christ; this was a desperate plea for God's attention to the need at hand! I thought, "Is my driving that bad that this man of God should be begging for this kind of divine intervention?" So for the next hour and a half, I was front row seat to Popie "pleading the blood" while I drove the Lincoln to church. We arrived safely and also returned safely home that night.

It didn't take very long to understand the prayer life that Popie had with God. His prayer wasn't to scare or intimidate, but he knew better than anyone I had ever known that the unseen battle that was raging could only be fought in prayer. I did drive Popie many times after this first white knuckled experience, and yes, he did "plead the blood" every time we left his driveway. By the way, we never one close call, accident, flat tire or mishap! Answered prayer!

***Kent Sexton – Conway, SC**
**Grandson***

I believe the greatest thing I remember about my grandfather, Popie, was the fact that he was always faithful to what he preached. He, to the best of his ability, strived to live a life of holiness. He also lived a life of dedication. No matter what time of day you visited, you would find him in some state of prayer or study most of the time. At breakfast, while mixing his honey and butter together his Bible was beside him. If you stayed over at night and got up late to raid the kitchen, you would find him in his study reading or praying. More than once as a child, I remember hiding under the dining room table when I was supposed to be asleep, listening to him as he prayed in his study. I am thankful that God chose to put me in his life and to see a living testimony of Godly character and faithfulness to the cause of Christ.

***Sheri Sexton – Asheville, NC**
**Granddaughter-in-law***

Popie was probably the sweetest man that I've ever had the privilege of knowing. I'm so very thankful and blessed that I got to know him and be a small part of his life. One thing that I will always remember as long as I live was when I lost my puppy and Popie knew how heartbroken I was about it. I remember talking to him and asking him if he thought our pets went to Heaven. With his sweet, soft spoken voice, he told me that whatever made me happy or brought happiness to my life would be in Heaven. Well needless to say, I believed every word he said.

***Debbie Hughes McCoy**
**Secretary to Dr. Ralph Sexton Jr. since 1980***

Oh my! Where would I even begin to say what Dr. Ralph Sexton, Sr. has meant in my life? I remember watching the *Send The Light* broadcast when I was young. We came one Sunday in 1974 for our first visit to Trinity Baptist Church, and I am still here in 2015! We were warmly welcomed by both Preacher, Sr. and Mrs. Sexton. They made us feel right at home, and we never felt like visitors.

My family and I loved hearing this sweet man of God preach. He was always so happy in Jesus, and everyone knew it. He was so gentle and easygoing, and he had such a heart for lost folks in our city. Everywhere he went he would tell people about Jesus, and he left tracts in the most unexpected places.

I started to work for his son, Dr. Ralph Sexton, Jr. in January of 1980. I began working at his dining room table, with a box of index cards for a mailing list. After a while, I was given a desk in the *Send The Light* office. I shared the office with Preacher, Sr.'s secretary, Mrs. Judy Proffitt. Preacher and Mrs. Sexton lived upstairs, and it was my joy to get to spend time with them each day.

When I came in to work, Preacher, Sr. always asked me if I wanted something to eat. He loved to feed people. It made him so happy. He would say, "Come upstairs and eat with me and my sweetheart." We sat around the kitchen table, and we had some of the sweetest times of fellowship.

One morning, after we finished eating our eggs, Preacher, Sr. drew me a little picture on a napkin. It was a little house on a hill with smoke coming from the chimney. A sign in the front yard said, "Home Sweet Home". He told me to keep praying, and God was going to send me the man He had picked out just for me. I still have the napkin, and 32 years later, I am still married to the man God picked out for me.

Preacher, Sr. was always very discerning, and he knew when things were not quite right. He would stop by my desk and ask me if things were alright between me and Jesus. My relationship with Him had to be right so that every other relationship would fall into place.

He taught me about keeping things in a "safe place". If someone told you something, you needed to keep your promise to them, and not share it with anyone else. He taught me about unconditional love. He was not always treated with respect and kindness, and he never got angry or acted ugly to anyone. I have seen him drop his head and never say a word in his own defense.

He taught me about living holy and being filled with the sweet Holy Spirit. I have never known a more amazing man of God.

He had such a wonderful sense of humor! He loved to laugh, and he loved to flip the lights on and off when he came into a room. He hid my shoes, as I would often go barefoot during the day. You could hear him laughing as he walked back upstairs.

I surely miss all of the things that made him so unique. If I was asked who had influenced me in my walk with the Lord, it would, without a doubt, be Dr. Ralph Sexton, Sr. I give him an A+, and I love him more than lunch from Long John Silvers!

***Mark Sexton – Grandson***

I meet new people all the time. When they realize I'm Ralph Sexton Sr.'s grandson, they tell me how much they loved him and miss him. People get wrapped up in obtaining material things here on earth, but when you go to heaven like Popie did, that's about as rich as it gets. I miss him.

***Loretta Parker – Asheville, NC***

It was 33 years ago, and I was a single 18 year old girl, expecting a baby, and scared to death. My parents loved me, but were disappointed in me and even ashamed. I knew they loved me, but it was a very difficult situation for them to accept.

My mother did the only thing she knew to do, call the pastor and she did. She made an appointment for us to go talk with Pastor Ralph Sexton and his sweet wife Jacque. We drove up the drive to the back of their home, my heartbeat so rapid you would have thought I was going to see a judge in a court of law! They immediately welcomed us in and off to the library we went. I could not tell you anything about the conversation EXCEPT this one comment, the one I will remember until I am called home.

Pastor Ralph said to me while hugging me, "Child you don't let Satan stop you from coming to church! You hold your head up high, you're one of God's little children!"

The love I felt was overwhelming, and I was not scared any longer. He had showed me what true Christ like love is all about! NO judgment, NO shame, just genuine Christ filled love.

***Mark Trammell – Mark Trammell Quartet***

Dr. Ralph Sexton, Sr. was my pastor during the beginning days of my now 40 years of music ministry. I'm convinced that his message "Bloom Where You Are Planted" is one of the key reasons that my family and I are still endeavoring to fight the good fight and pressing toward the mark. Growing in God was an essential teaching element that dwelt deep within the soul of this modern day saint.

I remember many nights during the early part of my ministry calling Bro. Ralph and even sometimes waking him from his sleep. He never once had anything other than encouragement and usually a brief story to remind me of the faithfulness of God.

To this day I still live on his last quote to me which was, "Mark, if we follow to the best of our ability the direction of our Master, not only will He reward us with indescribable peace, but He will also pick up the tab for our trip!" Very wise words from a very wise and Godly man.

***H.W. – Candler, NC***

In June of 1999, my father was at Mission Hospital on life support. I attended church service on Sunday morning and was walking out after service. I spoke with Popie and asked him if he felt that sometimes people hang on for those around them (you know sometimes we just don't want them to leave us). He said, yes, he did think that. I asked him if he would pray about my daddy. He prayed right there with people passing us, and in his prayer he asked God if he would release my father. Later that same day, my father left this world and went to Heaven. I have never forgotten this experience. I have often said that if Popie prayed for my leg to be broken, I would ask which one, so I could go ahead and have it put in a cast!

***Pastor Ricky & Jenny Rackley – Brevard, NC***

Wow! Ralph Sexton Sr. What a role model and mentor! Two things I remember that were an encouragement to me. Many times I remember I would run into Ralph Sexton Sr. around Asheville or when I was visiting Trinity. On numerous occasions he would come up to me and shake my hand and in his hand would be a $50 bill and he would tell me, "Young man keep preaching the Gospel." That was an awesome inspiration and testimony to me of his faithfulness to our Lord and Savior Jesus Christ.

In the early 90's (1993 or 1994), Brevard had a vote coming up for liquor by the drink. Dr. Randy Barton of Anchor Baptist Church and Rev. Tommy Owen headed up a campaign along with the churches of the county. The Sheriff, Milton Hubbard even spoke out against it. It was decided that those opposing the ordinance would march in a parade to show their opposition and hopefully keep it from being voted in. So they called Preacher Ralph and he agreed to be the Grand Marshall of the parade. He rode in a vehicle with two tall distinguished looking "bodyguards" walking alongside him through the whole parade. Rev. Ricky Rackley and Rev. Danny Pierson, members of Midway Bible Baptist Church, were those men. They would not have been honored any more if the President of the United States had been the in that car. That began a friendship between Ricky and Rev. Sexton that continued for several years.

When Ricky became pastor of Midway Bible Baptist Church a few years later, he had Rev. Sexton to come and preach homecomings and special services. The members loved Rev. Sexton as well. Midway even had a special service honoring Preacher Ralph giving him a plaque and a dinner for the many years of service to our Heavenly Father.

We still have the songbook that he had published to preserve the "old songs of Zion". Ricky and I were so honored to have him and Mrs. Sexton in our church! It was one of the highlights of our ministry and a memory that we keep in our hearts. They were a blessing and encouragement us, a young couple who considered them Heroes of the Faith.

***Victor Rigsby – Leicester, NC***

It has been my privilege to have had Pastor Sexton come by our shop on many occasions. As you know, he and Dick (Paul) McKinney were traveling companions, friends, and brothers in Christ. When Pastor Ralph had a nearby meeting to go to or if he just needed to get out and about, Paul would bring him by the shop (Smoky Mtn. Machining), and he would walk through the shop and just say a few words to us as we were working – always something encouraging. There was just something about his presence that was sweet and commanded our respect.

He lived the phrase that, "people don't care how much you know, until they know how much you care." He certainly cared about people and there are few left like him.

***Jackie West – Asheville, NC***

Ralph Sexton Sr., was a man that I truly counted as God's man. He was my hero, mentor, and friend. His words were always encouraging, challenging and inspiring. He was always willing to share Jesus with anyone that would listen and some that wouldn't. I loved him dearly.

***Sheila Sluder Bell – Asheville, NC***

Pastor Ralph and Jacque were very sweet and loving people that I met when I joined Trinity Baptist Church in 1996. Not long after joining the church, my grandmother Ida White Dungey was visiting and was talking to Jacque and she was telling Jacque that when Ralph lived at Buzzard Rock that they use to play together. Jacque asked her if they made mud pies and she said yes and they laughed and said they probably made mud pies and threw them at each other. Ralph and my Grandmother (Ida) played together as children and now they are in Heaven together.

I am thankful that I got to know and love Ralph and Jacque; they were two wonderful people and good Godly influence on my life the few years that I knew them.

Also when I think of Ms. Jacque, no matter what we were talking about, she would always say, "Just remember God keeps good records."

Just a few days before Popie was prompted to Heaven, a friend and I went by the house to see Popie. Of course, he was in bed, but Becky told him he had company so she helped him get into his wheel chair and brought him into the living room to visit. Of course, he rubbed his head to make sure his hair was laying down. He talked for just a few minutes before he was tired and went back to bed. I will always remember what he told us. He said, He said, "Stay close. Don't compromise. Love the Lord and each other."

Ralph and Jacque were very special people who I am thankful to have been friends with and can't wait for the day when we will all be together in Heaven.

***Laurel Styles – Asheville, NC***

I remember Ralph Sexton Sr. was always full of wit and a sweet spirit. He was soft spoken and kind hearted to all.

***Teresa Grooms – Candler, NC***

When I was 13 years old I started helping the Sextons at their home on Saturdays. The first Saturday my mom dropped me off in the driveway and left. I walked up the steps rang the doorbell, and soon Popie opened the door and said, "Just leave it in the basement," and he shut the door and walked away. I stood there looking around wondering what in the world I was going to do. (No cell phones back then!) Then Popie opened the door laughing and said come on in, Peanut. He continued to call me Peanut for years to come.

I so admired him and looked to him for guidance that every Saturday I went prepared with a list of "Can I do this and Can I go there?" questions. One day, Popie said, "Peanut, wherever you go and whatever you do, if it's ok for the Lord to come back and find you there, then it's ok for you to be there."

I am 51 years old today and have never forgotten that. It took me until I was an adult to realize how blessed I was to have such an amazing pastor. To this day I have never met anyone in comparison. I am blessed to have known him.

***Penny Andrews – Greensboro, NC***

It was on our first trip overseas to Israel back in 1993, and we were so excited. We were not only going to the Holy Land, but we were going with Bro. Ralph Sexton Jr., Squire Parsons, and Dr. And Mrs. Ralph Sexton Sr. My husband knew that Dr. Ralph's heart was weak, so he made it a point to carry their luggage and to be there if he was needed. Before we even left on our trip Dr. Sexton had written a book explaining about all the places we were going to see, and how they related to the scriptures. It just made it all come alive for all of us. Each morning we would go over that day's journey, and he would comment on it. Then we would have prayer and set out on our wonderful adventure.

Our group, The Gethsemane Quartet, sang in many services when he was preaching, as well as at Trinity Baptist Church in Asheville, NC. What a special blessing that was! Dr. Ralph was a very unique, and great man of God, and I am thankful I had the privilege of knowing him personally.

A grateful Heart,

Penny Andrews

***Becky Templeton – Daughter***

There is no way I can put into words all the memories of my Daddy and Mama of the past 27 years! That is how long it has been since Bob Terrell and Daddy wrote his life story *From The Mountains Came The Light*. As Popie would say, "Here it is in a nutshell!"

Daddy and Mama loved Jesus first and foremost, loved each other, loved their family and loved preaching and telling the world about Jesus! Nothing else mattered!

They worked side by side for almost sixty years. They lived what they preached. Daddy and Mama never compromised the things of the Lord! Daddy would always say, "If God said it, I will stand on it!"

Daddy had this great vivid imagination when preaching on Heaven. He would say, "Bananas in Heaven will be as long as a telephone pole with zippers in them for easy peeling! Grapes will be so big that after your squeeze all the juice out of them, you can use the hull for a shower cap! Watermelons will be as big as a wheelbarrow and no seeds!" Daddy would get so blessed telling these things, he would holler out, "I believe I could run to Goober Town, Arkansas and back!" You know to this day, I have never found Goober Town Arkansas on any map! Something tells me that the name of the street that Popie and Nana live on in Heaven is called Goober Town! What do you think?

Jimmy was driving Popie to a meeting in Greer, South Carolina one night and they were running a little late, so Jimmy had the pedal to the metal! Popie believed you should never be late to preach God's word and you should have a fresh smelling breath at all times. Daddy was a walking billboard for the Listerine mouth wash company. He carried quart size bottles of Listerine at all times in the car. Jimmy was driving about 65 mph down the highway and all of a sudden, Popie opened the car door and spit out a mouth full of Listerine. Jimmy hollered out and said, "Popie what are you doing?" Popie said, "Keep driving, son, we can't be late and that Listerine really burns!" Jimmy says to this day that when he thinks of that night, his heart starts racing! Jimmy said when they got to the church they had an hour to spare. Thanks, Popie.

Daddy and Mama took their youth group from the Jesus Saves Mission on a picnic one Saturday at the old Recreation Park. It was a very hot day here in the mountains and Daddy stopped to get a block of ice to chop up for their Cokes. They didn't have crushed ice in bags back then, so you had to buy it in blocks. When Popie got to the picnic he was carrying the ice to the table and he tripped and the block of ice went flying out of his hands and hit Mama in the back of her head and knocked her out cold! Daddy said when Mama came around she looked up at him, smiled and said, "Honey is it time to go?" I wonder If Mama meant was it time to go home or time to go to her Heavenly home? God bless that sweet angel. Being a Pastor's wife can be HARD at times!

Daddy had ways of getting the point across when he needed to. Jimmy and I were dating and Jimmy had stayed real late one night. We were sitting in the piano room at the Brevard Road house when we heard a loud sound hit the floor at the end of the stairs. I jumped up and ran to see what the sound was, and one of Popie's shoes was laying in the floor. I picked the shoe up and carried in to show Jimmy and I said, "I think it is time for you to go home!" Jimmy jumped up, grabbed his coat, and went running out the door. We dated for four years before we got married. I think Daddy lost a lot of sleep. Sorry, Popie.

My Daddy was a modern day prophet. He could preach prophecy so that a child could understand him. I can remember when I was around twelve years old at the little white church on State Street, Daddy said that there would be a day when we would pay a dollar for a loaf of bread. I thought Daddy had flipped his lid. I pay almost three dollars for a loaf of our favorite bread today. Daddy preached that there would be many wars in the world, which we have already seen. He said that there would be a one world government, one world religion and a one world money!.We are already headed that way! As Popie would say, "Buckle your seat belts, Honey! Be ready to meet Jesus; it won't be long until the trumpet sounds!"

My mother was a prayer warrior for Jesus. She would go into her office or bedroom and pray for two hours at a time! That little woman could touch Heaven when nobody else could! I asked Jesus would He please let one tenth of her mantle fall on me. He did. Hallelujah! Thank you, Jesus! We need more praying mothers like Nana today! Prayer changes things! Matthew 21:22 Amen!

On January 13, 2004, my Daddy went to live with Jesus. Daddy called for me to come into his room and he said, "Becky I am going to Heaven today and I want you to promise me that you will take care of Mama." I said, "Daddy you know I will, but please don't leave us!" I called for Jimmy to come and check Daddy and he said, "Go get Nana and Matthew!" Matthew came in with Nana, and Jimmy told them to start saying good bye to Popie and tell him it was ok to go on to Heaven. I called Ralph and said, "Hurry, Ralph, Daddy is getting ready to leave us!" We all held hands and Matthew said the sweetest prayer for Popie and all of us. Popie said, "Pull me up!"

I put more pillows behind him and Daddy said again, "Pull me up!" I thought Daddy was having trouble breathing, so I jumped in the bed and pulled him up against me.

Daddy said again, "Pull me up higher! Pull me up higher!" I said, "Jimmy, Popie is not talking to us, he is talking to the angels!" Popie looked at Nana and looked up towards Heaven and took his last breath here, which was his first breath in Heaven with Jesus. Home Free! Psalms 119:117, "Hold thou me up, and I shall be safe" Amen!

On November 29, 2009, Nana went to live with Jesus and her Sweetheart of 59 years.

Thank you, Daddy! Thank you, Mama! You were the greatest parents a daughter could ever have. Thank you for loving Jesus, my family and me. Thank you for being my heroes in Jesus and in my life. I love you beyond forever. I will see you again someday. Please tell our first grandbaby, Kalin Rebecca, that we love and miss her so much. It will be worth it all when we see Jesus! Love, Your Rebecca

***Randy Shepherd Crossfire Ministries – Asheville, NC***

Dr. Sexton Sr. inspired me in soul winning as he would ask many people that he would come in contact with outside the church walls, "Do you know Jesus Christ as your Lord and Savior?" What a blessing to have known this man of God.

***Lisa Hensley Carson***

I will always remember Popie coming into Ingles on Haywood Rd. and putting tracts in the cases of beer! When he finished doing that, he would wait in my check out line to pay for his groceries, no matter how long the line would be. The other cashiers would try to get him to come over to their line and he would say, "No thank you, I'm waiting in my little sisters line."

***Elizabeth Ingle – Granddaughter***

Being the youngest of five grandchildren, I was fortunate to get to spend numerous hours with my grandparents. As I look back at those moments, I see what a blessing they were to me and so many others.

There was such a humble spirit about them both. Nana had such a genuine smile and open arms to love you and Popie had such a fun sense of humor and unselfish heart. Most of all, their sincere walk for the Lord made the most impact in my life.

Popie made it a priority to share the gospel to whoever he came across with such a loving disposition and with a clear presentation of God's word. Nana made every attempt to make you feel welcome and loved; whether it be through inviting you in for a meal, a card in the mail or most of all, her dedicated prayer life. She knew the importance and commitment of prayer and she took it very seriously when a request was made.

I'm honored to get to share about special times I had with them.

Summer 1982: This was monumental in my life. Finally, the last grandchild to get to go with Popie to Santa Land in Cherokee, N.C. Matthew, my brother, and Kent, my cousin went together two years prior and I remember anxiously waiting my turn. Granted it was only 45 miles away, it was a tradition each grandchild anticipated. This trip was centered on quality time spent with Popie and me. I felt so proud to go on a trip in that big, blue Buick. Popie booked a hotel just so I could swim in an indoor pool and just a couple shops down from our hotel, is where he bought me my first pair of moccasins. The theme park was fun and we sure did laugh a lot, but the most I remember about that trip was after we ate at a restaurant by the river, he took me out for ice cream. I knew he would get his favorite butter pecan with two scoops. After we had walked down the sidewalk for only about ten feet, my ice cream toppled off my cone. Before I knew it, Popie said "I'm so grateful that kind lady gave me two scoops but I sure can't eat it all. Do you mind if I put some on your cone so we won't waste it?"

Spending the nights at Nana's and Popie's house: A night at Nana and Popie's was a treat. Whether it was all the grandchildren at once or just me, the ritual never changed. I loved it more when it was an unplanned stay. Nana would have me follow her to the upstairs linen closet to pick out my favorite blankets and she would also let me help her put sheets on the bed. I always picked the purple room because the bed was unbelievably comfy. After we all had devotions together in Popie's study, it was off to the kitchen for one of Nana's famous grilled cheese or maybe a bowl of cereal or even pimento cheese on saltines. I remember waking in the morning to the smell of eggs and bacon. Nana would holler to come downstairs for breakfast and I would slide down the big staircase rail. She had the kitchen table beautifully set with all the fixings and fancy glasses for the OJ. Popie would be reading his Bible in his notorious bath robe over his suit pants and dress shirt. It wouldn't be long you would start to hear knocks at the back door and people would come to visit to enjoy a cup of coffee. I use to think to myself, "Where did they get all that coffee?" It seemed to be brewing all hours of the day. If it happened to be a Sunday night spend-the-night, I would see the garbage truck parked in their driveway on

Monday morning and the sanitation workers would be seated at the breakfast table getting a quick bite to eat with a short devotion led by Popie. Popie and Nana never met a stranger and graciously opened their home on many occasions to love on others.

The Night Shift: My first nursing job was working nights at the old Saint Joseph's Hospital. The whole idea of me working 3rd shift was comical. I'm known to have some narcoleptic moments, but when I graduated RN school, it was the only shift open. Popie and Nana knew me well, so well, that they expected a nightly 2:00 a.m. call when I was on shift. I knew I could call them when I was having a tough night or a sleepy night or when I just needed to hear a comforting voice. I knew Popie would be up reading in his study or at the kitchen table eating a bowl of cornflakes. I would laugh because I guess I called so frequently that Popie would not answer the phone with a hello…he would answer and say "Hey sweetie, how is your night?" and soon after you would hear Nana pick up on the line and say, " How is my girl?" Conversations were short and always followed by prayer.

They never knew what that meant to me and how it encouraged me to get through some challenging nights. One particular night I was having a chaotic night and must have worried Popie on the phone because I can remember I was standing in a chair in a patient's room adjusting an I.V pole when I heard the elevator door ding in the lobby. It wasn't a patient's family member or staff member, it was Popie! He was wearing his overcoat over his pajamas, dress shoes, and his dress hat. He had come to bring me a strawberry milkshake. I was so surprised yet so worried that he had gone out in the middle of the night. He didn't stay but for a few minutes only to say he loved me and thought I might need something sweet to help me through the night. I had to hold back the tears because I thought, "Wow! That's a lot of love!" Of course I scurried to the phone to let Nana know that Popie was out on an adventure and he would be returning shortly. She said, "Honey, he said he was burdened about you and had to come."

Though the above memories might seem like random examples, they are were priceless memories to me. I could never thank my grandparents for all they did for me through my childhood and even into my married life. They adopted my husband Josh into our family with open arms. We loved fellowshipping with them and Josh loved the private talks with Popie especially when he would drive him to churches to preach.

We were blessed to have them be with us during the loss of our oldest daughter, Kalin Rebecca and the birth of our second daughter, Irely Faith. I can remember they added a crib to their house for Irely just in case she needed to nap. Nana was still here, but Popie didn't get to be here for the birth of our youngest daughter, Kaydon Ruth. Kaydon and Popie share the same birthday of September 14.

When I think of Popie, I remember images of him on his knees in prayer, eating cornbread in a glass filled with milk, combing his hair straight back, using yellow highlighters in his sermon notes, drawing stick figures, letting me eat liver cheese with the fat edges still attached when Nana wasn't looking, requesting for my mom to make chicken and rice, whistling to the tune of "I'm a Soldier," steak dinners at the Howard Johnsons, putting butter on anything edible, carving the turkey with an electric knife at family gatherings, bear hugging those he loved, and best of all, telling me to, "pray and press on."

When I think of Nana, I remember her singing throughout the house as she cleaned, playing the upright piano, calling my dad "Yank", showing me how to clean a wall mirror edge to edge, eating cottage cheese with pineapple, making her one and only egg shake, using scotch tape for a lint roller, decorating the entire house for Christmas, including the bathrooms, making her famous mac and cheese for the family, loving roses and opals, collecting angels, crocheting blankets, ironing handkerchiefs, using Vaseline for a nightly moisturizer, praying for the loss souls and best of all, encouraging me to bathe everything in prayer. Little did she know she was helping me prepare for my future as a Pastor's wife. Josh and I miss them so much and we are thankful for the example they set before us as we now have entered the ministry.

In closing, if you never meet my grandparents, they were exceptional in my eyes but they never wanted to shine above their Savior for He was the reason they wanted to "Send the Light" to so many. They were truly devoted to their marriage, serving Christ, and loving others. I know they walk each day with our Lord and their dream of strolling together in Heaven has come true. I look forward to the day I see them again. I pray you too, my friend, will be there.

***Judy Proffitt – Asheville NC***

In 1955, I started attending the Jesus Saves Mission, and that is where I became acquainted with the Sexton family. Ralph Jr. was about 8 years old and Becky was 5. We had a wonderful youth group and I learned to love the church and the Sextons.

While still in high school I began to type sermon outlines for Dr. Sexton. To me his name was "Preacher" and that is what I called him always.

When the *Send The Light* telecast ministry began, I volunteered to work with the mail. I continued to work as volunteer, until 1973 when I became the secretary and worked as such until 2004, when the ministry ended with Dr. Sexton's death.

Preacher and Jacque were a vital part of our family's life. He was our Pastor, mentor, advisor, and most of all, our friend. He was one of the kindest, most thoughtful, and caring Christians I ever knew.

Preacher and Jacque have shared many meals in our home and he was the only Pastor my children ever knew when growing up.

I have a lot of memories of seeing the church grow from the Old Mission, to the little white church on State street in West Asheville, to the rock sanctuary on Shelburne Rd.

This book, *From The Mountains Came The Light* is mostly printed word for word from Dr. Sexton himself. Bob Terrell, the author, and he went to lunch many many times. They would set the little tape recorder on the table and just converse. I took the tapes and typed them as they spoke, word for word. Then Bob took the typed pages and put it all in book form. I am honored to have had a part in making these pages come to life. I was fortunate to have spent so much time in their home and as I observed his life. I never saw one unkind deed or word. He truly lived as an example to the believers.

He always told me he wanted me to write a poem to be read at his funeral. I would tease him and asked if he wanted me to write it now, so he could edit or approve it. When the sad day came that we did have his service, the following poem was my tribute to him.

*<u>MY TRIBUTE To my friend, Dr. Ralph Sexton, Sr.</u>*

*I think I know how the disciples felt*
*On the Mount of Transfiguration;*

*For it has been my privilege and joy T*
*To observe a Saint in the making.*

*For many years I have witnessed a life*
*That was lived so true without malice or strife.*
*I never saw him angry, or heard him be unkind;*
*I never saw him judge another or any fault to find.*

*I know what kept him tender*
*It was the time spent on his knees,*
*And if one fell along life's way, He's say, but for God's grace, It could be me.*

*I never saw him without his Bible very near*
*He loved God's Word supremely,*
*To him it was most dear.*
*He had a vast knowledge of the Word*

*With scholars he could place,*
*But he kept the Gospel message simple,*
*So even a child could understand its Grace.*

*No respecter of persons could he ever be called*

*The richest to the poorest, he witnessed to them all.*
*He spoke God's word with boldness,*
*But love was on his face;*
*And you didn't have to know him long,*
*To sense the presence of God's Grace.*

*A spiritual giant has been taken from us*

*And no one will take his place*
*Though God will always have a witness,*
*To tell the world of His Grace.*

*But this gentle mountain man*
*Who could have had earth's fame;*
*Has graced our lives with his presence,*
*And we will never be the same.*

*When the angels came for his crossing*
*I am sure they were specifically told*
*What a valiant soldier and warrior,*

*They were bringing to the City of Gold.*

*He loved to preach about Heaven*
*And now he has found it all true.*
*The Saviour he loved,*
*And served with such faith,*
*Was there to welcome and greet him,*
*As he entered the beautiful gates.*

***Muzette Sexton – Daughter-in-law***

My first memory of my father-in-law was when I was a senior in high school. My Dad pastored a church in West Virginia. Bro. Sexton was the Evangelist for our annual Spring Revival. As was the custom, in that time, he stayed in the parsonage during the course of the revival.

He and I immediately bonded. He was one of the few adults in my childhood that engaged me in conversation. After all, in 1965, the old adage, "children should be seen and not heard," was very prevalent. He asked me what I enjoyed studying in school, how I liked West Virginia, and what my plans were for the future. I was totally smitten with him. I wrote, "Ralph Sexton is my favorite Preacher" in the front of my Bible. It didn't dawn on me that my Daddy was my Pastor.

During one of our talks, Brother Sexton told me that he had a son graduating from high school. "He wants to join the Marines," he continued, "but I am trying to get him to go to college first!"

The fall of 1966, I found myself in a small room of new freshmen at Trevecca Nazarene College. This handful of freshmen had been chosen to organize a "get acquainted" banquet. The upper classmen ask us to go around the room and introduce ourselves to each other. The boy sitting next to me said, "I'm Ralph Sexton."

"I know you!" I blurted out. Of course, what I knew was his name. He was Ralph Sexton, Jr. "So your Dad got you to come to college," I said. We had never met, so, of course, he had no idea who I was or what I meant.

The story is obvious after that. A year later, I married Ralph Sexton, Jr. I left my family behind and came to Asheville to live.

Popie, as our first child named Bro. Sexton, became my dearest friend. I loved him, and he loved me. He taught me so much of life and even more of Jesus.

Our relationship continued the same as it had begun. He would always ask, "How are your Mama and Daddy? Are you adjusting to living in Asheville?" He always put me at ease. I realize now, that his nature was to think of others first. What a perfect example of Christ he was to me. I don't believe our meeting that spring of 1965, was an accident. I believe God, "orders the footsteps of the righteous." How I thank God for putting Popie in my life.

***Beverly Sexton Parrish – Granddaugher***

In 2003, while my family and I were serving as missionaries in Central America, we made the decision to come home for the holidays, as we knew it would likely be our last Christmas with my grandfather, whom everyone called Popie.

Just a few weeks earlier, our world had been rocked by the unbelievable news that Popie had developed a large brain tumor. After all the years he had struggled with heart disease, surviving two massive heart attacks—the first being three months before I was born—it was a real shock to hear this diagnosis.

We came home to spend as much time with Popie as possible, but at last, the day arrived when we were to return to the mission field. I went to say goodbye to Popie on January 6, and as I entered the side door of his house, my heart was in my throat.

There were already a few other people there visiting, and Popie, always the consummate gentleman, was in his wheelchair (my first time to see him in it), wearing freshly-ironed blue pajamas and a warm robe, with his feet in leather slippers on the wheelchair footrest. He was at his usual spot at the table with his oversized Bible, marked and tattered from years of long use.

After a few minutes of visiting, he grew tired and I could see that he needed to rest. The visitors began to excuse themselves until the only people left with me were Nana, my cousin Thomas Freeman, and our longtime friend Squire Parsons.

I went and sat in the floor right in front of Popie's chair and put my head in his lap. My beloved grandfather laid his hands on my head, quietly comforting me with whispered prayers as I sobbed. I couldn't make out exactly what he was praying, and I'm not sure I would even remember, but it was the sweetest prayer ever—and prayed just for me.

Although I love music, I'm neither a musician nor a singer, but for some reason, Popie took my hand and said, "Sing 'Angel Band' to me. That was my precious Mama's favorite song." (Since I was a little girl, he had often told me how I reminded him of his mother that he loved so and talked of often.)

I loved that old hymn, and knew it well, so I wiped my eyes, cleared my throat, and began singing his requested song to him. After I finished the first verse, Squire, who had been sitting nearby, pulled up his chair and joined with me for my first and only duet with an award-winning professional singer! Squire's rich baritone filled the room, along with my joyful noise as we sang these words to this good and faithful servant of the Lord:

*Oh, Come, Angel Band*
*My latest sun is sinking fast, My race is nearly run,*
*My strongest trials now are past, My triumph is begun!*

*I know I'm nearing holy ranks Of friends and kindred dear;*
*I brush the dew of Jordan's banks, The crossing must be near;*
*I've almost gained my heav'nly home, My spirit loudly sings; The holy ones, behold, they come!*
*I hear the noise of wings,*
*O bear my longing heart to Him Who bled and died for me;*
*Whose blood now cleanses from all sin,*
*And gives me victory.*
*[Refrain]*
*O come, angel band, come, and around me stand,*
*O bear me away on your snowy wings*
*To my immortal home O bear me away on your snowy wings*
*To my immortal home.*

Author: Jefferson Hascall (1860)

The sweet presence of the Lord filled that room, and I encountered a grace that I hadn't previously known. I felt as though my heart would break as I kissed him goodbye before leaving. I knew it was the last time I would ever see him on this earth, and I had no doubt he knew that as well. We left it unsaid between us, but we both knew.

Early the next morning, I was on a plane with Dwight and our four children, headed back to our mission work in Costa Rica.

Seven days later, my parents called to tell me that Popie's healing had come, and he was at last in his heavenly home. Our hearts were broken and we would miss him terribly, but we were happy for him, that he was safely home.

# CLOSING THOUGHTS

This book tells the story of my father's life up to 1987. The Epilogue fills some of the years in between and up to his death in January, 2004.

We are indebted to the memory of Bob Terrell, for his labor of love. Bob made sure this story of a mountain preacher would live on!

A few years later, Bob was sick and spending more time at home. He approached me about continuing the storyline with another book.

This book has been on the shelf for many years. I am happy to announce it will soon be released.

*The Sawdust Trail* picks up the unique part of our ministry, the Tent Crusades. This book will cover the cities and people who have kept our heritage alive!

Thank you for your love, prayers, and friendship! May our Lord receive all of the honor for what He has done in all of our lives!

Yours in His service,

Leicester, NC
June 2016